Tinnitus

Questions and Answers

Jack A. Vernon

Oregon Health Sciences University

Barbara Tabachnick Sanders

American Tinnitus Association

Boston • *London* • *Toronto* • ⋯⋯ • *Singapore*

To Gloria E. Reich, Ph.D. — For lighting the way.

Executive Editor and Publisher: *Stephen D. Dragin*
Editorial Assistant: *Barbara Strickland*
Marketing Manager: *Stephen Smith*
Editorial Production Service: *Marbern House*
Manufacturing Buyer: *Chris Marson*
Cover Administrator: *Kristina Mose-Libon*

Internet: www.ablongman.com

Between the time Web site information is gathered and published, some sites may have closed. Also, the transcription of URLs can result in typographical errors. The publisher would appreciate notification where these occur so that they may be corrected in subsequent editions.

Library of Congress Cataloging-in-Publication Data

Vernon, Jack A.
  Tinnitus : questions and answers / by Jack A. Vernon, Barbara Tabachnick Sanders.
    p. ; cm.
  Includes index.
  ISBN 0-205-32685-4
    1. Tinnitus—Examinations, questions, etc. I. Sanders, Barbara Tabachnick.
  II. Title. [DNLM: 1. Tinnitus—therapy—Examination Questions.
  2. Tinnitus—diagnosis—Examination Questions. 3. Tinnitus—etiology—
  Examination Questions. WV 18.2 V541t 2001]
  RF293.8 .V47 2001
  617.8—dc21

                                                                00-064015

Printed in the United States of America
10 9 8 7 6 5 4 3 2 1   05 04 03 02 01 00

Contents

Appendixes

Preface

The nearer any disease approaches to a crisis, the nearer it is to a cure.
—Thomas Paine

The founding of the American Tinnitus Association (ATA) in 1971 came about through the efforts of Charles Unice, M.D., a doctor who himself had tinnitus. In 1975, the American Tinnitus Association prepared a periodic report known as the *ATA Newsletter.* Under the editorship of Gloria Reich, ATA's then executive director, the publication grew in size and scope. In 1988, a new name was chosen for it, *Tinnitus Today,* and it settled into a regular quarterly publication. In 1990, I was asked to write a question and answer article for *Tinnitus Today* consisting of my responses to questions that tinnitus patients wrote in. Many of the Q&As were published in the journal and many were not. I always took care to answer every letter personally. And I still do.

This book could not exist if it were not for your questions, and we thank you. The accumulation of questions asked and answered over these many years is included in this volume. Many of the answers have been modified from those that originally appeared in *Tinnitus Today,* necessitated by the advent of new information not available at the time of the original publication. Also, many of the responses are longer now than they were originally. We have more space in this book to expand answers and we have taken the liberty to do so.

Since 1994, Barbara Tabachnick Sanders has served as editor of *Tinnitus Today,* which included my Q&As. I could not help but notice that she rendered my column, and the whole of *Tinnitus Today,* an immeasurable service. Inasmuch as she had been such an intrinsic partner in the Q&A effort, it made sense that she continue her excellent service in this compilation effort and serve as this book's coauthor.

It is my hope that this volume will provide useful information to many tinnitus patients, especially those who remain untreated. It is my conviction that the cure for tinnitus, or at least for some forms of tinnitus, will be determined *and* available in the not-too-distant future, perhaps the next 5 years.

This statement is not a wild hope. Competent research teams are already at work in this area.

Both Barbara and I want to express appreciation to the American Tinnitus Association and its board of directors for making some of the materials in this book available to us.

Jack A. Vernon

When Jack Vernon asked me to write a book with him, I said yes so fast I forgot to ask him what the book would be about. But I could have guessed. He and I teamed up on his *Tinnitus Today* Q&A column in 1994, and we have been delighted about it ever since.

From the start of my association with Jack, I have been aware of my great good fortune: We live in the same geographic region, we both wandered into the same career field for one reason or another, and our lifetimes coincide. And despite our different backgrounds (me: writer; he: tinnitus pioneer), we became colleagues, then friends.

If you ask Jack, he will say that everything he knows about tinnitus he has learned from his patients. (He considers everyone who writes or calls him for tinnitus advice to be his patient.) And if you have ever spoken with Jack or if you've ever received a letter back from him, you might have the sense that you've found the best resource possible. Unequivocally, he has been my best tinnitus mentor.

A few things about our Q&A book: First, you will notice that the Q&As are grouped by topic. These groupings are intended to help you find specific interest areas quickly. Yet, inevitably, there is overlap. For example, we've included a question about *hearing loss* that leads to an answer about *tinnitus instruments*. Which chapter, the one on hearing loss or the one on tinnitus instruments, contains the needed information? In some form, you will find the answer in both.

You might also notice that there are no tinnitus *sufferers* in this book. There are, however, tinnitus *patients,* even though the people to whom we refer might not currently be patients. We made the philosophical decision to speak in positive and hopeful tones. It is a philosophy that also guides our day-to-day encounters with those who have tinnitus. We just can't help it; we are optimistic people. It is undeniable that tinnitus can create havoc, that it can be painful and troublesome, that it is often hard, terribly hard, to live with. And we know that a desperate few chose suicide as the solution to their tinnitus struggle. We know. It is why we wrote this book.

The American Tinnitus Association has graciously allowed us to include materials in this book that previously appeared in *Tinnitus Today.* We extend our thanks to this unique organization.

We also extend our thanks to our readers. Your observations about your tinnitus have led to scientific studies that have led to relief-giving treatments.

These observations are destined to lead us to a resolution of tinnitus once and for all.

And so we encourage you to stay optimistic (because things are much more promising than ever), to support tinnitus research (because it is the only way out), and, above all, to keep asking questions.

Barbara Tabachnick Sanders

Disclaimer: Throughout this book you will find the names of specific tinnitus-related products, organizations, and services. All company contact information is given in the appendixes. Note that our inclusion of this information is not an endorsement of the products and services. We offer these (and all the resources mentioned in the book) strictly as a service to our readers.   **JAV and BTS**

Acknowledgments

One nice thing about writing a book is the opportunity to thank those to whom we are indebted. On the other hand, one terrible thing about writing a book is that in the acknowledgments we always forget and thus omit some significant contributors. To solve this problem, I say from the outset that it is not possible for me to acknowledge all to whom I feel a deep debt of gratitude, and thus I will concentrate on only one person, Barbara Tabachnick Sanders. I first met Barbara about seven years ago when I started writing the Q&A column for *Tinnitus Today*, of which Barbara was the editor. Ever since that time, she has been putting my writing into proper English, and she has done the same with this book. If this book has merit, it is entirely due to her tireless efforts. If there are errors or shortcomings, they are mine.

JAV

With thanks: To my daughter Emily Tabachnick, a fine young editor, for always letting me know gently when I don't quite get it right and always enthusiastically when I do.

To my son, David Tabachnick, for keeping my computer, and therefore me, cool under fire.

To my father, Stan Pincus, who, after reading my first published article years ago, told me to not call him anymore. "Why not?" I asked. "*Write* to me instead," he said quietly. "Just write to me."

To my mother, Anita Pincus, whose 1985 book of extraordinarily comic poetry is still my reference book on life.

And to my husband, Stan Sanders, who learned about tinnitus long before I did—the hard way—and who will one day know that making meals and doing laundry month after month with grace and without complaint while his wife writes a book is the stuff of which long marriages are made.

BTS

Additional thanks to: William Brownell, Ph.D.; Peter Gillespie, Ph.D.; Dan Malcore; Billy Martin, Ph.D.; Mary Meikle, Ph.D.; Stephen Nagler, M.D.; Diane Shultz, M.A., CCC-A—gems all.

Illustrations and graphs: Stanley Rea Sanders

About the Authors

Jack Vernon was born in Tennessee, grew up in Virginia, and was a pilot during World War II. Thanks to the GI Bill, he was able to go to the University of Virginia, where he earned his B.A., M.A., and Ph.D. in psychology. His first research post was at Princeton University, a job that lasted 14 years. In 1966, he resigned this perfectly good job to move to Oregon and begin clinical research in tinnitus. He soon founded the Tinnitus Clinic at the Oregon Health Sciences University, the first tinnitus clinic in  the United States. Vernon thoroughly enjoys playing golf, despite the fact that he doesn't do it very well. He also loves woodworking, reading, and being with his wife, Mary.

Barbara Tabachnick Sanders studied fine art at Santa Monica College and California State University while freelancing as a writer. Writing won out. Her poetry and short stories appeared in *West* in the late 1970s. Her children appeared in 1980 and 1983. Since then she has authored more than 70 articles on parenting, tinnitus, and other health topics. She has been a feature writer for *Tinnitus Today* since 1993 and its editor since 1995. Sanders lives with her husband in Oregon, where she enjoys contra dancing, songwriting, and hiking the Cascades.

Glossary

Every field of study develops its own terminology to avoid confusion and ease communication among its practitioners. Users of this book would benefit from learning the following terms.

ABR: Auditory brainstem response, a hearing test that detects abnormalities in the hearing pathway between the cochlea and the brainstem.

acoustic neuroma: Rare tumor located on the eighth nerve between the cochlea and the brainstem. (This tumor can involve facial, vestibular, and auditory nerves.) It is almost always benign and very slow growing. This kind of tumor invades the eighth nerve and can cause deafness, tinnitus, facial paralysis, and loss of balance. Its cause is unknown, although some suspect a genetic origin. Unilateral (in one ear) tinnitus with no known cause can be a symptom of acoustic neuroma.

addictive: (usually referring to a drug) Producing a psychological and/or physical dependency. An addictive drug creates a need for the patient to take increasingly stronger doses in order to experience the same amount of effect as from a previous lesser dose.

afferent nerves: Nerves that begin in the sensory organs (eyes, ears) and transmit signals to the brain.

amplification: Procedure whereby auditory signals such as speech or music are increased in intensity. In tinnitus treatment, amplification usually refers to the use of hearing aids.

anecdotal report: Account based on personal experience. For example, an individual may associate consuming a food or medicine with onset or relief of physical symptoms such as headaches, tinnitus, or allergic reactions.

antidepressant: Medication used to decrease or control the human state of depression. Tricyclic antidepressants often cause or worsen tinnitus. Nontricyclics are generally recommended to assist the tinnitus patient with depression.

anxiolytic: Medication used to control the state of anxiety that is common in tinnitus patients. New research at the University of Buffalo has shown that the brain's limbic system (or emotion center) is activated during tinnitus perception. It is suggested that this might account for the anxiety frequently experienced by tinnitus patients.

audiogram: Chart of the patient's hearing acuity in both ears in the frequencies between 100 and 8000 Hz. (Some audiometric tests can measure hearing at frequencies as high as 12,000 Hz.) The decibels noted on an audiogram represent the quietest volume that can be heard at each frequency. This is the patient's threshold of hearing.

audiologist: A health-care professional, with a master's degree and sometimes a doctorate in audiology, who is trained to measure hearing, fit and dispense hearing aids, provide special tests, such as auditory brainstem response, and counsel on the use of cochlear implants.

auditory cortex: Part of the brain dedicated to receiving and interpreting neural signals from the eighth cranial nerves. There are two parts of the auditory cortex, one on the left side of the brain and the other on the right side. Each ear sends signals to both parts of the auditory cortex. The left side of the cortex is devoted to the interpretation of speech and music. The right side is devoted to interpretation of all other signals.

auditory nerve: Auditory branch of the eighth cranial nerve that leads from the cochlea in the inner ear to the auditory cortex in the brain.

auditory system: All the physiology and organs devoted to hearing, including the outer ear, ear canal, middle ear, inner ear, eighth nerve, and auditory brain center.

barotrauma: Damage to the inner ear caused by rapid and drastic changes in air pressure, such as from a very rapid airplane or scuba descent. The most common damage is a rupture of the round window membrane in the inner ear. This rupture allows fluids to leak out of the inner ear.

basic research: Research that adheres to scientific methodology and seeks knowledge about a fundamental aspect of nature. It is usually conducted in a laboratory.

biofeedback: Conditioning procedure whereby automatic or subconscious conditions, such as heart rate or body temperature, are brought under the control of conscious behavior.

cerumen: Earwax produced in the ear canal. Its purpose is to trap insects and to prevent them from damaging the eardrum. Earwax varies in color, although the color is not indicative of any special condition.

chronic: Referring to a health condition that is constant and severe.

clinical research: Type of research that adheres to scientific methodology and seeks information about an aspect of human health. Clinical research usually involves patients as test subjects.

cochlea: Inner ear hearing organ, it houses approximately 17,000 outer hair cells and 3700 inner hair cells (or cilia). These cilia are moved, bent, and sometimes destroyed by sound waves entering the inner ear and can be damaged or destroyed by ototoxic drugs.

cochlear implant: Surgically implanted electronic device that directly stimulates the eighth nerve fibers of the inner ear, which in turn send auditory signals to the brain. This permanent device is implanted only in ears that are totally deaf.

Cochlear implant circuitry allows the patients to receive some sounds; some patients even gain or regain speech comprehension. Many patients find relief from tinnitus with cochlear implants.

cognitive behavioral therapy: Counseling technique that helps people identify their unhealthy beliefs and expectations that might be prolonging unhappiness and other problems. Cognitive therapy is used to help the tinnitus patient regard the tinnitus as unworthy of attention.

conductive hearing loss: Hearing loss produced by malfunction or blockage of the outer ear or middle ear. The most common cause of conductive hearing loss is a fixation of the middle ear bones (or otosclerosis). Tinnitus associated with conductive hearing loss is usually low pitched. When conductive loss is corrected, the associated tinnitus often goes away or is significantly reduced.

control group: People who do not receive the treatment being studied in a research project. The results from the control group and the experimental group (the people who do receive the treatment) are compared to see if the treatment had an effect.

decibel (dB):   One-tenth of a bel, a unit of measure of sound intensity. It was named to honor Alexander Graham Bell, the inventor of the telephone. Sound intensity is measured on a logarithmic scale. For example, 90 dB is 10 *times* louder than 70 dB.

double-blind placebo-controlled study: Research study in which neither the patients nor the experimenters know which patient is receiving the active drug or treatment and which is receiving the placebo (the fake drug or procedure). Humans are easily influenced by expectations—their own and their doctors'. This type of study can eliminate the tendency for patients to report what they think their doctors want to hear.

ear canal: Portion of the ear that leads from the outer ear flap (pinna) to the eardrum. The ear canal is part of the outer ear.

efferent nerves: Nerves that originate in the brain and send signals to the glands and muscles. The ear is the only sensory organ that contains both efferent nerves and afferent nerves (ones that send signals from the sensory organs to the brain). Preliminary research suggests that the role of the efferent system is to reduce the intensity of the afferent system. Hyperacusis might be the result of a poorly functioning efferent system.

eighth nerve: Cranial nerve that leads from the cochlea to the area of the brain (the auditory cortex) that interprets auditory signals. The auditory and vestibular nerves combine to form the eighth nerve.

electrical stimulation: Alternating current (AC) and direct current (DC) used as a medical treatment. Electrical stimulation has been used in a variety of waveforms and polarities on various parts of the body, including the ear, to correct medical conditions. Negative DC applied to the ear can cause hearing damage and tinnitus. Positive DC can relieve tinnitus, but it causes tissue damage if sustained. Cochlear implants electrically stimulate the eighth nerve, which in turn transmits sounds to the brain.

ENT: See *otolaryngologist.*

eustachian tube: Tube that connects the throat to the middle ear so that air pressure in the middle ear remains equal to outside air pressure. Some people with sluggish eustachian tubes experience ear pain when they ascend and descend in airplanes.

experimental group: People who receive the drug or treatment that is being studied in a research project.

fMRI: Functional magnetic resonance imaging, a non-invasive, high-resolution scanning technology that is used to image human organ function. fMRI does not require exposure to radiation. This imaging technology is highly sensitive to movement. The patient's head must be held in place for a brain scan.

frequency: Number of cycles per second of sound waves. This equates to the perception of pitch. The human ear can hear the frequency range from 20 Hz or cycles (low pitched) to 20,000 Hz or cycles (high pitched).

habit forming: (referring to a drug) Producing withdrawal symptoms, such as headaches, upset stomach, and a feeling of malaise when use of the substance is discontinued.

habituate: To make an experience or sound so much a part of the subconscious experience that it does not reach one's conscious perception. When we hear the sound of a refrigerator motor and then become unaware of it shortly after, we have habituated the sound.

hair cells: Cochlear cells in the organ of Corti that interpret sound energy, convert it into electrical energy, and then send it to the brain. Outer hair cells receive the incoming sound energy. Inner hair cells send the signals into the auditory nerve and then on to the brain. Excessively loud sounds can damage or destroy outer hair cells. Also, the vestibular cells in the otoliths of the semicircular canals that electrically send balance information to the brain through the eighth nerve.

hearing aid dispenser: A professional who performs basic hearing tests and dispenses hearing aids.

hearing impaired: Having some form of hearing loss.

hearing instrument specialist: A professional who performs basic hearing tests and dispenses hearing aids, maskers, sound generators, and tinnitus instruments.

hearing loss: Amount of lost hearing measured in decibels. The faintest sound that a person with normal hearing can hear is between 0 and 20 dB. As hearing is lost, sounds need to be louder to be detected. A mild hearing loss is between 26 and 40 dB. A moderate hearing loss is between 41 and 55 dB. A moderately severe hearing loss is between 56 and 70 dB. A severe hearing loss is between 71 and 90 dB. A profound hearing loss or deafness is greater than 90 dB.

hearing threshold: Faintest sound level at which a person can hear a given frequency.

hertz (Hz): Unit of measure used to describe the frequency of sound waves. Ten hertz is a frequency of 10 cycles per second; 4000 hertz is a frequency of 4000 cycles per second. Ten cycles per second (or 10 Hz) is a much lower sound than 4000 cycles per second (or 4000 Hz). This unit of measure was named after Heinrich Hertz, the physicist who discovered radio waves.

homeopathy: Treatment of a disease or condition by administering very small and repeated doses of the remedy thought to cause the disease or condition. Based on Samuel Hahnemann's principle of *similars* or *like cures like.*

hyperacusis: Abnormal intolerance to ordinary sounds. Hyperacusis patients perceive almost all sounds as uncomfortably loud.

inner ear: Portion of the ear devoted to receiving and converting external sounds into neurological signals and then transmitting them to the auditory cortex. It includes the cochlea, semicircular canals, and hearing and balance nerves.

loudness matching: Matching the loudness of one sound to the loudness of a second sound. For tinnitus loudness matching, an external sound is introduced to the patient and gradually increased until the patient indicates that it is equal to the loudness of his or her tinnitus. The average loudness of tinnitus has been measured at 7 dB SL.

masker: Sound-emitting device used to relieve tinnitus, either ear level (like a hearing aid) or tabletop. The devices usually emit a 3000- to 12,000-Hz broadband sound, like the "shhh" of running water, a sound more aesthetically acceptable than the sound of the tinnitus. The ear-level devices are either in the ear (ITE) or behind the ear (BTE). The patient controls the masker volume. A masker can completely or partially cover up tinnitus. As a tinnitus relief device, it is most successful for people who have normal or near-normal hearing ability.

Ménière's disease (or Ménière's syndrome):   Named for and first identified by the French otologist Prosper Ménière. The symptoms of this condition are episodic vertigo, hearing loss, tinnitus, and a sensation of fullness in one or both ears.

middle ear: Section of the auditory system between the eardrum and the inner ear. The middle ear contains the ossicles (three small bones: the malleus, incus, and stapes) that transmit sound from the eardrum to the inner ear, the promontory, and the eustachian tube.

MRI: Magnet resonance imaging. A body imaging system that uses a magnetic field to minutely move atoms in the area of the body being studied. Low-energy radio waves record the changes in those atoms. The result of this process is a high-quality, soft-tissue image of the human body. The patient travels headfirst into the closed MRI tube for testing. These machines are notably noisy inside (up to 115 dB at head level). Patients are strongly advised to wear earplugs during the testing. Open MRIs are less claustrophobic and considerably quieter (below 85 dB at head level) than closed MRI machines, but have less resolution capability than the closed models.

noise cancellation: Technology that causes the elimination of a sound wave by the generation of an equal and opposite completely out-of-phase sound wave in the direction of the oncoming sound wave. Active noise cancellation has only been achieved for low-frequency sounds.

objective tinnitus: Sounds in the ear that can be heard by someone in addition to the person with the tinnitus. Pulsatile tinnitus is often objectively heard.

OSHA: Occupational Safety and Health Administration. Also Occupational Safety and Health Act of 1970. The organization, part of the U.S. Department of Labor, established the act to set on-the-job safety standards for all people in the United

States. OSHA noise exposure standards for workers in the United States are as follows:

90 dB maximum for 8 hours	105 dB maximum for 1 hour
95 dB maximum for 4 hours	110 dB maximum for ½ hour
100 dB maximum for 2 hours	115 dB maximum for ¼ hour

Many hearing health professionals believe that the allowable noise level is too high. The European occupational noise exposure standard is 85 dB for 8 hours.

otitis media: Inflammation of the middle ear, usually caused by infection and often accompanied by pain, hearing loss, and/or tinnitus.

otoacoustic emissions: Sounds that the ear naturally produces. There are three different kinds of otoacoustic emissions: (1) spontaneous emissions, (2) simultaneously evoked emissions, and (3) delayed evoked emissions. Spontaneous otoacoustic emissions (SOAE) can be picked up by sensitive microphones and are produced without any stimulation of the ear. They are otherwise not audible. Simultaneous evoked otoacoustic emissions (SEOAE) and delayed evoked otoacoustic emissions (DEOAE) are produced either by sending short sound bursts or sweeping tones into the ear. Otoacoustic emissions are not directly related to tinnitus.

otolaryngologist: A physician who specializes in the anatomy and diseases of the ear, nose, and throat (ENT). Also known as an otorhinolaryngologist.

otology: Study of the anatomy and diseases of the ear.

otosclerosis: Disease of the middle ear that eventually prevents the middle ear bones (the malleus, incus, and stapes) from effectively transmitting signals to the cochlea. Hearing impairment usually results. This condition can be corrected by a stapedectomy, a surgical procedure that removes one or all of the middle ear bones and replaces them with a prosthetic implant.

ototoxic: Substances that are damaging, or toxic, to the inner ear.

PET scan: Positron emission tomography, a scanning technology used to map the brain's neuronal activity and functional changes. PET scanning requires the use of injected radioactive materials. Although images from PET scanning are less precise than images from fMRI scanning, PET technology is superior in its ability to directly image chemical and physical processes. PET is also preferred for auditory studies because it is appreciably quieter than fMRI and therefore does not distort auditory test results.

pink noise: Band of noise composed evenly of all the tones from 200 to 6000 Hz.

pitch: Tonal aspect of a given sound that is measurable. The higher the sound wave frequency is, the higher the perceived pitch of the tone will be.

pitch matching: Matching the pitch of one sound to the pitch of another. In tinnitus pitch matching, two different pitched tones are presented to the patient, who selects the tone closer to his or her tinnitus. The selected pitch is then offered with a slightly higher pitch, and the patient chooses again. Increasingly higher tones are presented in this two-alternative, forced-choice manner until the patient repeatedly chooses the same tone. The average tinnitus pitch is 7000 Hz.

placebo: Inert substance that is given to usually half of the subjects in a controlled drug research study. In a double-blind, placebo-controlled drug study, neither the subjects nor the doctors who administer the drug and placebo know which patients are getting which substance.

presbycusis: Age-related auditory impairments that result in sensorineural hearing loss.

pulsatile tinnitus: Rhythmic, pulsing form of tinnitus usually in phase with the heartbeat and often audible to others.

recruitment: Abnormally rapid growth in perceived loudness of a certain sound. Recruitment is associated with hearing impairment.

residual hearing: Hearing ability in the speech frequencies that is available to a hearing-impaired person.

residual inhibition: Temporary cessation of tinnitus (complete residual inhibition) or temporary reduction of tinnitus (partial residual inhibition). This occurs when tinnitus is successfully masked with sound and then the sound is turned off.

sensorineural hearing loss: Loss of hearing caused by damage to the hearing mechanisms of the inner ear (cochlea) or the neural structures between the inner ear and the brain.

stapedectomy: Surgical removal of one, two, or all three diseased middle ear bones (the ossicles) and replacement of the bones with a prosthesis. The conductive hearing loss that often occurs because of the disease process (otosclerosis) is usually restored following this surgery. Presurgical tinnitus can improve after this surgery.

subjective tinnitus: Tinnitus that is only heard by the patient. It is the more common form of the disorder.

threshold shift: Measurable change in hearing ability, usually representing a decline in hearing.

tinnitus: Ringing, hissing, buzzing, humming, chirping, or other noise heard in the ears or head. Most cases of tinnitus are subjective, that is, perceived only by the person with the disorder and not generated by any outside noise source. In a survey of 4500 patients, 77% identified tinnitus as a single tone, 8% identified it as a "noise" sound, 13% identified it as a mixture of the two, and 2% identified it as a mixture of up to four different sounds.

tinnitus instrument: Wearable device that combines a tinnitus ear-level masker with a high-frequency-emphasis hearing aid, each with a separate volume control. A tinnitus instrument can completely cover up the tinnitus, or it can reduce the perceived loudness of the tinnitus to an acceptable level.

tinnitus retraining therapy (TRT):   Treatment for tinnitus that combines specialized directive counseling with exposure to a sound-enriched environment. Wearable in- or behind-the-ear sound generators are often part of the TRT protocol. Patients set the broadband sound devices at the point where the audible sound starts to mix with the tinnitus. The goal of this therapy is to retrain the brain to habituate the tinnitus. A TRT program can take up to 2 years to complete.

TMJ or TMJD: Temporomandibular joint disorder or dysfunction, a dysfunction of the jaw joint, jaw muscle, or both. TMJD can be caused by a misaligned bite, physical trauma to the head that damages cranial nerves and muscles, or a wearing down of the shock-absorbing disk in the jaw joint. Pain, tinnitus, dizziness, locking jaw, and swallowing difficulties are TMJD symptoms.

vestibular system: Portion of the inner ear that is devoted to balance (semicircular canal and vestibular nerve). Disorders of the vestibular system can produce dizziness, tinnitus, pressure sensations, and hearing loss.

white noise: Band of noise that includes all frequencies (from 20 to 20,000 Hz) detectable by the human ear.

Acoustic Neuroma:
Tumor on the Eighth Nerve

Q What would make my doctor suspect that I might have an acoustic neuroma? He wants me to have an MRI to test his hypothesis.

A An eighth nerve tumor is always suspected when tinnitus is in one ear only and when there is no known cause for the tinnitus. MRI is a modern imaging technique that provides a picture of the brain and is capable of detecting very small tumors, as small as 2 mm. If a tumor is detected when it is small, the patient requires a less invasive surgery to have it removed than if the tumor is large. As an acoustic neuroma grows on the eighth nerve (the hearing nerve), it invades more of the nerve, which can cause a hearing loss that begins in the high-frequency range. This is because the hearing nerve is laid down with the high-frequency nerve fibers on the outside of the nerve trunk and the lower-frequency fibers placed deeper within the nerve trunk. Acoustic neuromas also cause a loss of balance and, in many cases, tinnitus.

As an eighth nerve tumor grows, it can compress, deform, and displace the nerve, as well as interfere with the blood supply to the cochlea. Although these tumors are historically slow growing and almost always benign, they can grow big enough to physically impede brain function and cause death. The sooner they are diagnosed and removed (and there are options for removal or shrinkage), the better.

Note that the sound level inside the MRI tube is really beyond that which many tinnitus patients can safely endure, unless the patients are wearing earplugs.

Also see Chapter 33, MRI: Magnetic Resonance Imaging

Q I had acoustic neuroma surgery that left me deaf in one ear. I now wear a CROS hearing aid. Could the electronics in the CROS aid be the cause of the tinnitus in either or both of my ears?

A It is highly doubtful that the electronics of your CROS (*contralateral routing of signal*) hearing aid could have caused your tinnitus. Tinnitus can result from surgery of this sort. This hearing aid system sends sounds heard on the deaf side over to the good ear through a microphone worn on the deaf ear. The good ear essentially hears for both ears. The electronic component in this hearing aid is the same as in any hearing aid and does not generate enough energy to cause or affect tinnitus. Keep using your hearing aid. In time you will very likely learn to localize sounds. Also, with the CROS hearing aid, you will no longer have to put people on your good-hearing side or be surprised by sudden events that occur on your bad-hearing side.

Q The removal of a tumor on my right eighth nerve has left me completely deaf in that ear. Also, the tinnitus in that ear has gotten significantly louder. Is it common for tinnitus to become louder after eighth nerve surgery? And since I cannot hear in that ear, why do I hear tinnitus in that ear?

A It is not uncommon for tinnitus to appear louder after removal of an eighth nerve tumor. As hearing ability decreases, tinnitus perception often increases. Although you hear the tinnitus in your left (deaf) ear, the tinnitus sound is actually being perceived in your brain. The brain, in turn, is referring a signal of perception back to the ear. This is similar to the phantom limb phenomenon, whereby a person still feels pain in a limb that has been amputated. In this situation, and in yours, the brain is creating the perception.

Q I've heard of a treatment called *masking* that is used to cover up or hide tinnitus. This raises an important question for me: Is it safe to hide the signal of danger?

A No, it is not. Tinnitus can indeed be the signal of a very serious though correctable condition: an eighth nerve tumor (or acoustic neuroma). Eighth nerve tumors are almost always benign and are very slow growing. But slow growing or not, over time this kind of tumor can invade so much of the nerve that it can produce complete deafness. If left to grow, it can even cause death. According to research by Gale Neely, M.D., acoustic neuromas actually invade the eighth nerve.

Tinnitus is also a symptom of thyroid dysfunction, hypertension, allergies, and other physiological problems, some more serious than others. It is always recommended that a person with tinnitus consult with his or her primary care physician and have a thorough physical examination to rule out these health problems before moving on with treatments for the symptom of

tinnitus itself. Sometimes remediation of these health problems will eliminate or dramatically reduce the tinnitus. Other times the tinnitus persists
after the health danger has passed.

Q Several months ago, I removed an acoustic tumor from the left ear of
one of my patients. Initially, he did very well after the surgery despite becoming completely deaf on the operated side. Recently, however, he has
been complaining of tinnitus and is absolutely insistent that the tinnitus
is in the left ear only. In and of itself, this is not too strange. What *is* strange
is that the tinnitus is only present in the presence of noise. At night in bed,
his tinnitus quiets down and goes away almost completely. When he
wakes in the morning, he has no tinnitus at all. But the moment he hears
sound (in his good right ear) his tinnitus returns in the left ear. We have
experimented with him and found that sound introduced into his deaf left
ear does not induce tinnitus in that ear, but sound introduced into his good
right ear does induce tinnitus in the left ear. What a problem! Do you have
any answers or suggestions?

A It is *very* common for a deaf tinnitus patient to hear tinnitus in the deaf
ear. As the right and left auditory nerves travel up from their respective
cochleas to the brain, there are four places along the auditory pathway where
the two nerves and therefore the two ears are directly connected together. So
what is heard in one ear can have an effect in the opposite ear. Overall, the
auditory system is bilaterally arranged. (See Figure 2.1 on page 12.) Taking
advantage of this interconnection, we have introduced masking signals into
the good-hearing non-tinnitus ears of some patients and achieved tinnitus
reduction in their deaf ears because of it. Your patient, however, might try an
earplug in the right ear. This might cause a sufficient level of quiet and con-
sequent tinnitus relief in the left ear.

[The doctor reported back two weeks later: The earplug gave his patient almost complete tinnitus relief.]

Q I have been diagnosed with an eighth nerve tumor behind my right
ear and I'm nervous about having surgery to remove it. I have already lost
hearing on the right side and I have tinnitus. I also admit that I am dizzy
a good part of the day. In fact, I recently fell from the dizziness and broke
my ribs, so I know I must do something. Can the tumor be reduced in size
(it is 19 mm in diameter) by non-invasive treatments like radiation?

A Surgery is the surest way to remove an acoustic neuroma. This kind of mi-
crosurgery requires great skill because the hearing, balance, and facial nerves
are often all affected by the tumor. At one time we thought that these tumors
sat on top of or grew around the auditory nerve. Now we know that these tumors grow as part of the nerve. If the entire tumor is going to be removed, at
least some of the hearing nerve will have to be removed along with it.

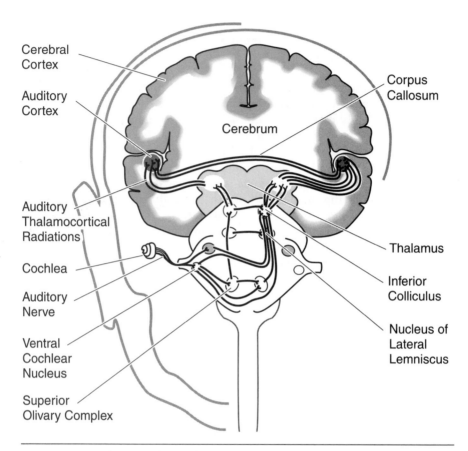

Cerebral Cortex

Auditory Cortex

Corpus Callosum

Cerebrum

Auditory Thalamocortical Radiations

Cochlea

Auditory Nerve

Ventral Cochlear Nucleus

Superior Olivary Complex

Thalamus

Inferior Colliculus

Nucleus of Lateral Lemniscus

FIGURE 2.1   *Auditory pathway, from the cochlea to the auditory cortex.*

The auditory nerve and the vestibular nerve are two branches of the eighth cranial nerve and consequently are intertwined as they leave the inner ear. The fact that you have dizziness and hearing loss means that both parts of the nerve are affected by the tumor. Your particular acoustic neuroma (also called a *vestibular schwannoma*) could either be located close to the inner ear or farther up the nerve path, since it is large enough to involve both the auditory and vestibular branches of the nerve. (See Figure 2.2.)

Some patients experience unwanted aftereffects from acoustic neuroma surgery, such as total deafness on the affected side, mild facial paralysis or tingling, balance problems, a continuation of the tinnitus, or sometimes a worsening of the tinnitus. If tinnitus is present before surgery, it can disappear after surgery. The reverse happens too. If tinnitus is absent before surgery, it might appear after surgery.

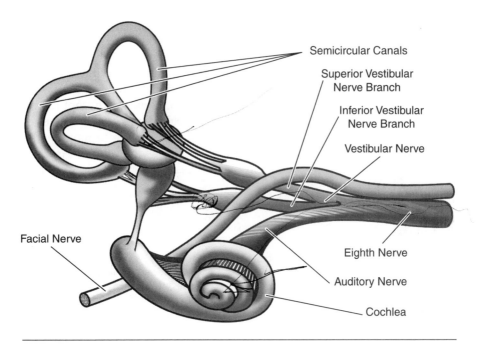

FIGURE 2.2 *Nerves in the inner ear.*

There are other therapies for this condition:

- *Fractionated radiotherapy:* small bursts of radiation given over a period of weeks.

- *Stereotactic radiosurgery:* single-dose precise beams of radiation. One form is gamma knife surgery: targeted beams of gamma rays and not a knife at all (and not surgery per se since no incision is made).

- *Proton beam surgery:* excision of tumors with radiation. In theory, this method involves less surrounding tissue than gamma knife surgery.

These radiation therapies are being used successfully to shrink tumors and correct malformations that had been otherwise inoperable in the conventional sense. But this radiation surgery can trigger its own side effects, from facial paralysis, hearing loss, and tinnitus to creating malignant cells from radiation-resistant benign cells. Research indicates that the smaller acoustic neuromas are more successfully treated with radiation than are the larger ones. Gamma knife surgery appears to offer a better outcome with respect to hearing preservation.

Some patients take a wait-and-see attitude about their acoustic neuromas because these tumors are historically slow growing. The age of the patient is a consideration too. An older patient with a very small tumor might choose to not undergo surgery at all. And it is true that some of these tumors appear to stop growing without outside intervention. Studies that followed those patients who took a wait-and-see approach, however, did not follow the patients' progress beyond a year to get the really long-term outcomes of the approach. If you take this approach, it would be wise to monitor the tumor with an MRI test every few months. The Acoustic Neuroma Association (www.anausa.org) offers a great deal of clear, lay-oriented information about this topic.

Resources _____

Gamma knife radiosurgery (noninvasive brain surgery): www.suttergammaknife.com/brain.html, 2/28/00

Gelfand, S. *Essentials of Audiology,* Thieme Medical Publishers, New York, 1997.

Thomassin, J. M., Epron, J. P., Regis, J., Delsanti, C., Sarabian, A., Peragut, J. C., and Pellet, W. Preservation of hearing in acoustic neuromas treated by gamma knife surgery, *Stereotact. Funct. Neurosurg.,* Oct. 1998; 70 Suppl 1:74–9.

3

Air Bags

Q I've read that our hearing can be damaged by the sound of exploding front air bags. I would imagine that the sound level of exploding air bags is even more dangerous to ears that already have tinnitus. What is the level of the sound produced when side air bags are added? And shouldn't we have the option of turning them off?

A Yes, the sound of inflating air bags is too loud for many healthy human ears to safely tolerate. The noise produced by a single front exploding air bag is estimated to be 160 decibels at the center of the explosion and 130 dB at head level. (Air bags deploy at approximately 200 miles per hour.) The addition of two side air bags to two front air bags can cause the noise inside a car to reach 178 dB. Sounds of this magnitude are far too loud for tinnitus patients, although it helps that the air bag noise is very brief (0.03 second, by one estimate). Keep in mind that a 140-dB sound is right at the human threshold for pain. We know of several patients who have sustained hearing loss, tinnitus, and/or hyperacusis after having been in very minor, very low-speed accidents during which their air bags deployed.

There have been concerted efforts to allow consumers to have air bag on–off switches installed or to give consumers the choice to disconnect air bags. (Many consumers would like to be able to decide if they want the devices installed in a new car at all.) So far, most of these efforts have failed. We suspect that air bag manufacturers have a very powerful lobby in Washington, D.C.

Lots of statistics are bandied about: the number of lives that have been saved because of air bags and the number of lives that have been lost because of air bags. The topic of auditory injuries from air bags is far down the list of those that the government is paying attention to. Moreover, the National Highway Traffic and Safety Administration (NHTSA) has stated that air bags do not cause hearing damage. We have seen differently.

The idea of an air bag on–off switch seems reasonable enough. It could be turned off or on at the drivers' discretion, say, off when driving in town where accidents might not be life threatening and on when driving on freeways.

Despite the fact that seat belts cannot quiet air bags, they can keep passengers pulled somewhat back, which can lessen the physical impact from a deploying air bag. Remember to use your seat belt. And if you want the rules to change, contact your congressional representatives.

Q As a result of an air bag explosion, I have high-pitched tinnitus and high-frequency hearing loss. I have suffered loss of concentration, loss of sleep, and loss of social enjoyment. Can tinnitus produced by an air bag explosion be relieved with masking?

A Undoubtedly, you were exposed to a lot of noise from the air bag. You were also exposed to a violent pressure change during the air bag explosion. It is hard to know which was responsible for the tinnitus. We have found that tinnitus induced by noise exposure is more readily relieved by masking. Tinnitus that is induced by head trauma or ototoxic medications is less readily relieved by masking. But it is never possible to predict in advance if masking will be successful. The only way to find out is to actually try it. Since your tinnitus is bilateral, it is likely that you will need masking devices for both ears.

Q I have tinnitus that I am able to control fairly well. However, I do not want it to get any louder. I have heard of people whose tinnitus was produced by the inflation of the air bag in their automobile. Should I disconnect the air bag in my car?

A People vary enormously in their susceptibility to hearing damage produced by loud sounds. Some people have tough ears; others have tender ears. There is currently no way to know beforehand, that is, before exposure to noise causes hearing damage, which people have which kind of ears. Tinnitus patients, though, are especially susceptible to loud noise exposure and run the risk of having their tinnitus worsened by it.

The federal government currently requires front air bags in all vehicles sold in the United States. Side air bags are still optional equipment. It is not, however, against the law to disconnect your air bag if you can figure out how to do it. Some people have disabled the fuses to their air bags and believe that this is sufficient. However, some air bags have built-in backup triggering mechanisms in case the fuses fail, so fuse disconnection might not solve the problem.

The National Highway Traffic and Safety Administration (www.nhtsa.dot.gov) allows some consumers to obtain permission from the federal government to purchase on–off switches for their air bags. There are four catches:

1. You need to fill out a form and indicate that you have a health problem other than tinnitus, since NHTSA does not recognize the connection between air bags and auditory damage.

2. You might have a very hard time finding a mechanic who will install the device. Many are fearful of liability if you are in an injury accident without an air bag.
3. Car manufacturers have made on–off switches for some but not all models, and car dealers will only install model-specific on–off switches. (Look on this Web site to find the manufacturer-made on–off switch vehicle list: http://www.nhtsa.dot.gov/airbags/manufli.html#sw13)
4. The switches are expensive ($300 to $400 each, installed) and they are good for only one use. (When a switch is in the *off* position and stops an air bag from exploding, the switch itself absorbs the electrical charge and is not functional again.)

Here are some other options:

Airbag Options, Inc.
2331 Gravel
Fort Worth, Texas 76118
877-4ASWITCH
E-mail: jay@airbag.net
Web: www.airbag.net

This company will send a technician to you to install a universal air bag control switch on site. The company requires that the vehicle owner have permission from the NHTSA for the switch. If the owner does not have the proper form from the NHTSA, the company will assist you in filing the appropriate paper work to qualify.

Airbag Service, Inc.
9675 SE 36th Street, #100
Mercer Island, Washington 98040
206-275-9124
Fax: 206-275-4112
E-mail: marketing@airbagservice.com
Web: www.airbagservice.com

Some of this company's U.S. franchises are equipped to install on–off switches and disconnect air bags.

Airbag Systems, Inc.
6110 E. Mockingbird Lane #102–107
Dallas, Texas 75214
800-205-0628
Fax: 214-265-1241
Web: www.airbagsystems.com

This company produces do-it-yourself air bag disconnection kits for your specific year, make, and model of vehicle. They also provide their own design of install-it-yourself on–off switch.

Q I developed hearing loss and tinnitus in both ears immediately following a car accident. Several days later, I noticed that conversations had an unusual sound to me, much like speeded-up speech. My hearing tests show an unusual hearing loss "notch" at 2000 Hz plus high-frequency hearing loss. My tinnitus is a low rumbling sound mixed with a high-pitched ringing sound. Could the deployment of the air bags be the cause of these problems?

A There is no doubt that the deployment of air bags can cause hearing problems, although we don't know for sure that it caused yours. James Saunders, M.D., published a study in 1996 outlining six definitive cases in which air bag deployments caused tinnitus and hearing loss. Some of the subjects also developed problems with disequilibrium.

Kathleen Yaremchuk, M.D., at the Henry Ford Hospital in Detroit, has undertaken a more comprehensive study and so far has collected data from 80 air bag-induced hearing-injured patients. The injuries being studied include tinnitus, hearing loss, and hyperacusis. Yaremchuk points out that air bag-injured people do not always notice their hearing loss immediately and some do not notice it at all. Consequently, she recommends a hearing test for anyone who has been exposed to an air bag deployment. If you want to participate in Yaremchuk's study by completing a questionnaire, contact her at the Henry Ford Hospital, Department of Otolaryngology, 2799 W. Grand Blvd., Detroit, Michigan 48202, 313-916-3282, E-mail: kyaremc1@hfhs.org.

It is possible that the crashing noises from the car accidents themselves cause the hearing damage. It is hard to know for sure in some cases. But in other cases the nature of the accident points to no other cause but the air bags. For example, a woman sustained profound hearing loss as the result of an air bag deployment in a car that bumped a parking median at 7 mph. There was no crash to make a noise.

It is likely that the speeded-up speech you are experiencing is due to your high-frequency hearing loss. If this is the case, *high-frequency emphasis* hearing aids might resolve this problem. If the tinnitus is the main problem, a tinnitus instrument (a combination masker and high-frequency emphasis hearing aid) is recommended. If the low-pitched rumbling is the main problem, it might be possible to customize a tape recording or CD for you. The fact that your hearing loss has recovered somewhat suggests that improvement could continue to the point that corrective measures may not be necessary.

Resources _____

Saunders, J. E. Automobile airbag impulse noise: Otologic symptoms in six patients, *Otolaryngol Head Neck Surg.*, Feb. 1998; 118(2):228–34.

Tabachnick, B. Air bag safety—air bag risk, *Tinnitus Today*, Dec. 1996; 21:4.

4

Alternative Treatments

When anecdotal reports about a drug or a treatment mount, they often get the attention of a researcher or two. With a little funding, the researcher is able to conduct an open study and then a double-blind, placebo-controlled study to prove or disprove the effectiveness of the treatment or the drug. If the treatment or drug is proved to be effective and safe by the standards of the American Medical Association (AMA) and can stand up to the further scrutiny of the U.S. Food and Drug Administration (FDA), it is moved off the *alternative* list and onto the *conventional* list. It is somewhat funny to realize that every accepted therapy of today was, at some point in history, an alternative therapy.

Some treatments, by their very nature, will never make that transition. Take mung beans. As a naturopathic physician once said, when challenged by a medical doctor to prove to his satisfaction that diet positively affected tinnitus, "I'm sorry. We cannot do a double-blind, placebo-controlled study on mung beans." The AMA's research standard ironically and similarly forbids a proof positive association between smoking and lung cancer. The reason is simple: We cannot do a double-blind, placebo-controlled study on smoking. Sometimes common sense needs to fill in the gaps.

In the United States, alternative treatments are those like acupuncture, homeopathy, cranial sacral therapy, and herbal therapies that have not been subjected to the U.S. "gold standard" of research, the double-blind, placebo-controlled study conducted in the United States. Many of these alternative approaches to health care have been studied in double-blinded tests outside the United States.

If you are considering an alternative therapy, investigate the treatment in every way that you can. Ask a medical doctor and a naturopathic physician for advice. If their advice differs, get third and fourth opinions. Go to the library and investigate through the Internet. Remember, though, that the Internet includes Web sites from both ends of the learning curve, from patients seeking advice to universities reporting research outcomes. Use discretion.

Q Lasers are being used for so many medical treatments and surgeries. Has anyone tried to use this technology for tinnitus?

A Lasers have been tried in clinics all over the world for the treatment of tinnitus. They have been tried alone, with IV (intravenous) ginkgo or other infusions, or in conjunction with prescribed weeks at health spas. When the laser therapy was isolated and studied scientifically, it did not appear to yield a positive (or, for that matter, a negative) effect on tinnitus. Low-power lasers (they are called *soft lasers* in Germany) were used on tinnitus patients in Poland, Japan, Germany, and Denmark. Japanese researchers reported some benefit from the laser treatments in an open study for their subjects. A double-blind study might help this approach bear more fruit.

Q I've read about "Transderm Scop" as a treatment for tinnitus. What kind of drug is it and what are the side effects?

A Scopolamine is an antivertigo drug. Transderm Scop is the brand name of a drug and conveyance system combined. Transderm Scop delivers scopolamine to the bloodstream through a patch on the skin (trans = through; derm = skin). A few patients have reported their experiences to us regarding use of this product. When they placed the patches on the mastoid bone (the bone on the side of the head directly behind the ear), their tinnitus was reduced. Some patients experienced unpleasant side effects. One patient was quite bothered by dizziness and dry mouth, although it helped her tinnitus. (She found it interesting that it caused the very symptom, dizziness, that it was designed to subdue.) Her doctor suggested that she cut the patches in half, which would cut the dose in half as well. When she did this, the treatment became manageable for her and the tinnitus was still quieted. Scopolamine is also used to prevent the nausea and vomiting associated with motion sickness. It is a rather strong medication (even when the patches are cut in half) and must be prescribed by a physician.

Q Does taurine play any possible role in the production of tinnitus? And if so, does it provide a possible treatment?

A Taurine is an amino acid that is found in high concentration in the heart, brain, and muscles. The organ of Corti (the part of the cochlea that houses the hair cells) has substantial quantities of it too. Interference with taurine function in the inner ear can lead to hearing deficits, and it is assumed that hearing losses usually have tinnitus as an accompaniment. High alcohol consumption, zinc deficiency, stress, cardiac arrhythmias, diabetes, and other disorders can cause taurine to be lost from the body's tissues.

Eighteen patients submitted to a double-blind placebo crossover trial to test the effects of taurine on their tinnitus. Nine patients were given 1 gram of taurine every day for 2 weeks; the other nine were given a placebo.

After 2 weeks, the taurine patients were given the placebo, and the placebo patients were given the taurine for an additional 2 weeks. (That's the cross-over part.)

Four (22%) of the 18 reported either a slight or a great improvement in their tinnitus with the taurine. No one displayed any negative side effects from it. For a natural chemical about which so little is known, it is surprising that even 22% of the taurine takers experienced tinnitus relief.

Q I read an article about DMSO and tinnitus in the *World Wide Encyclopedia of Natural Healing*. The article claims that 9 of 15 patients treated with DMSO experienced tinnitus relief. Would you recommend that I try this treatment?

A You might have a difficult time trying to purchase DMSO (dimethyl-sulfoxide). That article was published in 1974 and, since then, the FDA has changed its regulations regarding the substance. Stanley Jacob, M. D., at Oregon Health Sciences University, gets the credit for discovering the therapeutic properties of DMSO. In 1962, DMSO was sold as an industrial solvent and cleaner. In the same year, Jacob discovered that DMSO had analgesic properties. He soon learned that it was a free-radical scavenger, that it prevented permanent paralysis in animals with spinal cord injuries, that it reduced brain swelling in patients with head injuries, that it quickly entered the bloodstream through the skin, and that it could take other topically applied drugs with it. Jacob studied it further and found that it helped relieve bursitis and arthritis pain. By the mid 1960s, DMSO was available in health food stores and was nationally heralded as a wonder drug.

In 1965, researchers discovered DMSO's first negative side effect, abnormal changes in the eyes of animals. It was right at that time that the FDA began requiring double-blind placebo trials for all medications, including over-the-counter curatives like DMSO. Unfortunately, DMSO could not be tested in this way due to its very distinctive, very strong garlic odor. The patients (and their doctors and family members and possibly their neighbors) would all know if they were taking DMSO. The DMSO bandwagon in the United States came to a grinding halt.

In 1975, Chilean researcher Aristides Zúñiga Caro conducted the clinical trial to which you refer. In this nondouble-blind study, 15 patients who had had tinnitus for at least 6 months received daily injections of DMSO in combination with lidocaine and other chemicals. Also, once every 4 days, patients received another combination of chemicals that included DMSO. This mixture was sprayed directly into the ear canal. Some patients initially experienced unpleasant side effects, such as rapid heartbeat and heavy headedness, but the symptoms all ended within a few days. After 30 days, 9 out the 15 test subjects claimed that their tinnitus was gone. Two others said that their tinnitus was diminished, and four others said that their tinnitus had become occasional. The patients gave the same reports when they were surveyed a year later. To date, there has been no further study of this compound for its use as a tinnitus relief agent.

In 1978, DMSO was approved by the FDA for the treatment of interstitial cystitis, a painful bladder inflammation. Today, it is available by prescription, but for that condition only. DMSO is prescribed in many countries to treat arthritis and other conditions. It is also available in the United States to veterinary physicians for treating horses and dogs.

Despite DMSO's seemingly limited availability, people are able to acquire it. (We searched the Internet and found a "distributor" in less than 1 minute.) If you do purchase this product, be exceedingly cautious. Industrial-grade DMSO is not the same in purity as the pharmaceutical grade nor is it made under the same production scrutiny. If impure DMSO is applied to the skin, it will carry the impurities into the bloodstream. Be careful.

Q I've heard that there is a new treatment for tinnitus in Israel, but I don't know what it is exactly. I wonder if it involves medicine or devices like maskers. Have you heard from anyone who has gone there and tried it?

A The treatment to which you refer is offered at Hadassah Medical Center's Tinnitus Clinic by Dr. Zecharya Shemesh. It is highly individualized and somewhat hard to describe. We know that it does not involve surgery nor the use of sound devices or the introduction of external sound. We know that each patient is seen by Shemesh, who by all accounts is a kind and caring doctor. And we know that each patient is evaluated with blood tests and medical screenings. Ultimately, as part of this treatment, each patient is given a medicine to compensate for any metabolism deficiency or excess as determined by Shemesh. This is the part of the protocol that is somewhat scary. The patient is never told and cannot find out what the medicine is. After several weeks of evaluation and one-on-one time with Shemesh, the patient goes home. When a refill of the medicine is needed, Shemesh mails an unmarked bottle of pills to the patient. Are they homeopathic drugs? Antianxiety drugs? The medical peril of such a practice is mind-boggling. Shemesh has said that the Israeli government does not allow him to reveal the details of the protocol.

A few people have told us that the treatment in Israel helped them with their tinnitus. We have also heard from a few people who said that they enjoyed the time they spent with Shemesh in Israel, but felt that their tinnitus was no better because of it. When this treatment becomes known for the world to study and try, then there will be more to discuss.

Q When I was in Germany recently, I was seen by a Professor Rodegra who treats tinnitus with hyperbaric oxygen. He claimed that this treatment increases the circulation of blood in the ears. I didn't have enough time on my trip to actually have the treatment. Is there a hyperbaric oxygen chamber anywhere in the United States where I can try this treatment?

A   Yes and no. You can contact the Undersea & Hyperbaric Medical Society (301–942–2980, www.uhms.org) and they will direct you to a nearby hyperbaric oxygen (HBO) facility. However, Leon J. Greenbaum, Jr., Ph.D., their executive director, is quick to advise that there are no acceptable data to support the use of HBO to treat tinnitus and that it is not a reimbursable treatment in the United States (meaning that the expense will be the patient's alone). Nevertheless, a few physicians will probably treat tinnitus patients with HBO, even though it is not approved for that use.

During hyperbaric oxygen therapy, the patient rests in a sealed chamber. The air in the HBO chamber slowly changes from the normal mix of gases that we breathe (with 21% oxygen) to 100% oxygen. The air pressure in the chamber is then increased to two to three times normal. Although this pressurization happens slowly, it can cause ear discomfort. The depressurization process is also done at a gradual rate.

HBO treatment is used for crush injuries, decompression sickness from scuba diving, carbon monoxide poisoning, and several other conditions. (Williard C. Harrill, M.D., from Baylor College of Medicine, suggests that hyperbaric oxygen therapy can itself *cause* barotrauma to the inner ear.) As for tinnitus, HBO therapy has been evaluated in several clinics outside the United States. Patients who had had hearing loss or tinnitus for more than 3 months at the time of HBO treatment had less positive results than patients whose tinnitus or hearing loss was more recently acquired. In one German study, 6.7% of patients who had had tinnitus for less than 3 months experienced "excellent" improvement and 44.3% expressed noticeable improvement with HBO therapy.

Q   **I have been taking *Ginkgo biloba*, 160 mg per day, and it has helped my tinnitus. How long can I continue taking ginkgo and are there any side effects from taking it?**

A   Tens of thousands of people take *Ginkgo biloba* to relieve their tinnitus. Untold numbers of people have used it through the ages. (It has been used in Chinese medicine for at least 5000 years.) Today it is estimated that millions around the world use ginkgo for circulatory ailments, including dementia and Alzheimer's disease.

There is one rare side effect that in certain cases can be serious. Because ginkgo has a blood-thinning property, it might alter bleeding time, especially if it is taken along with coumadin, high doses of aspirin, or other blood-thinning medications. If you are taking any of these drugs, ask your doctor to give you a bleeding-time test. If the results are normal, there should be little concern about taking this herb, although it is probably best not to take two blood-thinning agents at the same time.

Years ago, tinnitus patients began reporting tinnitus relief when they took ginkgo. Several open trials were started, one notably by Dr. Ross Coles in England in 1986. This trial seemed promising, and so a 30-patient placebo study was initiated. But the results of the study did not overwhelmingly point to ginkgo as a useful tinnitus relief agent.

Another open trial began in 1991 by Susan Seidel, an audiologist, tinnitus patient, and tinnitus self-help group leader in Maryland. When Seidel asked her group members if they would be interested in taking *Ginkgo biloba* as part of an open trial for tinnitus relief, 50 people in her group agreed to try it. Hundreds more joined in over the years.

In 1999, Seidel examined the data. Six hundred and thirty patients in her study took 120 mg (40 mg three times per day) of *Ginkgo biloba* (24% ginkgoflavonoids extract). Patients took the herb daily for an average of 3 years. Each participant completed a tinnitus severity and quality of life survey before starting the ginkgo and another survey after having taken ginkgo for 3 months. Patients ranked their experiences on a scale of 1 to 10. On average, both the tinnitus severity ratings and the quality of life ratings improved by two notches. Seidel's 630 study participants continue to take the herb because they say it helps them feel better and sleep better. These comments are, of course, anecdotal and not specific to tinnitus. But their comments are consistent with those we have heard from many other patients over the years.

In 1999, researchers Drew and Davies conducted a double-blind, placebo-controlled study on ginkgo at the Medical School in Birmingham, England. This extensive, yearlong, 1115-patient study showed that ginkgo had no greater therapeutic effect than the placebo for tinnitus relief. Many people were helped and not helped by the ginkgo, and many were helped and not helped by the placebo. On the other hand, the researchers also note that, out of the approximately 540 patients in the study who took 50-mg ginkgo tablets three times a day (150-mg daily total) for 12 weeks, there were essentially no adverse responses to the herb. Therefore, the researchers feel that it is safe for patients to take ginkgo if they are in reasonably good health and not taking antithrombotic medication.

Drew and Davies offer this additional observation. In a recent study, ginkgo was shown to be effective for short-term memory loss when it was given in single 120-mg daily doses, but *not* effective when given in divided doses of 50 mg three times per day. Perhaps we would see more success with ginkgo for tinnitus if it were studied using different dosing schedules.

Q **It's the strangest thing, but I get tinnitus relief from using a heating pad around my neck. Do you know why that is?**

A The heating pad does a great deal to relieve stress and tension—not only muscle stress and tension, but psychological stress and tension too. We know that some people can make their tinnitus worse by physically tensing their necks, jaws, and other extremities. When you lie down and relax with (or without) the heating pad, you are working on stress reduction, which is probably contributing to your tinnitus reduction.

In a nonplacebo research study, 26 tinnitus patients were given an unspecified relaxation therapy. Prior to the treatment, the patient's mood was evaluated and the tinnitus loudness and annoyance levels were assessed. The goal was to help patients passively accept their tinnitus, rather than to actively resist it. Nine of these patients (35%) reported significant tinnitus improvement with relaxation techniques. Perhaps if the therapy had been combined with a soothing sound stimulus the success rate would have been higher.

Q I have recently heard about a special enzyme that is recommended for the relief of tinnitus. What is the name of this enzyme and how does one use it?

A The enzyme formula is called Wobenzyme-N (named for the inventors of the therapy, Wolf and Benitez) and was identified by Michael Schedler, M.D., a German ear, nose, and throat specialist as a treatment for tinnitus. It is available over the counter in the United States and by prescription in Germany. Wobenzyme-N contains trypsin (48 mg), chymotrypsin (2 mg), bromelain (90 mg), papain (120 mg), pancreatin (200 mg), and rutin (100 mg) derived from plant and animal sources. The primary action of these combined enzymes is as an anti-inflammatory agent.

When Schedler originally tried this combination of enzymes for his own shoulder pain, he noticed that it not only alleviated his pain, but also quieted his longstanding tinnitus. He tested the compound on his tinnitus patients, but he did not place a double-blind placebo control on the study and has, to date, only anecdotal information about it. Schedler reports that 50% to 60% of his patients had a reduction of their tinnitus while using the enzymes.

Schedler recommends that tinnitus patients take ten Wobenzyme-N tablets with a glass of water three times a day on an empty stomach. He has observed that for some people as few as two to three tablets three times a day can work. In any case, it is best to start at the lower daily dose and work your way up. Schedler notes that it can take 3 to 4 weeks before relief will occur. This product is currently sold over the counter in the United States and can be ordered from Naturally Vitamins (1-888-4Vitamin, www.naturallyvitamins. com).

Note that, as of this writing, the claims about Wobenzyme are just claims. We have written to Schedler for further information about the testing of this product but have not heard back from him. We hope that this anti-inflammatory product will be properly studied for its usefulness in relieving tinnitus.

Q I've heard about acupuncture, but I don't know what it is. Can you explain it?

A Acupuncture treatment involves the insertion of very small needles under the skin at certain points in the body. This treatment is intended to correct the flow of the body's life force, or Qi (pronounced "chee"), which the Chinese believe is responsible for our health and well-being. The Chinese have identified more than 400 meridian points on the body where the pathway of the Qi comes to the surface.

Acupuncture treatments will likely not hurt you. (Remember that this treatment has been used in China for more than 2500 years.) The U.S. government's National Center for Complementary and Alternative Medicine has funded research to study acupuncture further. As is the case regarding most tinnitus treatments, we have heard from several patients who found acupuncture helpful for relief of tinnitus and from several patients who said it was ineffective.

Swedish researcher Alf Axelsson studied 20 male tinnitus patients for 16 weeks. He tested their response to acupuncture with and without electrostimulation. In this study, all patients thought they were getting the full treatment. When the electrical stimulation was taking place, a light went on where the patients could see it. The light was rigged to go on even when the electricity was not turned on for the placebo group. This might be as close to a placebo study on acupuncture as can be done.

The results of the study: More patients preferred the acupuncture with the electrostimulation than without it. One patient dropped out of the study after the first week because he experienced longstanding improvement after one treatment with the electrostimulation and acupuncture. Some patients also responded favorably to the placebo (non-electric) acupuncture.

Q I've read that there is new objective evidence that acupuncture is effective in relieving pain. In as much as both pain and tinnitus can be phantom sensations, wouldn't it be reasonable to try acupuncture to relieve tinnitus?

A The article you mentioned discussed some compelling evidence about acupuncture as a relief-giving treatment for pain. This report was originally made at a 1999 meeting of the Radiological Society of North America. A research team headed by Dr. Huey-Jen Lee, from the University of Medicine and Dentistry of New Jersey, produced light pain in the upper lip of 12 patients. The researchers then used acupuncture to reduce the pain sensation. The patients' responses were measured with fMRI (functional magnetic resonance imaging), which depicts neurological events as they occur in the brain. When these patients were experiencing pain, parts of their brains appeared to light up when viewed with fMRI. (This is nearly identical to the Buffalo study on tinnitus patients whose brains lit up during the tinnitus experience when viewed with PET scans.)

Following the acupuncture, the researchers reported that the patients' pain had subsided to varying degrees. The report also indicated that the relief was greater when light electrical stimulation was employed along with the acupuncture.

[Q] I read about Dr. John's Special Ear Drops, which contain glycerine, water, isopropyl alcohol, niacin, shark oil, extract of ginger, ginkgo, echinacea root, chrysanthemum, lycci berries, myrrh oil, garlic oil, and zinc. Is it safe for me to put these drops in my ears? And if I put them in there, where do they go?

[A] Three of the substances included in the drops (ginkgo, niacin, and zinc) have produced some anecdotal relief of tinnitus when taken orally. So far, though, there has been no study on this liquid preparation of herbs for tinnitus relief.

The eardrum is not permeable, so substances cannot seep through it to the other side and into the middle ear cavity. However, the eardrum is vascular. So there is bound to be some absorption of the herbal preparation into the bloodstream through the eardrum. The amount of ginkgo, niacin, and zinc in the drops is a fraction of the amount needed orally to produce an effect.

The ear canal is a somewhat confined place. Its average length is 2.57 cm. The canal begins at the outside of the ear and ends at the eardrum or tympanic membrane. Along the walls of the ear canal are small glands that produce earwax to keep insects and other foreign matter from reaching and damaging the eardrum. When there is a middle ear infection, it is the eardrum that hurts.

We have heard from one patient who said that the drops quieted his tinnitus. This might have happened as a result of the drops loosening some clogged earwax that had been touching the eardrum. It is hard to say what effect the drops could have had. We have also heard from 12 patients who said that the drops did not help their tinnitus. And we have heard no reports of worsened tinnitus as a result of these drops.

[Q] Can minerals affect tinnitus? I've read specifically about zinc and magnesium for tinnitus relief. Can these minerals really help my ringing? If so, how much of them should I take?

[A] Zinc is found in high concentration in the inner ear, which might be why researchers continue to test its usefulness for hearing disorders. Researcher G. E. Shambaugh decided to study zinc for its effect on tinnitus. He discovered that, out of a group of 115 tinnitus patients, 79 (69%) patients were zinc deficient. When these 79 zinc-deficient individuals were given zinc supplements, 12 (15%) patients had a marked reduction of their tinnitus and 29 (37%) patients reported some tinnitus relief.

Concurrently, Japanese researchers, Ochi et al., found that the blood zinc levels of 121 tinnitus patients were quite low. When these patients were given 34 to 68 mg of zinc per day for 2 weeks, their blood zinc levels were significantly higher and their subjective degree of tinnitus was significantly lower. The recommended dietary allowance (RDA) for zinc is 15 mg per day, although other sources recommend 50 mg of zinc per day for optimal health.

Magnesium is an interesting mineral as it relates to the ear. Israeli researcher J. Attias et al. studied the effect of noise exposure on 300 normal-hearing military recruits. Half of these soldiers took 167 mg of magnesium daily for 2 months. The other half took a placebo. All this occurred during repeated noise exposure. The magnesium group experienced significantly less hearing loss and less severe hearing loss when it did occur than did the placebo group. Tinnitus was not measured in this study. However, we have heard from patients who experienced tinnitus relief when they took magnesium supplements.

Q Sometimes I think I notice a difference in my tinnitus—sometimes it's better, sometimes it's worse—when I eat different foods. How does my diet affect my hearing?

A Our diet affects all aspects of our health. For example:

- Diets too rich in fats not only make us gain weight, but they can cause arteries to clog and our circulation to be compromised.
- When we are under unusual stress, we use up our stores of B vitamins. A deficiency of these vitamins has been associated with a variety of neurological problems, including tinnitus. A study in Israel demonstrated that people exposed to extreme loud noise and who had vitamin B_{12} deficiencies were more inclined to experience noise-induced hearing loss and noise-induced tinnitus.
- Monosodium glutamate (MSG), a food additive, depletes vitamin B_6 from our bodies and is a common allergen.

According to Rich Barrett, a naturopathic physician, sufficient nutrition is more of a problem in older patients who tend to have less efficient absorption capacity and a less adequate diet than younger patients. He has had patients whose sensorineural hearing loss improved with zinc supplementation to their diets. (Zinc picolinate is a more absorbable form.) Zinc is especially useful for older patients, he believes, particularly if they have a loss of taste and smell, which is a sign of zinc deficiency.

Barrett and fellow naturopath Rita Bettenburg treat tinnitus patients, but not just for their tinnitus. "The whole person must be treated. It is the basis of naturopathic philosophy," says Battenburg. Naturopathic treatments aim to increase the patients' nutritional status and circulation and to tone the nervous system. And sometimes it helps the tinnitus. Other times it does not.

When tinnitus patients seek help, Barrett and Bettenburg recommend a specific diet:

- Low-fat, low-sugar, high-complex-carbohydrate diet
- Protein not to exceed 12% to 15% of the daily diet

- Vegetarian cleansing or a short fast
- Inclusion of sesame seeds, black beans, celery, oyster shell, pearl barley, adzuki beans, yams, lotus seeds, chestnuts, and grapes
- Avoidance of spices, alcohol, and coffee

They also use a variety of herbal medicines, including ginkgo biloba (they prefer the tincture, a liquid form); supplements such as vitamins A and D; omego-3 fatty acids, magnesium, zinc, and calcium; and a variety of homeopathic aids, the choices of which depend on how the patient describes the tinnitus symptom. (If the tinnitus is louder in the morning, then one homeopathic medicine is prescribed. If the tinnitus is associated with headaches and sensitivity to noise, then a different homeopathic medicine is prescribed.)

If you are allergic to a specific food, your tinnitus could respond negatively to its consumption. You can do an elimination–challenge diet to test the suspected food. (For 7 to 14 days, you limit your foods to those that are the least likely food allergens. You then reintroduce foods one at a time and monitor your reaction to them. This is best done with the guidance of a physician, medical or naturopathic.) If consuming a certain food causes the tinnitus to get louder and the elimination of that food from your diet causes the tinnitus to get quieter, then by all means do not eat that food!

Q **Has anyone tried Chinese medicine (tinctures, decoctions, herbs) for tinnitus, that is, besides the Chinese?**

A As a matter of fact, tinnitus researchers in China compared the effects of Western medicines such as valium, nicotinic acid, B vitamins, and carbamazepine with traditional Chinese medicines including Rhizoma Gastrodiae, Ramulus Uncariae cum Uncis, Poriae Cocos, Flos Chrysanthemi, Radix Polygoni Multiflori, Fructus Liquidambris, Radix Rehmanniae, Rhizoma Alismatis, Radix Scrophulariae, Fructus Lycii, Radix Glycyrrhizae, Semen Plantaginis, and Semen Vaccariae.

The researchers gave 32 patients alternating doses of the Chinese medicines and the Western medicines. A control group of 27 tinnitus patients were given the western medicines only. Of the 32 Chinese–Western medicine patients, 11 (34.4%) reported an absence of tinnitus, 16 (50%) said they were improved, and five (15.6%) reported no tinnitus relief. Of the 27 Western medicine-only patients, five (18.6%) reported an absence of tinnitus, 10 (37%) were improved, and 12 (44.4%) reported no tinnitus relief.

Tempting as it might be to go to the health food store and purchase these preparations ourselves, we need to remember that these herbs are in fact drugs and that their healing powers lie in their being properly combined and prescribed. In the United States, naturopathic physicians dispense Chinese medicines.

Q Can homeopathy offer help for my tinnitus? I've tried everything else.

A Researchers in England wanted to know the answer to this question. So in 1995 they conducted a double-blind placebo crossover study to test the effectiveness of a homeopathic preparation called Tinnitus manufactured by Natura, Pretoria South Africa. The ingredients of this preparation are sodium salicylate *(Natrum salicylicum)*, ascaridole *(Chenopodium anthelminticum)*, conine *(Conium maculatum)*, and quinine *(Chininum salicylicum)*, all at a dilution of D60. Homeopathic preparations are always very dilute.

Only 28 patients participated in the study, which in hindsight could have limited the usefulness of the test results, or so the researchers thought. Nevertheless, the results showed that the homeopathic product was significantly more likely than the placebo to produce tinnitus relief. (Six out of the 28 responded favorably to the homeopathic preparation; none out of 28 responded favorably to the placebo.) While this preparation was not helpful for a majority of the tinnitus patients, the researchers concluded that it was probably effective enough to warrant further research, if not of the specific preparation itself, then of certain components of the remedy.

Q I received a letter about Tinnitabs™, a "natural formula" for the relief of tinnitus. Do you have any comments to make about this so-called "amazing" product?

A The letter is actually an advertisement for Tinnitabs. The statements about tinnitus relief are from the author's own experience, not from actual research. The product contains five natural homeopathic ingredients that are intended to trigger the natural healing processes in the body. According to the letter, a bottle of 250 tablets costs $19.95 with a money-back guarantee. Tinnitabs is available by mail order from the distributor, Vital Choice Products. The product's active ingredients (in a lactose base) are the following:

Chininum salicylicum, 6X	*Phosphorus*, 12X
Hydrofluoricum acidum, 12X	*Platinum metallicum*, 30X
Kali bromatum, 6X	

We asked Vital Choice Products why these five substances were chosen. They stated that the ingredients were selected from the U.S. (homeopathic) Pharmacopoeia's thousands of listings, 200 of which are noted specifically to help tinnitus. All substances listed in this reference are considered safe when they are taken individually. It is also commonplace to mix homeopathic substances, and the resulting combination products are generally considered to be problem free. Boericke and Tafel, the manufacturer of Tinnitabs, confirms that this particular combination of homeopathic ingredients was not double-blind placebo tested prior to its distribution as Tinnitabs.

Tinnitabs has been listed with the U.S. Food and Drug Administration (FDA), which neither gives nor denies approval to any homeopathic drug or drug combination. We asked them why, and they admitted it is because they have very limited resources to monitor these products. They are also not concerned about the safety of these ingredients because they are usually very dilute. Consequently, Tinnitabs and other homeopathic substances can be marketed to the public in the U.S. without having to submit to the FDA's review or testing processes, which *is* required for new over-the-counter and prescription drugs.

But does Tinnitabs work for tinnitus? So far, we have heard from one patient who said that it helped and from several patients who said that it did not help. No one has reported that it made tinnitus worse.

Q I have read that Cimicifuga 6C four times a day helps tinnitus. I've also heard that Carbo vegetabilis 6C helps tinnitus. Do you know anything about either of these preparations? Are they safe and do they work?

A These are two more homeopathic substances cited as tinnitus relief agents. As millions of people do, we paged through the Internet and came across several sites that offer homeopathic, naturopathic, and prescription medicines for sale. One site, www.MotherNature.com, sells both Cimicifuga (black cohosh) and Carbo vegetabilis along with other homeopathics for tinnitus. These products are more than likely safe. The only concern is that the company touts these substances as "sure" alternatives to the frustrating problem of tinnitus. Be cautious about any product, service, medication, or therapy that bills itself as a sure solution.

Q Can niacin help my tinnitus?

A In the early days of modern tinnitus treatment (the 1960s), niacin was the treatment of choice for tinnitus. Niacin (also known as vitamin B_3) is a peripheral blood vessel dilator. When taking it, you will probably flush and blush to a considerable degree, a natural and harmless reaction. It is easy to imagine that when a niacin taker blushed he or she thought that the chemicals were getting into the head region, and more specifically into the region of the ear and the tinnitus. A placebo effect might be at play with this substance. However, when tinnitus patients used nonflush niacin, a few also said that it helped to bring their tinnitus noises down.

Michael Seidman, M.D., is an ENT physician at the Henry Ford Hospital who has done considerable study of alternative and complementary therapies for tinnitus. He concedes that there is no clinical proof that niacin works to quiet tinnitus, nor is there an agreed upon standard dose to take for tinnitus relief. Still, some people report relief with it, so he suggests that patients follow this protocol: Begin with one 50-mg tablet twice a day for 2 weeks. If there is no improvement, increase the dosage to 100 mg twice a day for 2 weeks until a maximum of 500 mg twice a day is reached at 3 to 4 months. If the tinnitus does not respond to this niacin regimen, then the niacin should be discontinued. (Doses of niacin above 1000 mg per day can cause liver damage.)

Seidman does not recommend the use of nonflush niacin over standard niacin because of a greater incidence of liver problems.

Q **Can you comment on the auditory training for autism and how it is used for tinnitus relief?**

A In auditory training, the clinician determines which pitches (or tones) are most disturbing to the autistic patient. These pitches are filtered out of recordings of speech and music. (Autistic patients seem to favor Mozart's music.) Then these filtered recordings are repeatedly played to the autistic patients in an attempt to reach their balance mechanism through the inner ear and enhance their balance and coordination. Auditory training therapy was developed by Alfred Tomatis, M.D. Auditory integration therapy, a variation, was developed by Guy Bérard, M.D.

Do autistic children have tinnitus? Many are verbal enough to indicate that they do. Many more are supersensitive to sounds and sometimes display discomfort in only moderately noisy environments. Audiologist and auditory training specialist Judith Belk, Ph.D., says that music therapy has not been used specifically for tinnitus although it probably would be soothing.

The term *auditory training* is also used by those who teach techniques and tips to hearing-impaired people—techniques like lip reading and tips like asking for the topic that's being discussed so that one can better follow the conversation. This is not the same auditory training!

For more information about autism, see Chapter 27, Hyperacusis.

References _____

Axelsson, A., Andersson, A., and Gu, L.-D. Acupuncture in the management of tinnitus: A placebo controlled study, *Proceedings of the Fifth International Tinnitus Seminar,* Reich, G. E., and Vernon, J. A., eds., American Tinnitus Association, Portland, OR, 1996.

Balch, J. F., and Balch, P. *Prescription for Nutritional Healing,* Avery Publishing Group, Garden City Park, NY, 1997.

Barrett, R. A naturopathic treatment of tinnitus, *Proceedings of the Fifth International Tinnitus Seminar,* Reich, G. E., and Vernon, J. A., eds., American Tinnitus Association, Portland, OR, 1996.

Bensky, D., Gamble, A., and Kaptchuk, T. *Chinese Herbal Medicine-Materia Medica,* Eastland Press, Seattle, 1986.

Bettenburg, R. Introduction to naturopathic treatment, *Proceedings of the Fifth International Tinnitus Seminar,* Reich, G. E., and Vernon, J. A., eds., American Tinnitus Association, Portland, OR, 1996.

Cook, A., ed. *Alternative Medicine Sourcebook,* Omnigraphics, Detroit, 1999.

Drew, S. J., and Davies, W. E. *Ginkgo biloba* in the treatment of tinnitus: Preliminary results of a double-blinded placebo-controlled trial involving 1115 subjects, *Proceedings of the Sixth International Tinnitus Seminar,* Hazell, J., ed., Tinnitus and Hyperacusis Centre, London, 1999.

Habets, B. *The Tinnitus Handbook, A Self-Help Guide,* United Research Publishers, Encinitas, CA, 1996.

Harding, N. J., Donaldson, I., and Davies, W. E. Taurine and its potential in the treatment of tinnitus, *Tinnitus 91—Proceedings of the Fourth International Tinnitus Seminar*, Aran, J. M., and Dauman, R., eds., Kugler Publications, New York, 1991.

Kau, R. J., Sendtner-Gress, K., Ganzer, U., and Arnold, W. Effectiveness of hyperbaric oxygen therapy in patients with acute and chronic cochlear disorders, *ORL J. Otorhinolaryngol Relat. Spec.*, Mar.–Apr. 1997; 59(2):79–83.

Mirz, F., Zachariae, R., Andersen, S. E., Nielsen, A. G., Johansen, L. V., Bjerring, P., and Pedersen, C. B. The low-power laser in the treatment of tinnitus, *Clin Otolaryngol.*, Aug. 1999; 24(4):346–54.

Ochi, K., Ohashi, T., Kinoshita, H., Akagi, M., Kikuchi, H., Mitsui, M., Kaneko, T., and Kato, I. The serum zinc level in patients with tinnitus and the effect of zinc treatment, *Nippon Jibiinkoka Gakkai Kaiho*, Sept. 1997; 100(9):915–9.

Rogowski, M., Low-power laser in the treatment of tinnitus—a placebo-controlled study, *Otolaryngol Pol.*, 1999; 53(3):315–20.

Seidel, S. Ginkgo—More fact than fiction!, *Proceedings of the Sixth International Tinnitus Seminar*, Hazell, J., ed., Tinnitus and Hyperacususis Centre, London, 1999.

Shiomi, Y., Takahashi, H., Honjo, I., Kojima, H., Naito, Y., and Fujiki, N. Efficacy of transmeatal low power laser irradiation on tinnitus: A preliminary report, *Auris Nasus Larynx*, 1997; 24(1):39–42.

Yang, D. J. Tinnitus treated with combined traditional Chinese medicine and Western medicine, *Chung Hsi I Chieh Ho Tsa Chih.*, May 1989; 9(5):270–1, 259–60.

5

Barometric Changes:
The Effect of Changing
Air Pressure on Tinnitus

Q Is there any information about the effect of altitude on tinnitus? I now live in Kansas, but I'm anticipating a move to Colorado.

A Some time ago we conducted a study in which we deliberately altered the pressure in the ear canal of 639 tinnitus patients. For 128 (20%) patients, the decreased air pressure produced a change in the perceived tinnitus. The tinnitus was reduced for 108 (17%) of these patients; the tinnitus was exacerbated for 20 (3%).

As for where we live relative to sea level, the higher the elevation, the lower the barometric air pressure. So moving to the higher altitude in Colorado might help you. We recommend a trip to the anticipated locale first to see if the altitude change has any effect on your tinnitus.

Q Can weather conditions affect tinnitus? My tinnitus fluctuates rather markedly, and the fluctuations seem to be related to the weather conditions.

A There is one patient who was so adamant about his tinnitus and weather conditions that we asked him to keep written records of the intensity of his tinnitus. He charted it through various weather conditions, such as relative humidity, temperature, wind, and rain. After keeping records for more than 7 months, he found a relationship between his tinnitus intensity and changes in the weather. Interestingly, the relationship appeared to be related to the presence of a change and not to the presence of any particular weather condition.

Q I've noticed that anytime it is cold and humid my tinnitus goes up in intensity. Conversely, anytime it is hot and dry my tinnitus is reduced sometimes to total absence. Do heat and humidity really affect tinnitus?

A Several tinnitus patients have concluded that outside temperature and humidity do have a great deal to do with their tinnitus. However, since the ear is a pressure detector, not a detector of temperature or humidity, we suspect that the reason your tinnitus is affected by weather is due to pressure changes. If you plan to record weather conditions that occur during your tinnitus fluctuations, be sure to note barometric pressure levels and the direction of the changes (high to low or low to high). You might want to spend extended time in a desert location to test the observation.

6

Biofeedback

Q What is biofeedback and how does it work in the management of tinnitus?

A Biofeedback is a training technique by which we can learn to alter our blood pressure, muscle tension, heart rate, and other bodily functions that are not normally within our control. This is accomplished at first with devices that measure electrical signals from the muscles, sweat gland activity, skin temperature, brainwave activity, and heart rate. The goal of biofeedback is for the patient to learn how to relax tense muscles and to relax in general for overall good health.

Electrodes are attached from the electromyograph and thermal biofeedback device to the patient's forehead and neck. The electromyograph biofeedback instrument measures the electrical activity of muscles as they contract. It then converts the electrical signals from the muscles and translates them into visible or audible signals, a flashing light or a beeping tone, for the patient to observe. The flashes or beeps are synchronous with the frequency of muscle contractions.

The thermal biofeedback instrument measures skin temperature. When we are under stress, our blood vessels become constricted and our skin temperature is cool. Thermal biofeedback training helps people overcome this response, decrease their blood vessel constriction, and ultimately increase their skin temperature. Eventually, patients learn to control their muscle tension, heart rate, and skin temperature when they are not hooked up to the devices. This enables them to achieve a relaxed state when they need to. Biofeedback training can also teach people to control their heart rates, sweat gland activity, and even brainwave activity.

But does this help tinnitus? It can. The most notable positive effect has been the improvement in some patients' ability to sleep. In a study conducted in Israel, 43.5% of tinnitus patients who received biofeedback therapy reported improved sleep versus less than 5% of the control group in the study. Another study conducted in Sweden demonstrated mood improvement and tinnitus relief as a result of biofeedback training. Patients who were most likely to respond to this therapy were those with normal hearing, jaw fatigue, low-severity tinnitus, fluctuating tinnitus, and those with nighttime bruxism (teeth grinding).

Resources

Dobie, R. A review of randomized clinical trials in tinnitus, *Laryngoscope,* Aug. 1999; 109.

Erlandsson, S. I., Rubinstein, B., and Carlsson, S. G. Tinnitus: Evaluation of biofeedback and stomatognathic treatment, *Br. J. Audiol.,* Jun. 1991; 225(3):151–61.

Podoshin, L., Ben-David, Y., Fradis, M., Gerstel, R., and Felner, H. Idiopathic subjective tinnitus treated by biofeedback, acupuncture and drug therapy, *Ear Nose Throat J.,* May 1991; 70(5):284–9.

The Brain's Involvement
in Tinnitus

Q Since tinnitus is a symptom similar to pain, why not treat tinnitus with pain medication?

A Pain is a signal that something is wrong in the body. Severe tinnitus is also a signal that something is wrong, often in the auditory system and maybe elsewhere in the body as well. Pain and tinnitus are very much alike in this regard. Pain and tinnitus have something else in common. Both are perceived because certain areas in the brain have been triggered to express that perception.

Pain medication is designed to target and quiet the brain's many pain centers. Now, if it turns out that the brain center responsible for tinnitus is also the brain center responsible for the perception of pain, then the use of a pain medication might be helpful for tinnitus.

Q Why do some medical professionals consider tinnitus to be the same as pain? I know I can differentiate between these two things!

A They probably do not consider pain and tinnitus to be the same thing any more than we do. They might be looking at these two phenomena as neurological events. In this context, both of these events are phantom sensations. Consider the experience of those who still feel pain in amputated limbs. That is an example of a phantom sensation. Tinnitus is not a real "sound" event stimulated by external sound energy. Therefore, it is a phantom sensation.

Researcher Aage Møller, Ph.D., compared the pathophysiology (or what could be physically wrong) in cases of severe tinnitus and chronic pain. He believes that these two events, pain and tinnitus, are both caused by changes in the central nervous system as a consequence of the plasticity (changeability) of the central nervous system. This means that the brain can alter its function either because of specific input or because of a deprivation of input. In either case, the result can be chronic pain or chronic tinnitus.

Q **Do we know anything about the biochemistry of tinnitus, or is tinnitus assumed to be an event that only involves the nervous system?**

A Chemical changes take place in the body when the nervous system is active. However, we don't quite know where one event (the chemical change) leaves off and the other event (the nervous system activation) begins. We don't even know if one event is the result of the other.

Regarding tinnitus, it is well known that exposure to loud sounds can produce tinnitus. It is also known that exposure to loud sounds produces an increase in brain activity in the dorsal cochlear nucleus, one of the structures along the auditory pathway to the brain. However, when this was studied, no chemical changes were found. We would have expected to see some alteration in amino acid or oxidative energy metabolism, changes that normally occur in the brain during neural activity.

Q **I've noticed an increase in references to the brain regarding tinnitus. This really makes sense, since it's highly likely that all sensations ultimately end up in the brain. If this is the case, doesn't it then make sense to attempt to relieve tinnitus by treating the brain in some way?**

A It clearly does. William Martin, Ph.D., from Oregon Health Sciences University, conducted a very interesting study along these lines. A surgical procedure was done to relieve movement-disorder symptoms like those of Parkinson's disease. In this surgery, electrodes were implanted in deep brain tissue (the *medial nucleus* or mid-thalamus) in 30 patients. After surgery, all 30 patients were able to control their previously uncontrollable movement disorders by activating the implanted deep brain stimulator with remote control devices.

The patients were then sent questionnaires that asked if they had hearing loss and/or tinnitus. Eight of the 30 patients responded that they had hearing loss, but that activation of the implants did not change their hearing in any way. Seven of the eight also reported that they had tinnitus. And three of the seven indicated that they experienced a marked reduction in the loudness of their tinnitus when they activated the deep brain electrode. (The other four patients noted no improvement in their tinnitus when they activated the electrodes.)

We would not have guessed beforehand that a deep brain electrode implant in the thalamus would have had an impact, let alone a major impact, on tinnitus. The auditory cortex, not the thalamus, would seem to have been the correct target. And it still might be. But it is clearly not the only target.

Learning more about the brain, we realize that placing electrodes in the thalamus is not really a farfetched idea. All sensory stimuli, with the exception of odors, are processed through the thalamus before they are directed to their respective parts of the brain. For example, visual signals go through the thalamus on their way to the visual cortex, and auditory signals go through the thalamus on their way to the auditory cortex.

Another new study might shed light on the connection between tinnitus and the thalamus. Rudolfo Llinas, M.D., Ph.D., from New York University Medical School, presented a new theory about neurological disorders and their origins. He believes that two parts of the brain (the thalamus and the cerebral cortex) normally fire their electrical impulses in a synchronous way. But when these two parts of the brain are out of phase with each other, disorders like Parkinson's, severe depression, and tinnitus appear. To test this theory, a surgery was developed to implant electrodes into the thalamus of a patient with severe depression. This permanent pacemaker-like implant was directed at a specific region of the thalamus to regulate it. Amazingly, it alleviated the patient's depression. Llinas has not yet tried this procedure on tinnitus patients.

We are very optimistic about neurological work of this sort. And, at the same time, we need to express some caution. The cortex of the brain is so very complex that serious side effects are always possible when an artificial stimulation is introduced to it. (The cortex of the brain is made up of so many neuron connections that if we were to count the connections, or synapses, at the rate of one per second, it would take us 32 million years to count them all.)

Q Do MRIs or other brain scans reveal evidence of tinnitus?

A Very recently some investigative work by Richard Salvi, Alan Lockwood, and Robert Burkard, at the State University of New York at Buffalo, has revealed the brain area involved in the *perception* though not the *production* of tinnitus. The researchers found tinnitus patients who could shift the intensity of their tinnitus by changing their gaze (called *gaze-evoked tinnitus*). Using positron emission tomography (PET) brain scanning technology, Salvi et al. were able to compare images of the patients' brains taken during the periods of loud and soft tinnitus. The comparison allowed them to see which area or areas of the brain were active during the changes in tinnitus volume.

This research bears a resemblance to recent work that was done with epilepsy. Similar scanning techniques led to identification of the part of the brain involved in epileptic seizures. This in turn led to the kind of surgical ablation of brain tissue that has brought some forms of epilepsy under control.

Q Have the researchers in Buffalo discovered the brain area that is the source of the tinnitus?

A The researchers in Buffalo identified the portion of the brain in the auditory cortex that is involved in the perception of tinnitus. They also showed that the limbic system is involved in a patient's experience of tinnitus. The limbic system is the brain's emotion center. This connection might explain why many tinnitus patients feel anxious or in other ways emotional about their tinnitus. This is very important and promising work and, yes, it might well lead to a cure for some kinds of tinnitus. The American Tinnitus Association funded the research seed (or starter) grant for the preliminary work for this study.

We think it would also it be incredibly interesting, not to mention helpful, to study the perceptual area of the brain during a patient's residual inhibition (the temporary cessation of tinnitus after masking sound is turned off). When we eventually learn what goes on in the brain during residual inhibition (and we *will* learn that), we will theoretically know which areas of the brain to target with medications or procedures to quiet the tinnitus for greater lengths of time.

Q Have other researchers used imaging to study the brain's activity during the experience of tinnitus? If so, have they been able to use this information to find a treatment that works?

A Functional brain imaging technology keeps taking enormous strides forward. In doing so, it gives us the opportunity to study many processes in the human nervous system. Although scientists have not yet made the leap and found a cure for tinnitus because of PET (positron emission tomography) scanning, we have discovered a major advantage to its use. It provides us with a way to objectively evaluate—to essentially see—the effectiveness of tinnitus treatment methods.

There are many things that lead tinnitus patients to report positive effects from a treatment, such as unconsciously wanting to please their healthcare providers. But neuroimaging devices, like PET scans, cannot be fooled. In one study, Mirz et al. used PET scanning to see what the brain did during periods of measurable tinnitus reduction. The patients were scanned while their tinnitus was being masked, while they were having IV injections of lidocaine, and while using masking plus IV lidocaine. The researchers discovered tinnitus activity in the right prefrontal cortex of the brain. This was a little bit surprising for two reasons: (1) It was not in the typical auditory areas of the brain, and (2) it was only on the right side, regardless of the perceived location of the tinnitus.

Mirz et al. cite another study in which brain activity was mapped with PET scanning during auditory hallucinations. In these cases, the right cortex was again the site of activity. These researchers suggested that the right cortex could be the brain region responsible for all phantom auditory sensations.

From their work with lidocaine and masking, Mirz et al. came up with some fascinating suggestions:

1. Severe, disabling tinnitus is associated with brain activity in areas that are functionally linked with other cortical areas that process memory, attention, and auditory signals.

2. There are regions of the brain that normally engage in interaction with the environment and keep us distracted. The failure of these regions to divert attention and habituate internal sounds results in severe tinnitus.

We believe that this objective evidence—this tantalizing visualization of tinnitus—will lead the tinnitus research community right into a cure.

Q I find it very interesting that we've now identified the brain area responsible for generating tinnitus. What problems or consequences might result from deadening this area?

A Yes, finding the brain areas that are involved in the *perception* (not the generation) of tinnitus is a very important discovery. And if we were able somehow to deaden or remove these brain areas, it might mean the end of tinnitus. Or it might mean that other brain cells would eventually take over this function, since the brain is very plastic, or adaptable. Or it might mean that the patient would lose the ability to perceive certain sounds. Or it could mean that the tinnitus would simply change the way it sounds and be perceived elsewhere. Taking out the tinnitus brain perceptual area could lead to many things. The first step is to test these theories through research.

Q Do these PET scans show us exactly which parts of the brain to cut out in order to cure tinnitus? How would the surgery be done?

A The PET scans do show which areas of a patient's brain are involved in the individual's tinnitus perception. We have learned that the locations vary from person to person, but often the limbic system is affected. Scientists still do not know if these active areas are generating the tinnitus or are just affected by its presence.

The ultimate cure for tinnitus could well be highly specific and restricted brain surgery. Most likely the surgery will be performed not with a scalpel, but with lasers or fine radiological beams (like in gamma knife surgery).

There is one catch: If the cortical area of the brain devoted to the hearing system is the area that needs to be excised, its location would present surgeons with a big challenge (as if brain surgery is not challenge enough). The auditory cortex is very inconveniently located in the side walls of a cavelike fold in the brain that extends back into the temporal area. It is well protected and difficult to access. Since removal of the brain area responsible for epilepsy has suppressed some forms of epilepsy, it is logical to think that removal of the brain area responsible for tinnitus could do the same for tinnitus.

We hope that one day tinnitus doctors will scan the brains of tinnitus patients using PET scanning technology, or subsequent generations of PET, and indicate to the neurosurgeons which specific areas to remove. It is one of many hopes for the future. We are just not there yet.

When considering the central nervous system, Hallowell Davis and Richard Silverman said in their book *Hearing and Deafness*, "Remember that everything is more complicated than you think."

Resources

Lockwood, A. H., Salvi, R. J., Coad, M. L., Towsley, M. L., Wack, D. S., Murphy, B. W. The functional neuroanatomy of tinnitus: evidence for limbic system links and neural plasticity, *Neurology*, Jan. 1998; 50(1):114–20.

Makarenko, V., and Llinas, R. Experimentally determined chaotic phase synchronization in a neuronal system, *Neurobiology*, Dec. 22, 1998; 25(26):15747–52.

Martin, W. H., Shi, Y.-B., Burchiel, K. J., and Anderson, V. C. Deep brain stimulation effects on hearing function and tinnitus, *Proceedings of the Sixth International Tinnitus Seminar*, Hazell, J., ed., Tinnitus and Hyperacusis Centre, London, 1999.

Mirz, F., Pedersen, C. B., Ishizu, K., Johannsen, P., Ovesen, T., Stodkilde-Jorgensen, H., and Gjede A. Positron emission tomography of cortical centers of tinnitus, *Hearing Research*, 1999; 134:133–44.

8

Causes of Tinnitus

Q Is tinnitus a signal of impending deafness or hearing impairment or possibly a very serious condition?

A Tinnitus is *not* an indicator of impending deafness. It is, however, easier to say what tinnitus is not than what it is. We know that it is a signal that something is, or was, wrong somewhere in the auditory system. The "something wrong" could be as simple as debris on the eardrum or as serious as a tumor on the hearing nerve.

Q I have been diagnosed as having "noise-type" tinnitus. Frankly, I thought tinnitus was tinnitus. Are there different kinds of tinnitus and do the different kinds have different causes?

A Noise-type tinnitus is the kind of tinnitus that is best matched by a band of noise rather than a single tone. A single tone would be like the sound of a single key on a piano. A noise-type tinnitus is like the sound of many keys on the piano played simultaneously, although usually not pleasingly.

Patients with noise-type tinnitus most often describe the sound they hear as a hissing sound. Audiometrically, this means that the center of the bandwidth of the noise is in the high frequencies. Statistically, tonal tinnitus is more prevalent than noise tinnitus.

In a sample of 1544 patient, 76% had tonal tinnitus, 21% had noise tinnitus, and the other patients had tones and noises combined. When these same 1544 tinnitus patients were asked to rate the severity of their tinnitus on a 10-point scale (where 10 was the most severe tinnitus imaginable), those with noise-type tinnitus had an average rating of 5.5, while those with tonal tinnitus had an average rating of 7.5. From these results, we concluded that tonal tinnitus is perceived as being more disturbing than noise tinnitus.

At one point, we thought that the description of tinnitus might be related to the cause of the tinnitus. But after years of data collecting we know that that is not the case. Some people with noise-induced tinnitus have noise-type tinnitus and others with noise-induced tinnitus have tonal tinnitus. Some people with tinnitus caused by taking ototoxic drugs have the noise type; others have tonal tinnitus.

Q **Right after my husband had a stroke, he began to hear the sound of running water in his right ear. Soft music helps him get to sleep, but I want to know if there are other people who developed tinnitus after having had a stroke.**

A We have not heard of other cases of tinnitus that were produced by stroke. But we do know of several different parts of the brain, such as the thalamus, the limbic system, the frontal lobe, and of course the auditory cortex, that are involved to varying degrees in the perception of tinnitus. If the stroke involved any one of these areas, especially the auditory portion of the brain, it is reasonable to assume that tinnitus could be produced. A stroke is essentially the death of brain tissue caused by a lack of blood flow and insufficient oxygen to the brain, and any part of the brain could be affected by it. Fortunately, your husband has found that playing soft music helps him get to sleep. Because the quiet music works, he could test a tinnitus masker in his right ear to see if it could help him during the daytime.

Q **Which should I see for my tinnitus: an otologist, an otolaryngologist, or an audiologist?**

A The majority of health insurers require that you see your primary care physician (PCP) first for any health concern. Then you can ask for a referral to a specialist. Even if this is not a requirement, it is a good idea to be examined by your PCP to have common health problems like high blood pressure or thyroid dysfunction ruled out. Tinnitus can be a symptom of these conditions.

Your primary care physician can then refer you to an ear, nose, and throat doctor (an ENT or otolaryngologist) or to an otologist (an ears-only doctor) who can identify more specialized conditions, such as damage to the eardrum or debris resting against the eardrum, middle ear problems like otosclerosis, and acoustic neuroma. These often have tinnitus as a symptom.

At this point you might be referred to an audiologist for basic and advanced hearing tests. An audiologist can closely analyze the presence and scope of any hearing loss and determine if other hearing disorders are present. Because audiologists receive training in counseling, their bedside manner is often quite palatable to tinnitus patients.

Q **In some of the reading I have done, reference is made to *peripheral* and *central* tinnitus. What do these terms mean?**

A *Peripheral* tinnitus refers to tinnitus originating in the inner ear. *Central* tinnitus refers to tinnitus originating in the brain. However, as yet no tests

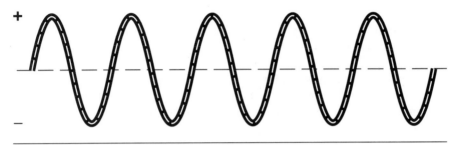

FIGURE 8.1 *Two sinusoidal sound waves "in phase" (one on top of the other)*

are available to differentiate true peripheral from true central tinnitus. The classification system is based more on educated guesswork than on measurable facts. If someone has tinnitus because of extreme noise exposure, it is reasonable to assume that the locus of damage is in the inner ear. We might then say that this tinnitus is peripheral. But even in a case as clear-cut as this, more than likely we will discover that all tinnitus is a brain phenomenon—not initially perhaps, but eventually.

Also, the location of the perception of tinnitus does not necessarily tell us the location of its origin. For example, tinnitus that is perceived in the head does not necessarily mean it is a central tinnitus. The in-the-head localization of tinnitus is just as likely to be due to equal neurological input from both ears. We can duplicate this with external sounds. When two sounds are totally equal in loudness and pitch, are in phase (the sine curves of the sound waves are identical), and are delivered to the ears through headphones, the sounds are not perceived as two separate sounds in the ears, but rather as a single sound in the head. (See Figure 8.1.)

Q My doctor refers to many different types of tinnitus, such as sensory tinnitus, conductive tinnitus, and central tinnitus. Do these different types mean that different treatments are necessary for each type?

A For now the attempt to classify tinnitus in this way is an academic exercise only. No evidence is available to support the different classifications. We hope that eventually classifications are established and that, once done, they will direct clinicians to treat specific types of tinnitus with the appropriate therapies.

Here is what we do know about some tinnitus "types": Conductive tinnitus can be the result of otosclerosis. It is sometimes resolved by surgery (stapedectomy) that removes the diseased middle ear bones and replaces them with prosthetic middle ear bones.

Central tinnitus refers to subjective tinnitus that originates in the brain, although we do not know in which part of the brain. We do know that medications (like benzodiazepines) exert an effect on the brain. These drugs could be tested once someone's tinnitus was definitively identified as central tinnitus.

Q I have had tinnitus for 5 years. About 2 years ago, I was diagnosed with diabetes for which I take 28 units of insulin every day. Is it possible that the stress of tinnitus brought on my diabetes? Or could the diabetes have caused my tinnitus?

A It is very unlikely that your tinnitus caused your diabetes. It is also highly unlikely that any tendency you had for diabetes caused your tinnitus. It *is* entirely possible that the stress and tension produced by the diabetes could have exacerbated your tinnitus. Consider this too: The incidence of diabetes in the patient population at the Oregon Hearing Research Center's Tinnitus Clinic is approximately 5%, the same as for the general population. In early 2000, the Portland VA Medical Center initiated a study to investigate the incidence and experience of tinnitus in diabetic patients. We will be learning more soon.

Q I've read that tinnitus could be caused by an injury to the auditory nerve. How does one injure the auditory nerve, and how would such an injury cause tinnitus?

A Physical trauma to the head could injure the auditory nerve. A tumor on the auditory nerve and the subsequent surgery to remove it would undoubtedly cause some damage to the auditory nerve.

Here's how the nerve helps us hear. Sound waves enter the ear and ultimately stimulate the hair cells in the cochlea. The hair cells then stimulate nerve cells in the auditory nerve that travel up to the auditory cortex, the hearing part of the brain. It is possible that an injured auditory nerve produces what would be similar to a short circuit between the nerve fibers. If the insulating cover, or myelin sheaf, on each nerve fiber breaks down, it could produce a *locked interaction* between fibers, causing a continuous signal that could be perceived as tinnitus. The myelin covering of these auditory nerve fibers is exceptionally thin and susceptible to injury.

A second possibility is related to the *spontaneous activity* in the auditory nerve. We would assume that the auditory nerve would be quiet so that it could receive messages from the ear. Instead, this nerve actually produces more noise on its own than any other nerve in the body! Nerve injury might change this spontaneous activity, either causing more or less of it. This could be a physiological basis of tinnitus.

Several patients have had their auditory nerves cut in an attempt to end their tinnitus. The unfortunate result of this surgery demonstrates a third connection between the auditory nerve and tinnitus. Most of these patients continued to hear their tinnitus after the surgical severing, and in many cases the tinnitus got louder.

Q I have been diagnosed with palatal myoclonus, a spasm in the roof of the mouth (although I wasn't really aware of it). I also have a "clicking" tinnitus and I wondered if these two conditions are related.

A They often are. A clicking sound is frequently the first symptom of palatal myoclonus (which literally means *palate spasm*). It is believed that one is born with this condition. Palatal myoclonus, which is extremely rare, cannot be surgically corrected, but it has been treated successfully with carbamazepine, tryptophan, and injections of botulium toxin directly into the tensor palatini muscle near the eustachian tube. A middle ear myoclonus is a spasm in the tympanic cavity and can be surgically corrected. Discuss these treatment options with your ENT physician.

Q Can tinnitus be so severe as to cause the inner ear to hurt and, in turn, cause headaches?

A No, tinnitus does not cause pain. Tinnitus is a symptom, much as pain is a symptom, of something that has gone wrong somewhere in the body. These three symptoms (tinnitus, pain in the ear, and headache) could all be the result of the same problem or of three separate problems. It is certainly possible to have two unrelated things wrong with us at the same time.

Here is how symptoms, even of different origins, can affect each other. Tinnitus (caused by X) is so disturbing that the patient cannot sleep. The stress from the sleeplessness causes louder tinnitus as well as chronic headaches (caused by Y). The lack of sleep makes the patient irritable and more sensitive to small annoyances. These reduced tolerances for pain make the ear pain (caused by Z) seem more annoying. If your headaches are persistent and frequent, it is wise to consult with a neurologist.

Q I experienced severe dehydration that I believe caused my tinnitus. According to what I've read, dehydration produces extra histamines, which are the body's water regulators. Do histamines produce tinnitus?

A We know of another patient whose tinnitus was the result of extreme dehydration. His dehydration not only produced tinnitus, but it also produced severe hearing loss, so much so that he qualified for a cochlear implant. If someone is extremely dehydrated, it seems reasonable that the endolymph and perilymph fluids of the inner ear could be compromised and that such a compromise alone could cause hearing loss and tinnitus. (We need these fluids to have healthy ears.) It is not likely that increased histamines would cause these negative effects, primarily because the ear is protected from blood flow or blood pressure changes in so many ways. New research does suggest that histamines might boost circulation in the vestibular part of the ear.

Q How long will it take for tinnitus to fade away if it is going to do that?

A Sometimes tinnitus just fades away. When this happens, the tinnitus is usually short lived, perhaps only a few weeks old before it begins to decline.

If you have had your tinnitus for a year or more, it probably will not fade away on its own. However, if your hearing is temporarily impaired (for example, due to an excessive amount of earwax that is discovered and then removed), and the hearing returns to normal, your tinnitus will probably reduce and go away altogether within weeks of resolving the problem.

Q We live in an atmosphere of hundreds of radio, television, telephone, and microwave signals. Has anyone considered the possibility that we, who hear tinnitus, might actually be hearing electromagnetic signals?

A We are sure it has been considered. But at this time we cannot measure such things. Speculatively, tinnitus is probably not the perception of electromagnetic signals. When tinnitus patients were taken into a radio-frequency-shielded room at the OHRC Tinnitus Clinic, their tinnitus was not eliminated or even reduced. In fact, the room was sound shielded so that the tinnitus appeared louder than normal, just as it would in any very quiet environment. We really do not know the long-term or, for that matter, the short-term effects of microwaves, low-level x-rays, and other electrical waves that are all around us. The perception of tinnitus could be one of the effects of one of these invisible forces.

A related and equally unexplained noise phenomenon has been reported around the world, but most commonly in the United States and Europe. It is referred to as "the hum." This low-level hum has been reported in every state in the United States, with a concentration of reports in New Mexico (Taos, New Mexico, is known for its "Taos hum"), Arizona, California, Washington State, Colorado, Michigan, and along the East Coast.

In response to complaints from a high number of hum hearers in Taos, a team of University of New Mexico investigators decided to try to identify the cause. They measured local geological waves, electromagnetic radiation, and other possible environmental sources for the hum. But they found none that corresponded to the ultra-low-frequency (30 to 80 Hz) rumble that was described by the hearers.

Researcher James P. Kelly, Ph.D., at the Division of Otolaryngology at the University of New Mexico, has continued to study this noise phenomenon and offers an interesting theory regarding the hum. All normal-hearing ears emit sounds (evoked otoacoustic emissions) in response to outside sounds. And many people's ears just produce sounds anyway (spontaneous otoacoustic emissions). These are ultraquiet sounds that cannot be heard by the person whose ears are making the sounds. Nevertheless, Kelly and his team of researchers are investigating the possibility that otoacoustic emissions and the Taos Hum are related. Perhaps something environmental *is* triggering these otoacoustic emissions and therefore the hum.

A good "hum" information Web site:

www.eskimo.com/~billb/hum/hum1.html

Q My tinnitus started 6 years ago. As I now look back, it started at the same time that we purchased a new television set. Several weeks ago, my son asked if I could hear the 16,000-Hz signal that the TV produced. I said I could not hear any such signal. And for reasons best known to him, my son set about building us a new TV set. However, instead of using the transformer that produced the 16,000-Hz signal, he used liquid crystal technology that emits no audible sound.

After using our new modified TV for less than a week, I realized that my tinnitus had gone from a 7 on a 10-point scale to a 2. Some days it's a 1. It has remained that way for almost 2 months. I am convinced that that old TV signal was exacerbating my tinnitus, and I now wonder how many other people are experiencing the same thing. Have you heard of other patients whose tinnitus has been exacerbated by the transformer signal coming from a TV set? (Incidentally, my hearing is down 80 dB at 8000 Hz.)

A Several people have told us that they can hear the horizontal oscillations of their TVs. No doubt it is true. At birth, we have no hearing damage and can hear up to 20,000 Hz. Even though your hearing is down at 8000 Hz, this does not mean that your hearing is also down at 16,000 Hz or at even higher frequencies. It is clear that you have the ability to hear some very high frequencies, some "islands of hearing" perhaps.

No, we have not heard of this as a cause of tinnitus—yet. It does make one wonder how many patients have the same tinnitus trigger and are unaware of it. It is a temptation to recommend abstentious TV behavior to those patients who do not know what caused their tinnitus.

TVs currently come in three different electronic varieties: CRT (cathode ray tube), LCD (liquid crystal display), and plasma (found in the new flat screen models). The cathode ray tubes are the ones that oscillate in the superhigh-frequency range and constitute the bulk of TVs today. Rear-projection big screen models also use CRTs. Plasma screens (new thin-film technology) and LCDs are essentially silent, relatively new, and still expensive to purchase. Fortunately, the demand for this quiet technology is pushing manufacturers in that direction. (We don't want to kid ourselves. The demand for LCD technology is not because it is quiet, but because LCD technology takes up very little space relative to CRTs. This enables the construction of less bulky TVs. The quiet component is a bonus.) Sony and Magnavox make TVs using LCD technology.

Computer monitors currently use either CRTs or LCD technology. Laptop computers and flat panel monitors are all LCD. Standard, boxlike monitors all use CRTs.

Some hyperacusis patients have reported that the sounds from their computers are so annoying that they need to wear ear protection when they work with them. We had assumed that the only sounds that these sound-sensitive patients could not tolerate were the sounds from the computer (that is, the big box that contains the hard drive). Indeed, some people with hyperacusis and tinnitus have rewired their computers and set them up in nearby sound-insulated closets.

We are bombarded with superhigh-frequency sounds all the time, and for most people there is no ill effect. (Incidentally, high-frequency sounds lose intensity very rapidly as they travel. This is probably why elephants mumble in such low frequencies—they communicate across great distances!)

Resources

Bento, R. F., Sanchez, T. G., Miniti, A., and Tedesco-Marchesi, A. J. Continuous, high-frequency objective tinnitus caused by middle ear myoclonus, *Ear Nose Throat J.*, Oct. 1998; 77(10):814–8.

Bryce, G. E., and Morrison, M. D. Botulinum toxin treatment of essential palatal myoclonus tinnitus, *J. Otolaryngol.*, Aug. 1998; 27(4):213–6.

Diehl, G. E., and Wilmes E. Etiology and clinical aspects of palatal myoclonus, *Laryngorhinootologie*, July 1990; 69(7):369–72.

Kelly, J. P. Interdisciplinary Investigation of Low Frequency Hearing, University of New Mexico Health Sciences Center, 2/4/00, www.unm.edu/~jpatk/unmotorsch.html

9

Cochlear Implants: Surgical Implants That Restore Hearing

Q I've read about cochlear implant patients who have had their tinnitus relieved by the implant device. I've often said I would gladly sacrifice the hearing in my left ear if that would relieve my tinnitus. Can you tell me more about this implant procedure?

A If you have any usable hearing at all, you are not a candidate for a cochlear implant. To currently qualify, you must either have a hearing loss in both ears that is so severe it cannot be helped by hearing aids (a 90-dB loss or greater) or you must be completely deaf.

The cochlear implant utilizes alternating current (AC) electrical stimulation to activate the eighth nerve. The normally functioning inner ear naturally stimulates the eighth nerve with its own electrical activity and by the additional electrical activity caused by incoming sound waves. The AC stimulation in the cochlear implant attempts to replace the lost electrical potentials normally generated by the inner ear.

A cochlear implant is a miraculous invention. The surgery to implant it, however, is an invasive, permanent, and expensive ($50,000 per ear) procedure. An electrode-embedded wire is threaded through and implanted inside the cochlea. In the process of the surgical implantation, all remaining cochlear hair cells are destroyed. A magnetic receiver–stimulator is also implanted on the inside of the skull so that a magnetic transmitting coil can attach to it on the outside of the skull.

It is really not known if the electrical stimulation from the implant relieves the tinnitus or if the additional background sounds brought in by the

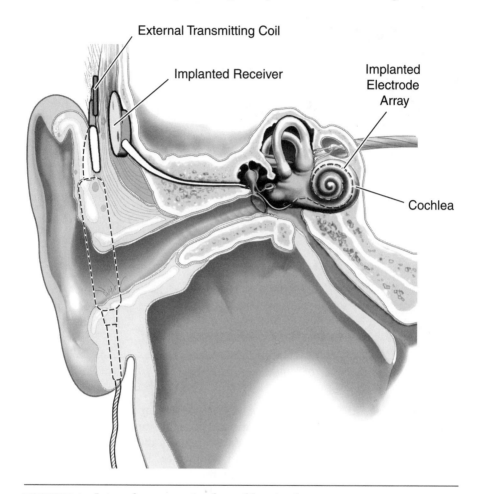

FIGURE 9.1   *Internal components of a cochlear implant.*

implant act as a natural masker to the tinnitus. Most, but not all, cochlear implant patients who had tinnitus before the implantation experience tinnitus relief after the implantation. There are also a few cochlear implant patients who did not have tinnitus before surgery, but who developed it after surgery.

Figures 9.1 and 9.2 show a cochlear implant cross section and the cochlear implant magnetic transmitting coil, respectively.

Q **I have a cochlear implant that I had hoped would not only provide hearing, but also tinnitus relief. My tinnitus is a head noise, something like a musical roaring. My hearing has improved, but my tinnitus has not. Do you have any suggestions?**

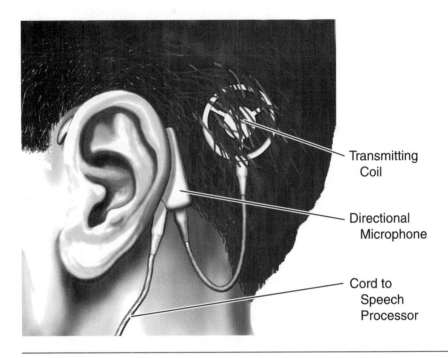

Transmitting
Coil

Directional
Microphone

Cord to
Speech
Processor

FIGURE 9.2   *External view of a cochlear implant.*

A   The House Ear Institute in Los Angeles reports that a majority of the patients implanted with the cochlear implants obtain tinnitus relief from the electrical stimulation and/or the reinstated hearing ability provided by the instrument. The odds were certainly in your favor. Recently, we reported about a patient in Israel who got tinnitus relief by playing masking sounds into his cochlear implant. (The masking sounds were those provided from the Moses/Lang CD available from the Oregon Hearing Research Center.)

Since describing the success with the patient in Israel, a cochlear implant patient in California tried similar masking, but without success. Nevertheless, we still recommend that you try masking through your implant. Several other companies, like Personal Growth Technologies and Petroff Audio Technologies, produce CDs that might help.

Masking through a Cochlear Implant

A patient who lives in Israel had cochlear implant surgery. Unfortunately, the surgery did not alleviate his tinnitus. (He actually believes that it made it worse.) To test out an idea, we sent him a Moses/Lang masking sampler CD. We wanted to see what would happen if he played the masking tracks through his cochlear implant.

(continued)

In the exchange that follows, we asked him the questions and he provided the answers.

Q: When you play the Moses/Lang CD through your cochlear implant, do you still detect the tinnitus in the implanted ear?

A: No, the tinnitus in the implanted ear is completely masked.

Q: When the tinnitus in the implanted ear is completely masked, can you hear any tinnitus in the opposite un-implanted ear?

A: Yes, the tinnitus in the un-implanted ear is not affected.

Q: Which track on the Moses/Lang CD is most effective in masking your tinnitus in the implanted ear?

A: Track 5 is best, although I do experience some masking from several other tracks. [Track 5 is a band of noise from 6000 to 14,000 Hz. The pitch of the patient's tinnitus has not been measured, but it is likely high, somewhere in the same 6000- to 14,000-Hz range.]

Q: When the tinnitus in the implanted ear is masked, does residual inhibition occur?

A: I am not sure. I need more time to experiment with it.

Q: When you played the Moses/Lang CD into your implanted ear, what did you hear?

A: It's hard to describe. But as best as I can explain it, I heard a sound, a noise, not necessarily a pleasant sound, but it's better than the tinnitus.

Q: When the masking sound is present, are you able to appreciate other sounds such as speech or music?

A: The answer is yes. But a very strange thing happens. Speech and music sound much clearer while the masking noise is present as opposed to when the masking noise is absent.

Q: Are you sure that it's not because you are learning how to better appreciate sounds with the cochlear implant?

A: No, it is not a matter of training. I have tested this effect many times by simply turning the masking sound off. Each time I turn it off, speech and music are not as clear as when it is on. I have repeated this test many times and the effect is always the same.

The patient was able once again to play the violin and could play compositions by Vivaldi rather well with the CD masking sound present. From this interchange we conclude that it is possible to produce effective tinnitus masking and tinnitus relief for at lease one patient using a specific bandwidth of masking sounds played into the patient's cochlear implant.

Resources

Tabachnick, B. From Volta's battery to cochlear implants—A chronicle of electrical stimulation, *Tinnitus Today*, June 1995; 20(2):7–12.

Vernon, J. Masking of tinnitus through a cochlear implant, *J. Am. Acad. Audiol.*, June 2000; 11(6):293–4.

10

Cognitive Therapy and Counseling

Q I've been told that counseling could help me deal with my tinnitus. But, to tell you the truth, I don't know how counseling could ever make me forget about this noise. Can it really work?

A Therapist and author Richard Hallam wrote, "It is essential in therapy to lend yourself to persuasion." If you try counseling, it would help move things along if you believed that it could help. Counseling, in and of itself, is not always a satisfactory solution for people with tinnitus. But when it is paired with masker or sound generator therapy or with needed medication (like an antidepressant), the two therapies together can be greater than the sum of their individual parts. Sometimes the counseling component makes other therapies successful.

Q My doctor has suggested that I try cognitive behavioral therapy. How is that going to help my tinnitus?

A Cognitive behavioral therapy is a form of counseling that helps patients work on their maladaptive behaviors and negative thinking patterns about their tinnitus. According to Robert Sweetow, Ph.D., director of audiology at the University of California, San Francisco, "A common characteristic shared by tinnitus patients is an unhealthy (though not abnormal) attitude to this unwanted auditory annoyance which leads to a maladaptive reaction. A reaction is a learned behavior, and all behaviors are subject to modification." Cognitive behavioral therapy appears to be most effective when it is used along with other tinnitus treatments, such as masking, medication, relaxation therapy, or tinnitus retraining therapy.

See a psychologist or a tinnitus specialist or call the American Tinnitus Association for a referral to a health professional who offers this kind of counseling. Richard Hallam's book, *Living with Tinnitus: Dealing with the Ringing in your Ears,* is a very clear and approachable layperson's guide to cognitive therapy. (Hallam's book is out of print. However, you can ask Amazon.com and other on-line booksellers to search through used book databases for it.)

Q My ENT suggests that I try cognitive therapy for my tinnitus. Do I have to have this exact form of therapy to be helped? I was in counseling years ago, before I ever had tinnitus, but it wasn't specifically cognitive therapy.

A Most tinnitus patients can benefit from some form of counseling. Cognitive behavioral therapy happens to suit the struggles and thinking patterns of tinnitus patients, so it is often mentioned and used. The goal of cognitive therapy is specifically to bring the patient to the point where he or she regards the tinnitus as unworthy of attention.

Tinnitus can, without question, produce a great deal of stress. However, people experience stress about other things in life. Tinnitus patients tend to think of the tinnitus as the one and only cause of their anxiety, lack of concentration, or other problems. Therapist Richard Hallam thinks this is not fair. He discovered in his counseling practice that when tinnitus patients overcame their difficulties with relationships, work, and childhood traumas they were better able to let go of their attention to their tinnitus.

Robert Sandlin, Ph.D., former tinnitus clinic director, discovered this same phenomenon with his patients. He described one such patient who had had tinnitus for many years and who had been unable to cope with it. Through the course of Sandlin's history taking during his first visit with the patient, he learned that she actually did get relief from her tinnitus while she was in the shower. The relief was so great that she was taking 12 or 13 showers a day.

Sandlin immediately prescribed a tinnitus masker for this patient, who used it avidly. The patient felt that the masker was tremendously effective and described her experience with it as being released from agony. However, after about 6 months she found that she was suddenly unable to mask the tinnitus no matter what level of masking sound she chose. In fact, she reported that the tinnitus was worse than ever. Through continued conversations with the patient, Sandlin learned that she was experiencing a difficult interpersonal relationship problem. Her inability to mask the tinnitus started when the relationship problem began.

We encourage you to take advantage of any counseling opportunity. If you can find a therapist who is willing to explore the intricacies of tinnitus and with whom you feel a rapport, you will be on the road to manageable tinnitus.

Resources

Hallam, R. *Living with Tinnitus: Dealing with the Ringing in Your Ears,* Thorsons Publishers Limited, Wellingborough, England, 1989.

Hogan, K. *Tinnitus: Turning the Volume Down,* Network 3000 Publishing, Eagan, MN, 1998.

Sweetow, R. W. The role of cognitive-behavioral therapy in tinnitus perception, *Tinnitus Today,* March 1998; 23:1.

11

Demographics: How Many People Have Tinnitus?

Q Exactly how many people have tinnitus? I've read so many different numbers.

A Perhaps as many as 40 million people in the United States have tinnitus to a minor degree. A smaller but still alarming number of people have severe, quality-of-life-disruptive tinnitus. In the United States, the number of people with severe tinnitus is estimated to be anywhere from 2% to 5% of the population, or 5 to 13 million people. We may never know exactly and the surveyists don't agree. They do come close enough to each other to provide a fairly accurate sense of the extent of the problem.

Gallaudet University's 1990 survey showed that 2.6% of the U.S. population had severe tinnitus. The National Institutes of Health survey stated that 4% of the U.S. population had a severe form of tinnitus. Dr. Ross Coles's study showed that 0.5% to 2.8% of the English population had severe tinnitus. If you average the percentages, you get 3%. If you multiply that times the current population in the United States (275,000,000), you arrive at more than 8 million people in the United States who have severe, chronic tinnitus. The percentages are believed to apply to all industrialized countries where people work in factories, ride motorcycles, and play music too loud.

Q Does everyone have tinnitus to some degree?

A In 1953, two researchers, M. E. Heller and M. Bergman, put 70 adult test subjects with normal hearing and no tinnitus into a soundproof room (willingly we presume) for 5 minutes. When the subjects emerged, they were each asked to describe what they had experienced in the soundless chamber. Ninety-four percent described tinnitus, exactly as hearing-impaired adults with tinnitus describe their tinnitus. Depending on the situation, we might all have tinnitus.

Resource

Brown, S. C. *Older Americans and Tinnitus: A Demographic Study and Chartbook,* Gallaudet Research Institute, Washington, DC, 1990.

12

Dentistry and Tinnitus

Q The sound of my dentist's drill is so shrill and noisy that it makes my tinnitus louder for many weeks. Do you know where I can go to have my teeth filled without having them drilled?

A If you want to avoid the high-pitched dentist's drill, you might be able to take advantage of micro air abrasion dental technology. This is a new way to clean out tooth decay and has a few advantages over high-speed drilling. For one thing, the micro-abrasion machinery is very quiet. The air abrasion is also pain-free, so patients do not require novocaine or other anesthetics. The drawback to the air abrasion treatment is that, at least for now, it can only be used for small cavities. The standard dental drill is still necessary for root canals, bridge and cap work, and for repair of deep cavities.

The obvious solution is to have your teeth cleaned and checked every 6 months. Frequent visits to the dentist can keep dental damage to a minimum. (Dentists refer to this as "micro-dentistry.") And if a cavity is caught while it is small, it can be treated with this quiet technology.

Ask your dentist where you might find a quiet dental drill in your area, or ask a local dental school for a referral. Or contact this distributor: American Dental Technologies, Inc., 5555 Bear Lane, Corpus Christi, Texas 78405, 800-320-1050, 361-289-1145; Fax: 361-289-5554, www.americandentaltech.com.

Q Can I prevent damage to my ears—and an increase in my tinnitus—if I have general anesthesia for dental work? Will earplugs be helpful awake or asleep?

A Earplugs will block some of the air-conducted sound that goes through the ear canal. But the majority of the sound from a dental drill is conducted to the inner ear by the bones in the face and head. So, yes, earplugs will help, but only a little. As for general anesthesia, it will only prevent your awareness of the sound. Sound is energy that travels into your ears whether you are awake or asleep.

You could ask your dentist to drill in short spurts, 5 seconds on and 10 seconds off. (To our knowledge, no dentist has refused to do this for a patient when the patient asked.) The exacerbation of tinnitus by loud sound is a time-intensity function. Although you cannot control the sound intensity of the high-speed drill, you can control the length of time that you are exposed to it.

Q   As a consequence of my fear of dental work due to my tinnitus, I have neglected my teeth and now considerable work is needed. Some of the necessary work involves removing old fillings, and some involves drilling and filling new cavities. Will laser dentistry work or should I have general anesthesia?

A   Laser and air abrasion dental devices are much quieter than the conventional high-speed drill. But their range is limited. They will only work for cleaning out small cavities and removing some fillings. The smaller the job is, the better the chance that this quiet form of dentistry can be helpful. And whether you are awake or anesthetized, sounds are still conducted to your inner ear.

Recently, however, a patient reported that he had undergone extensive jaw surgery that involved sawing away part of the jawbone. When the anesthesia wore off, the patient's hyperacusis and tinnitus were not worsened. This patient reported his experience to another hyperacusis patient who needed dental work. The second patient had the dental work done under general anesthesia and suffered no exacerbation of his hyperacusis. For your consideration.

Q   I am a dentist and have had tinnitus for many years. I wonder if my exposure to the high-speed drill caused my problem. I want to investigate the possible connection. Is there any literature on this topic?

A   In the late 1970s, a dentist (and tinnitus patient himself) conducted an informal survey of all the dentists in Oregon, Washington, Idaho, and Northern California. He found that *every* dentist who had purchased the high-speed drill that became available in 1955 had high-frequency hearing loss and tinnitus. To prevent your tinnitus from becoming worse, wear ear protection (earplugs and if necessary earmuffs) any time you use the high-speed drill.

Q   I had tinnitus many years ago when I was a musician with a rock group. Since my retirement, the tinnitus has gradually faded away. Recently, I had my two front teeth capped, a procedure that involved the implantation of two steel rods. After the procedure, my tinnitus started up again. A friend has suggested that the steel posts are causing an electrical short circuit that is stimulating my ears and causing tinnitus. Is this possible?

A Possible, yes. (Anything is possible.) Probable, no. It is doubtful that there is an electrical short circuit associated with your teeth. It is much more likely that the intense sound of the drilling reinstated your tinnitus. You previously demonstrated that excessively loud sounds, like those you experienced during your rock band days, induced tinnitus for you. Since you had the dental work done only a week ago, the exacerbated tinnitus may be temporary. Wait a month. If the tinnitus has not decreased by then, see a tinnitus clinician. Call the American Tinnitus Association for their national and international lists of health providers who specialize in tinnitus.

[This patient's tinnitus gradually faded away in a month's time. If only all musicians and audience members could be as fortunate.]

Q I've heard that some people had their metal fillings removed to relieve their tinnitus. Do you think that can really help? Has there been any research on this?

A Common amalgam dental fillings are made of a mixture of silver, mercury, and other metals. This material (primarily the mercury) is suspected by some to cause health problems, including fatigue, anxiety, and tinnitus. But connections have not yet been scientifically demonstrated. Researchers in Sweden evaluated 1023 women to determine the connection, if any, between amalgam fillings and the symptoms of tinnitus, hyperacusis, TMJ, and headache. They found no associations between the amalgam fillings and any of the disorders, but they did find that tinnitus, hyperacusis, and TMJ dysfunction correlate with each other.

You can certainly choose to remove and replace your current amalgam fillings with tooth-colored resin fillings for front teeth and gold fillings for the back teeth, where stronger chewing surfaces are needed. But be prepared for the noise of the dental equipment that will be used, and discuss your need for short periods of drilling with your dentist.

Resource

Rubinstein, B., Ahlqwist, M., and Bengtsson, C. Hyperacusis, tinnitus, headache, temporomandibular disorders and amalgam fillings—an epidemiological study, *Proceedings of the Fifth International Tinnitus Seminar*, Reich, G. E., and Vernon, J., eds., American Tinnitus Association, Portland, OR, 1995.

13

Depression

Q Is tinnitus merely annoying or does it do real harm?

A If you are asking if tinnitus itself does real harm to the auditory system, the answer is no. If you are asking if it does harm to other systems, the answer is yes. It can disrupt the quality of life and interfere with sleep, concentration, and productivity. It can induce anxiety and depression as well as stress and tension. For most people with severe tinnitus, it is not merely annoying. It is greatly and constantly annoying. Tinnitus is itself a symptom that something has done harm to the auditory system or the part of the brain involved in tinnitus perception.

Q Can antidepressants help my tinnitus?

A Most of the tricyclic antidepressant drugs can worsen tinnitus. Nortriptyline (brand names: Pamelor or Aventyl) might be the exception to this rule. It is a tricyclic antidepressant that does not appear to exacerbate tinnitus. It is also easily measured in blood samples, and the correct dose can be quickly evaluated. Nortriptyline has very few negative side effects, and it produces a slight sedative effect, so it helps patients sleep. For these reasons, researchers chose to study it for its effectiveness as a tinnitus relief agent.

Mark Sullivan, M.D., Ph.D., et al., at the University of Washington, conducted a double-blind placebo-controlled study of nortriptyline with 19 patients, all of whom had tinnitus and depression. The results: Patients on this drug felt better. However, since the patients' tinnitus loudness was not measured before or after the study, they do not know if the drug actually quieted the tinnitus or if it sufficiently relieved the depression so that the patients were able to handle their tinnitus better. The researchers also admit that the improvement could have been the result of the patients' response to the compassion of the caregivers administering the drug. Many patients who took nortriptyline found that their depression and insomnia were particularly relieved. The nortriptyline group did show greater tinnitus relief than the placebo group, but the difference between the two groups was small. If you choose to try nortriptyline, note that high doses of vitamin C could inhibit the effect of the drug.

For people with depression and tinnitus, Robert Dobie, M.D., suggests the use of a new class of antidepressants called selected seratonin reuptake inhibitors (SSRIs). This includes drugs like Prozac, Zoloft, and Paxil. In addition to their tendency to not aggravate tinnitus, this class of antidepressants has fewer and less troublesome side effects overall than the tricyclic antidepressants.

Test your tinnitus. If it becomes louder when you first start taking an antidepressant, stop taking it immediately. The tinnitus increase is almost always reversible when the offending drug is stopped within 2 days of use. Report the reaction to your physician and ask for another medication.

Q   **Can depression make tinnitus worse? And if so, what can be done about it? I have had bouts of depression for many years, long before the tinnitus appeared.**

A   In many cases, tinnitus is the cause of the depression. However, your depression preceded the tinnitus, so a treatment for depression is indicated. Since most tricyclic antidepressant drugs can temporarily worsen tinnitus, how does one treat depression without making the tinnitus worse? Ask your doctor to suggest a nontricyclic drug, like Wellbutrin, for depression. Although nortriptyline is a tricyclic antidepressant, it produces relatively few negative side effects and is often effective for the depression associated with tinnitus.

The Berkeley *Wellness Letter* included an article entitled "A Better Treatment for Depression" and discussed the effect of a plain old plant called St. John's Wort on the condition of depression. (The word *wort* comes from the old English word for plant, and this particular plant was named for St. John because it blooms around June 24, the birthday of St. John the Baptist.)

Unlike most herbal remedies, St. John's wort or *Hypericum perforatum* (active ingredient: hypericin) has been studied extensively, although not in the United States. St. John's wort is used extensively for depression in Germany. One estimate indicates that in 1994 German physicians prescribed 66 million daily doses of St. John's wort for depression. Another study published in the *British Medical Journal* reviewed 23 studies of St. John's wort, three of which were directed at depression. The results indicated that St. John's wort was somewhat more effective than the usual drugs, including Prozac, that are prescribed for depression. However, St. John's wort is generally not effective for very serious cases of depression. Present-day AIDS researchers are also studying this herb for its possible antiviral activity. These studies contained no reports of serious side effects from the herb. The minor side effects reported include gastrointestinal discomfort, fatigue, dry mouth, slight dizziness, and sunlight sensitivity.

The Berkeley *Wellness Letter* suggests that St. John's wort should not be taken in conjunction with other antidepressants, the blood-thinning drug Coumadin, some oral contraceptives, and a few other medicines known to interact negatively with this herb. The U.S. National Institutes of Health is planning an extended study of St. John's wort.

If your depression is severe, it is not likely that St. John's wort will relieve it. On the other hand, if your depression is mild to moderate, consider trying this herb for at least 4 weeks. The recommended dose is 2 to 4 grams per day.

Q I recently learned about SAMe for depression and it has worked wonders for me. Not only has SAMe relieved my depression, but I'm convinced that it has also lowered my tinnitus. Do you think someone will conduct a study of SAMe for tinnitus patients?

A It is exciting that you have found some depression and tinnitus relief with SAMe. It is common for tinnitus to produce depression. When a patient is able to truly relieve his or her depression, any accompanying tinnitus will often appear lessened.

As for studying it, if enough patients report success with a medication and this information makes its way to an interested researcher, the researcher might conduct an open study of the drug. (An open study is a drug trial on a group of patients who know what drug they are taking.) If the results from the open study are favorable, the researcher might take the next step (funds permitting) and conduct a double-blind-placebo-controlled study. This is a much more formal study in which neither the patients nor their dispensing doctors know who is taking the placebo and who is taking the active drug.

SAMe (*S*-adenosylmethionine) is a molecule that is part of every living cell and is constantly being produced. This substance is currently being studied all over the world for its use to help relieve depression and repair arthritis. SAMe supplements are available over the counter and over the Internet (www.drugstore.com).

A 1994 study in Italy demonstrated that SAMe's effectiveness in relieving depression was superior to the placebo and equal to standard tricyclic antidepressants. The only difference was that SAMe had relatively few and infrequent side effects. (Mild stomach upset was reported.)

This substance has not been approved by the FDA. But it might happen when proper research studies are done in the United States to test the usefulness and safety of the substance. Nevertheless, the FDA permits SAMe to be sold as a dietary supplement as long as the marketers do not state that it has therapeutic uses. No one else yet has reported its effectiveness for tinnitus.

Resources

Bloomfield, H., Nordfors, M., and McWilliams, P. *Hypericum and Depression,* Prelude Press Health-Center.com—Antidepressants. http://www.health-center.com/pharmacy/antidepressants/1/22/00

Cowley, G., and Underwood, A. What Is SAMe, *http://newsweek.com/nw-srv/issue/01_99b/printed/us/so/he0101_1.htm,* 3–26–00

PDR for Herbal Medicines, 1st ed., Medical Economics Company, Montvale, NJ, 1998.

Sullivan, M., Katon, W., Russo, J., Dobie, R., and Dakai, C. A randomized trial of nortriptyline for severe chronic tinnitus. Effects on depression, disability, and tinnitus symptoms, *Arch. Intern. Med.,* Oct 11, 1993; 153(19):2251–9.

Worry wort, *Wellness Letter,* University of California, Berkeley, May 2000, 16:8.

14

Drug Perfusion:
In-the-Ear Drug Treatment

Q My ENT physician recently told me that drugs for the relief of tinnitus were being dispensed directly into the inner ear. How do they get the drugs in there? Can you tell me more about this procedure?

A It might help to first understand how we hear. Sound energy enters the ear and vibrates the eardrum. The eardrum then vibrates the middle ear bones (the malleus, incus, and stapes). The stapes is attached to the cochlea, our inner ear hearing organ, at the oval window. The oval window is a part of the cochlea that faces the middle ear space. (See Figure 14.1.) The vibrating middle ear bones send the sound energy through the oval window and into the cochlea. The hair cells in the cochlea receive the sound signal and send the message through the auditory nerve to the brain.

The round window is also a part of the cochlea that faces the middle ear space and could be viewed as a pressure release valve for sound that enters the inner ear. The round window is recessed in a niche, called the *round window niche,* and is covered with a membrane.

Researchers have recently discovered what they believe is the most important function of the round window: It sits in the perfect location on the cochlea to receive drugs by way of perfusion! Unlike the oval window, which sits directly next to the stapes and in the direct path of sound, the round window is the window of choice for direct drug delivery.

Drugs can be given to patients for the treatment of inner ear disorders by perfusion. (To *perfuse* is to pass or seep through slowly.) These drugs are dispensed so that they perfuse through the round window membrane and into the inner ear. The tympanic membrane can be reflected, or lifted up, to allow drugs into the middle ear space. But if we were to reflect the membrane of the round window, the perilymphatic fluid in the inner ear would leak out. This could seriously damage the ear and possibly destroy all hearing.

Also see Chapter 32, Ménière's Disease.

68

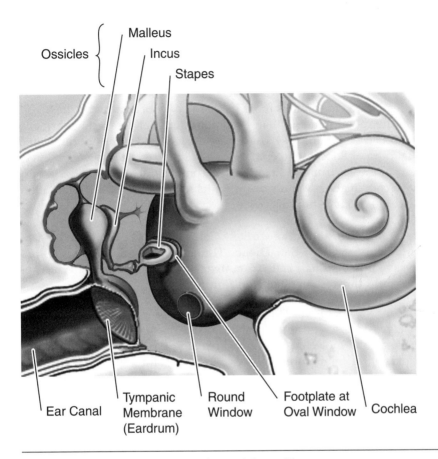

Ossicles {
  Malleus
  Incus
  Stapes
}

Ear Canal | Tympanic Membrane (Eardrum) | Round Window | Footplate at Oval Window | Cochlea

FIGURE 14.1 *Oval and round windows of the cochlea.*

To avoid this, a very tiny catheter (tube) was developed to fit through a reflected eardrum and the middle ear space and to rest in the round window niche right against the round window membrane. A micropump has also been developed to work in conjunction with the catheter to deliver exact and timed doses of medication to the round window.

In a study of 20 patients, this approach was used to deliver drugs through the round window membrane. Five of the 20 patients had Ménière's disease and were treated with perfusions of the antibiotic gentamicin. Four of the five experienced complete remission of their vertigo. The fifth patient reported that the vertigo had been considerably reduced. The drawback was that three of the five patients had increased hearing loss as a result of the perfusion, and one became totally deaf in the treated ear because of the ototoxicity of the antibiotic.

The other 15 patients in this study had tinnitus and were given lidocaine by microcatheter to the round window. Of the 15, two experienced a

50% or more reduction of tinnitus volume. These data are not very encouraging. But it is possible that the lidocaine used in this study did not contain a sufficient amount of epinephrine to prevent the blood vessels in the very vascular round window membrane from carrying the drug away before it could be effective in the inner ear space.

By its nature, lidocaine is more liable to be carried away by the blood vessels in the round window than is gentamicin. Therefore, epinephrine, a drug that constricts blood vessels, is absolutely required in the lidocaine mix. The usual ratio of lidocaine to epinephrine is 1 : 100,000. However, to effect anesthesia of the eardrum, we had to use a composition of 1 : 1000. It is possible that a combination of these drugs in the same ratio placed at the round window could produce tinnitus relief.

Q I read an article about the work of Col. Richard D. Kopke at the U.S. Naval Medical Center in San Diego. The article described Dr. Kopke's work to save inner ear hair cells from toxic or damaging agents. What application could this research have on tinnitus?

A Dr. Kopke's work is very important. Loud noise and certain drugs such as aminoglycosides, a type of antibiotic, damage the ears by causing the production of harmful molecules known as free radicals. Kopke's procedure involves placing a miniature catheter (or tube) through the tympanic membrane and through the middle ear until the tip of the catheter rests on the round window of the cochlea. This precise delivery system places the medicine exactly where it is needed. In this case, the catheter delivers antioxidant drugs into the inner ear to counteract the free radicals caused by loud noise and ototoxic drugs.

Kopke is part of a research team that first demonstrated success with this technique on animals and then tried it on three people, with apparent success in all three. Clearly, the delivery of a drug to the exact position where it is needed will offer significant advances for noise-induced and drug-induced damage to the ear. It is also very possible that any action that prevents or corrects ototoxicity or ear damage will also prevent or correct tinnitus. It is also entirely possible that the hearing damage initially sustained by the three test subjects was temporary and would have resolved without the antioxidant perfusion. Skepticism aside, it is a very exciting development. Overall, the developments in this field of micro-targeted delivery of medications to the inner ear seem to be heading us toward safer surgical procedures and maybe, in time, hearing restoration.

Resources

Feghali, J. G., Lefebvre, P. P., Staecker, H., Kopke, R., Frenz, D. A., Malgrange, B., Liu, W., Moonen, G., Ruben, R. J., and Van de Water, T. R. Mammalian auditory hair cell regeneration/repair and protection: A review and future directions, *Ear Nose Throat J.*, Apr. 1998; 77(4):276, 280, 282–5.

15

Drug Side Effects

Q I recently had a bad cold and my doctor put me on E-Mycin. After the first day of taking the drug, my tinnitus got louder. By the end of the 10-day therapy, my tinnitus was almost unbearable. I've been off the E-Mycin for 7 days now and the ringing is just as loud as it was on the last day I took the drug. Will it return to its usual level or will it stay at this level?

A Your tinnitus will very likely return to its original level, but it will take time—a lot of time. Sometimes a reversal can take months to correct itself. Don't get discouraged by the slow progress. From now on it is essential that you tell your physician about your tinnitus before he or she prescribes a medication. At the first sign of increased tinnitus after starting a medication, always contact your physician and ask for a substitute drug. Generally, the sooner you stop taking an offending medication, the more rapidly you will recover from its side effects.

Q I've been prescribed a diuretic (Bumex) for my hypertension and edema. But it seems to be making my tinnitus worse. I thought that if my high blood pressure were brought under control the tinnitus would go down. Why am I having the opposite reaction?

A Bumex (bumetanide) is a powerful *loop diuretic* that is often prescribed for the exact health problems that you describe. And as is the situation with a loop diuretic, tinnitus can be one side effect of its use because it reduces or impairs hearing. However, researchers Halstenson and Matzke studied bumetanide and found it to be less ototoxic than furosemide, another loop diuretic, even though bumetanide is 40 times more potent than furosemide milligram per milligram. It is important to note that the combination of loop diuretics and certain antibiotics can significantly and permanently damage hearing.

If your health condition can tolerate some experimentation, you might want to consider a natural herbal diuretic, like one with Uva ursi, dandelion root, and juniper berries in it. But before you make any changes to your routine of medication, consult with your doctor.

Q If I am taking two drugs at the same time and both drugs have tinnitus listed as a possible side effect, am I guaranteed that my tinnitus will get worse?

A Not everyone who takes a medication will experience negative side effects from it. The combining of drugs can create a different set of problems and side effects, including the possibility that one drug will prevent the other drug from being effective. Let your doctor know the names and dosages of all prescription, herbal, and over-the-counter medicines that you are taking.

Quite often, negative side effects will disappear over time if you continue taking the drug. Side effects also tend to be temporary, so stopping the drug will usually put an end to the unwanted effects. It is best to discuss all the potential side effects of a drug ahead of time with your physician before he or she prescribes it and, most certainly, before you take it.

The *PDR Companion Guide* includes the percentages of patients who have observed side effects following use of prescription and over-the-counter drugs available in the United States. The guide lists specific side effects, like tinnitus, then lists the drugs that cause the side effects. We need to remember that when a drug is reported to cause a specific symptom in 2% of the test population, this means that it does not cause the symptom in 98% of the population. Also note that the percentages for tinnitus listed in the guide represent the number of people who reported *new* cases of tinnitus, not a worsening of existing tinnitus. Admittedly, it is a strong possibility that the drugs listed could exacerbate tinnitus too. But, to be fair, the drugs were not included on the list for this reason. (We have included the 2000 *PDR Companion Guide* tinnitus side effects listing in the appendix of this book.)

Looking at the list, we noticed that the PDR statistics for drug side effects were reported differently from drug to drug. So we asked the PDR publishers why this was so. They told us that drug companies report their side effects data to the PDR in different ways. Some companies supply the PDR with results from research studies, while other companies supply the PDR with reports from patients, both of which the PDR publishers find acceptable.

Q Which drugs will make my tinnitus worse? And what if I have no choice but to take one of them?

A Many antibiotics (such as streptomycin and gentamicin), several chemotherapy agents, and plain old aspirin can make tinnitus worse. Some do so permanently (like chemotherapy agent cisplatin) and others do so temporarily (like aspirin).

Sometimes the condition for which a medicine is given is serious enough that a specific drug must be used regardless of the risk of tinnitus exacerbation. If a necessary drug does adversely affect your tinnitus, talk to your doctor immediately. He or she might be able to trim down the dosage or shorten the length of time that you will need to take it. The sooner you go off the drug, the quicker the tinnitus can go back to its original level.

In the case of chemotherapy, there are other drugs that can (and probably should) be given along with the chemo drugs that will dramatically reduce the ototoxic effect of the chemotherapy agents without reducing their effectiveness against the cancer.

We like to assign blame to the medicines that we take or the foods that we eat when the tinnitus goes up. But we are not always correct with our guesses when we do. We need to remember that tinnitus can fluctuate without a detectable rhyme or reason.

Q I am concerned specifically about the cancer drug cisplatin. My mother will be given this shortly for her treatment, but I read that it almost always produces hearing loss and tinnitus. Is this a risk that cancer patients must take?

A Fortunately, this is not a risk that cancer patients must take. It has been found that 38% of patients who are treated with the chemotherapy compound cisplatin will experience hearing loss and tinnitus as a result. This effect, however, can be minimized by the addition of 4-methylthiobenzoic acid or thiosulfate without reducing the anticancer effect. Other compounds, like amifostine, are being used experimentally as chemotherapy *pre*treatments. Amifostine pretreatment was shown to significantly reduce the incidence of tinnitus and some other undesirable symptoms associated with cisplatin. Still other drugs like *nerve growth factor* and *neurotrophin 4/5* are being studied because of their ability to totally prevent hearing damage from cisplatin.

Q I've noticed that several drugs on the PDR list of "drugs that cause tinnitus" are medications that are frequently prescribed to tinnitus patients. How is this possible?

A The degree and type of symptoms that we experience when taking drugs are very often dose dependent. It is a common enough occurrence that a drug, like caroverine, taken at one dose level will help a disorder, but taken at another (stronger) dose level will cause problems, including a worsening of the symptom that it had earlier helped. Also, some drugs, like aspirin, are benign when taken in small doses, but are almost guaranteed tinnitus producers when they are taken in large doses. It is an undisputed fact that some people are sensitive to some medications (as well as to foods, pollens, perfumes, etc.) and other people are not. For now, it is an inexplicable fact of life.

The following adverse reactions were some of the ones listed for lidocaine in the 2000 PDR: lightheadedness, nervousness, euphoria, dizziness, drowsiness, blurred vision, and tinnitus. Although tinnitus is listed as a side effect, it is well established that an intravenous injection of lidocaine will eliminate tinnitus in 75% to 89% of patients for 30 minutes or more.

Q My doctor has recommended that I take an aspirin a day as a heart problem preventative. Right now, my tinnitus is bearable, but I do not want it to get any louder. Will an aspirin a day increase my tinnitus?

A In laboratory studies, it took approximately 24 aspirin tablets (two to three times the manufacturer's recommended daily dose) to induce tinnitus in test subjects. Salycilate, the active ingredient in aspirin, is the culprit. Theoretically, if you already have tinnitus, any amount of aspirin could aggravate it. The chances are good, however, that a single aspirin will not increase the loudness of your tinnitus. In the event that it does, know that aspirin-induced tinnitus always resolves when the aspirin is discontinued.

About 10 years ago, we used aspirin to deliberately induce tinnitus in some non-tinnitus test subjects. We learned a number of things right away.

1. It took a great deal of aspirin to induce tinnitus.
2. We could not study the patients with aspirin-induced tinnitus because any sound we delivered to them, even the quiet tones from a simple hearing test, masked their tinnitus and then put it into extended residual inhibition.

Since then, we have wondered what would happen if tinnitus were purposely made louder with aspirin and then we attempted to mask it. Would the masking cover the entire tinnitus or just the aspirin-induced increase? And would the tinnitus that was worsened by aspirin and then successfully masked go into extended residual inhibition? Such an experiment might be worthwhile for those who cannot be masked in the usual fashion.

Q I've had pulsatile tinnitus for 6 years now and I cope very well with it. Recently, I had an ankle injury and was told to take Celebrex for the inflammation. After 3 days, my tinnitus went crazy, so I went off the drug immediately. It took 2 weeks for the tinnitus to return to normal. Do anti-inflammatory drugs usually provoke tinnitus?

A Celebrex (chemical name: celecoxib) is a nonsteroidal anti-inflammatory drug that is often used to treat the pain of arthritis. Its list of side effects includes dizziness, headache, nausea, and bloating, but not tinnitus. This omission does not mean that it is innocent. It just means that no one has yet reported tinnitus as a side effect. Let your physician know. He or she is the one who can report this information to the drug company, who in turn reports it to the PDR publishers who will include it in their drug interaction books.

As for anti-inflammatories, some do and some do not cause onset and presumably an increase in tinnitus. Naprosyn and Ponstel are nonsteroidal anti-inflammatories that do not list tinnitus as a side effect. Ask your physician if there is another drug that can be substituted for Celebrex, preferably one that does not list tinnitus as a side effect—remembering of course that tinnitus is not listed as a side effect for Celebrex!

Q My tinnitus greatly increased in loudness after I took Viagra 8 weeks ago. Is it likely to return to its original level if the medication is stopped? If so, how long do I need to be off Viagra before the tinnitus will return to its original level?

A Unfortunately, Viagra has not been on the market long enough for us to know the answer. As a general rule, if a medication increases tinnitus and you quickly cease taking the medication, the tinnitus returns to its original level over time. The length of time that it takes is highly variable from person to person and from medication to medication. Although we do not yet know the normal tinnitus recovery time for Viagra (if, in fact, Viagra is the cause), we *do* know that the degree to which one stresses over these situations can increase tinnitus. Therefore, we encourage you to try some form of tinnitus relief as a way to decrease stress and possibly speed the recovery process. A final thought: Is it possible that there was another situation or medication that could have led to your increased tinnitus? We ask that only because, considering the wide use of this medication, we have heard from relatively few people who have had a similar reaction.

Q I'm 75 years old and have had constant tinnitus in both ears for about 10 years. It was not a problem until 3 weeks ago when I took 25 mg of Viagra. Four hours later, I awoke with very loud tinnitus that lasted several hours. It has settled down, but it is still louder than before. Is Viagra known to increase tinnitus?

A According to the 2000 *Physicians Desk Reference*, tinnitus is a side effect of Viagra, but in less than 3% of the cases. As you probably know, tinnitus can get louder on its own. This event could be such an occasion. The only way to determine whether or not Viagra caused the tinnitus increase is to try it again. Also, be sure that there is not another event, such as noise exposure or unusual stress (positive or negative), that may be causing the tinnitus increase.

[This patient tried Viagra two more times and experienced no increase in his tinnitus.]

Two other patients commented that their tinnitus became louder immediately after using Viagra. (We did not ask them if the result was worth the price.) There are a number of reasons why we probably have not heard from more male tinnitus patients who have taken Viagra.

1. Patients could be reluctant to comment about their use of this drug.
2. People are much more likely to speak up when something goes wrong than when something goes right.

Q   **I have had manageable cochlear Ménière's disease with some tinnitus, hearing loss, and fullness in the ear. Then this summer I took three 2-week-long regimens of Biaxin, Prilosec (an acid suppressor), and Pepto-Bismol tablets. Since this summer, the tinnitus has been extremely bad. Can I determine medically if hair cells have been damaged or destroyed?**

A   Tinnitus is not listed as a side effect for Biaxin in the *Physicians Desk Reference*. On the other hand, Prilosec does list hearing loss as well as tinnitus as possible side effect for 1% of those who took it. Fortunately, these side effects often disappear when the drug is discontinued.

Pepto-Bismol contains salicylates, a known tinnitus inducer. The instructions on the Pepto-Bismol label state that, if you take Pepto-Bismol with aspirin (which is sodium salicylate) and your ears start to ring, discontinue taking both since you would be getting a double dose of salicylates. Salicylate-induced tinnitus is temporary and will decline in time to its original level. Alka Seltzer, Anacin, Ascriptin, Aspergum, Bufferin, Doan's pills, and Excedrin are other common over-the-counter drugs that contain salicylates.

Tinnitus associated with Ménière's disease is often maskable because it is commonly in a mid- to low-frequency range. If you had your hearing tested before you started the medications, have another hearing test now to determine if any more hearing loss and therefore hair cell damage has occurred. If you do have additional hearing loss with your increased tinnitus, it could also be temporary.

Q   **I've read that some artificial food flavorings contain sodium salicylate. This is the ingredient in aspirin that makes tinnitus worse. The report estimated that the average person consumes about 125 mg of sodium salicylate daily in the form of artificial flavorings. Could this be affecting my tinnitus?**

A   One baby aspirin contains 80 mg of sodium salicylate, which is usually not enough to influence tinnitus. The estimated 125 mg of sodium salicylate from a day's worth of artificial flavors probably would not have an effect on tinnitus for most people. If, however, 125 mg of sodium salicylate does make your tinnitus louder, the effect would be temporary. Consider avoiding artificial flavorings for a short while and see if this makes difference. Also, pay attention to other substances that contain salicylates, like Alka Seltzer or Pepto-Bismol, that you might consume through the course of a day.

Q What anti-inflammatory medications can tinnitus patients use? I've read several anecdotal reports about patients who used cortisone for other reasons and found that it relieved their tinnitus too. Will cortisone shots help or worsen tinnitus?

A Drug side effects vary greatly from patient to patient. Some patients are excessively sensitive to medications and experience all sorts of side effects, whereas others never experience any side effects. The over-the-counter drug Advil (ibuprofen) is not likely to exacerbate your tinnitus. But if it does, the exacerbation will be temporary. It is also unlikely that cortisone shots will exacerbate your tinnitus. Some patients have reported a temporary reduction in their tinnitus after taking cortisone.

Cortisone is frequently administered to reverse sudden-onset hearing loss. Many physicians are aware of this treatment and prescribe it when a patient arrives at a clinic within days of the condition's onset. Although these physicians do so knowing that cortisone has not been clinically proved effective for this condition, they prescribe it anyway because it works. (If more than a week has passed since the onset of the hearing loss, cortisone is usually not effective in reversing the damage.)

When you try a new medication, evaluate your tinnitus at the same time. Use a 10-point grading scale and judge the loudness of your tinnitus under the same environmental conditions every day. If you find that there is the slightest increase in your tinnitus while taking a medication, inform your primary care physician to see if an alternative medication is available. One of the best anti-inflammatory medications is aspirin. It might be possible for you to gain the anti-inflammatory effect from aspirin at a level below what would increase your tinnitus. If you try aspirin, discontinue it at the first sign of any tinnitus increase.

Resources

Balch, J. F., and Balch, P. *Prescription for Nutritional Healing,* Avery Publishing Group, Garden City Park, NY, 1997.

Halstenson, C. E., and Matzke G. R. Bumetanide: A new loop diuretic (Bumex, Roche Laboratories), *Drug Intell. Clin. Pharm.,* Nov. 1983; 17(11):786–97.

Madasu, R., Ruckenstein, M. J., Leake, F., Steere, E., and Robbins, K. T. Ototoxic effects of supradose cisplatin with sodium thiosulfate neutralization in patients with head and neck cancer, *Arch. Otolaryngol. Head Neck Surg.,* Sept. 1997; 123(9):978–81.

16

Drugs That Help

Q I've heard that Xanax can help tinnitus. What kind of drug is it and how much do I need to take to get relief?

A Xanax is an anxiolytic (antianxiety) medication. It was tested in an open trial after a few patients who were taking it for anxiety happened to mention that it reduced their tinnitus. In 1993, Xanax was double-blind placebo-control tested for its effects on tinnitus. In this study, 76% of the patients who took 1.5 mg of the drug daily experienced a 40% or more tinnitus volume reduction. The placebo group reported a 4% volume reduction. The study lasted 12 weeks and most of the subjects reported relief after 8 weeks. The actual measurement of the tinnitus loudness before treatment averaged at 7.5 dB above hearing threshold. The actual measurement of the tinnitus loudness after treatment averaged at 2.3 dB above threshold, a significant drop. This double-blind study has not been duplicated, but the medication is nevertheless widely and successfully used for tinnitus relief.

If your physician consents to a trial of Xanax for you, try the following dose schedule that was used in the study. *Remember:* no alcohol at all with Xanax.

1. For the first 2 weeks, take 0.5 mg in the evening. This is not enough Xanax to relieve tinnitus for most patients, but it will determine whether the drug produces too much of a drowsy effect for you.
2. For the next 2 weeks, take 0.25 mg in the morning and again at noon and 0.5 mg in the evening. For some patients, this is enough to reduce tinnitus.
3. If the tinnitus was not reduced during phase 2 or if it was reduced only slightly, take 0.5 mg of Xanax three times a day for the next 2 weeks.
4. To taper off Xanax, take 0.5 mg twice a day for 3 days and then 0.5 mg once a day for 3 days; then stop altogether.

Q I have been on Xanax for 6 weeks and my tinnitus is all but gone. Should I continue on this drug?

A With your prescribing physician's concurrence, you can continue taking Xanax at your present dose level for 1 more month and then taper off. Wait 1 month, and at the end of that time go back on the Xanax, but only if necessary.

If you do go back on it, you can start taking it at the dose you previously found effective for tinnitus relief. Xanax is not addictive, but it can be habit forming. Therefore, you will still need to taper off the drug slowly each time that you discontinue it. Discuss the dosing schedule with your doctor.

Xanax is a benzodiazepine drug. Benzodiazepines are antianxiety drugs that promote mental and physical relaxation by reducing nerve activity in the brain. Benzodiazepine use can result in a physical dependency, especially for those who have or have had problems with alcohol, so caution is advised. It is also important to note that benzodiazepines have been associated with the emergence or worsening of manic depression. However, it is not known if these drugs cause the depression or fail to prevent it. If depression occurs during the course of benzodiazepine treatment, it is prudent to discontinue taking the drug. Other benzodiazepine drugs are flurazepam (Dalmane), oxazepam (Serax), diazepam (Valium), triazolam (Halcion), clonazepam (Klonopin), and chlordiazepoxide (Librium).*

Q I have followed the Xanax dose schedule, but I've only experienced slight relief from it. What should I do next?

A Some patients who have gotten only minor relief from 0.5 mg three times a day have found significant tinnitus relief by increasing the dose to 0.5 mg four times a day. Consult your prescribing physician about this possibility. But do not do this without his or her permission.

Q I recently obtained a generic form of Xanax that did not relieve the tinnitus nearly as much as the name brand. Have others reported the same thing?

A Even though the generic brand of a drug should contain the same ingredients as the name brand, patients have reported noticeable differences in the way the generic drug works versus its name brand counterpart. In your case, it would be wise to request the name brand from your pharmacist.

We have also heard from a tinnitus patient who had taken Xanax and was helped by it. However, the side effect of drowsiness was quite bothersome to her, so she tapered off the drug and stopped. A few months later, she

*Proprietary drug names are capitalized, and generic drug names are in lowercase.

decided to take Xanax again and was incredibly relieved that the drowsiness did not return. Only when she went to purchase another refill did she learn that her second try with Xanax had actually been with a generic form of the drug. (She had been given the name brand the first time.) To test out her idea that the generic and the brand were different, she tried the name brand again and found that it again made her sleepy. In her case, the "weaker" generic form of the drug gave her the tinnitus relief she wanted, but without the side effects she could not tolerate.

Q I have given the drug Xanax a full and precise trial, but I've experienced no relief from my tinnitus. What other drug might I try?

A Many drugs have been studied all over the world for their effect on tinnitus, and many have been found to be useful. Drs. Denk, Felix, Brix, and Ehrenberger worked in Austria with the drug caroverine. (Caroverine is an antispasmatic drug made in Austria that has been used in Europe and Japan for several decades.) In this double-blind, placebo-controlled study, the drug was administered as a slow, single intravenous infusion to 30 patients. Another 30 patients received a placebo infusion. If the tinnitus faded, the usage was stopped. If too much was given and the tinnitus got louder, the loudness was reversed by the immediate administration of glutamate. The researchers considered the caroverine successful if the patient rated it as such and if the patient's tinnitus loudness matching measurement showed a 50% or more reduction. Of the 30 patients who received IV caroverine, 63.3% experienced measurable relief. Of the 30 who received the placebo, none experienced relief.

The positive effect lasted for hours, days, and even months for some of these patients. Denk et al. speculate that the varied duration of tinnitus relief experienced by the patients in this study could be related to the variety of tinnitus causes. (There is no way to know this, but it is an interesting speculation!)

The researchers reported no severe side effects (some slight headaches only), and in no case did the therapy have to be stopped before completion. Some patients who had a successful experience with IV caroverine were able to have their tinnitus stabilized by oral caroverine. This is another promising study that we would like to see repeated.

Q Does arthritis cause tinnitus? In my case, it seems that the tinnitus and the arthritis started at the same time. I am also taking furosemide and I wonder if it could be making my tinnitus worse.

A Arthritis does not cause tinnitus. However, the high doses of aspirin that people often take to relieve arthritis *can* cause tinnitus. Furosemide is a loop diuretic that piqued the interest of tinnitus researchers Guth, Risey, and Amedee at Tulane University some years ago because of the way the drug affects the ear. In 1986, Guth et al. learned that furosemide reduced the activity of the hearing nerve and reduced the *endocochlear potential* in the inner ear, that is, the natural electrical voltage that makes our hearing system work. (Guth refers to the endocochlear potential as the inner ear's battery.) The researchers found this interesting because the endocochlear potential increases when tinnitus increases, at least in animal studies. They wondered if the reduction of the endocochlear potential would have an opposite effect and if a reduced cochlear potential would reduce tinnitus.

To test this, they gave 80-mg intravenous injections of furosemide to 40 tinnitus patients in their clinic. Of these 40 patients, 20 reported a temporary lessening of their tinnitus after the furosemide injections. They continued with a double-blind study of these patients. Twelve of the 20 "positive furosemide responders" were given oral doses of furosemide; the other eight were given another diuretic that does not affect the ear. Because both drugs cause frequent urination, the subjects could not tell which drug they were taking. With doses varying from 80 to 160 mg per day, 10 of the 12 patients responded positively to oral furosemide.

Since that time, Guth et al. have tested IV furosemide on a total of 180 patients, 85 of whom reported a reduction in tinnitus because of it. All 85 were put on oral furosemide. The researchers note that patients on the oral drug have had side effects no worse than increased urination. (They looked for decreased potassium levels, which can result from furosemide use, but found no cases of it. This might be because the patients took potassium supplements while they were taking the furosemide.)

The researchers also note that the 50% response rate to IV furosemide has held up over time. Their theory—perhaps more of a musing than a theory—is that half of all people with tinnitus have peripheral (inner ear) tinnitus and that the other half have central (brain) tinnitus. Since furosemide affects only inner ear chemistry and not brain chemistry, the researchers wonder if this drug could have specific usefulness for patients with peripheral tinnitus. The bigger wonder is why this drug has not been studied more.

Note that furosemide interacts quite negatively with aminoglycosides, a group of antibiotics. In fact, many diuretic and aminoglycoside combinations can cause profound and permanent hearing loss.

Q **I think I have tried everything for my tinnitus without success: ginkgo, sleeping pills, meditation, vitamins, and antidepressants. Finally, I called a local audiologist who had just read a study about fluoxetine (Prozac) for tinnitus. According to the study, three patients took Prozac for 1 week and their tinnitus went away. Based on this, I asked my family physician for a prescription for Prozac. After taking 10 mg of Prozac daily for 5 days, my buzzing stopped completely. I have been on this medication for 9 days now and the buzzing has not returned. To be thorough, if I am subjected to a sudden loud noise, the buzzing will return, but just for a**

few minutes. Here is my question: I have read that the positive effects of Prozac tend to disappear after continued use. Have you heard of this experience with Prozac?

A   Some health-care professionals refer to "Prozac poop-out," but they cite only anecdotal cases. One of these accounts referred to a patient who had taken Prozac for 10 years before its effectiveness declined. In none of these cases did a clinician increase the dosage or suggest that the patient take a hiatus from the medication and then return to it.

The Oregon Hearing Research Center conducted a very brief open study of Prozac with 25 patients and found that 5 of the 25 patients experienced tinnitus relief, 7 had their tinnitus increase, and 13 experienced no change at all. There is every reason for you to continue taking Prozac since it is helping, and at the same time be careful to avoid loud sounds. If the effectiveness of Prozac does wear off for you, consider going off the drug for 1 month and then back on it again, but only if your prescribing physician agrees to such a plan.

Q   I had taken Prozac for more than a year, which actually helped my tinnitus. My physician retired, so I stopped taking the drug when my prescription ran out. The nurse later told me that I should not have stopped taking this particular drug so suddenly. I did not know what else to do. What did I do wrong?

A   Prozac, like many other drugs, including Xanax, can be habit-forming. Thus, for some patients the sudden cessation of this drug could cause unpleasant withdrawal symptoms like nausea, lightheadedness, and a general feeling of malaise. With drugs of this nature, it is best to taper off gradually to avoid the withdrawal symptoms. It is a very individualized process. Some people need to taper off habit-forming drugs *very* slowly. Other people, like you, have no problem tapering off this drug quickly.

As for your doctor, you can contact his or her office again and ask for a referral and for your medical records to be forwarded to a new doctor. Since you found tinnitus relief with Prozac once, it would be nice if you could experience that relief again.

Q   I've heard the term *calcium channel blockers* and that they are a kind of drug that is being used to help tinnitus? Do they work?

A   Calcium channel blockers are a group of medications that are used to treat high blood pressure, abnormal heart rhythms, bleeding between the brain and the skull, angina (chest pain), and even migraines. Simply, calcium channel blockers stop calcium ions from crossing cell membranes. This action relaxes the arteries, which causes the arteries to dilate, which improves the blood supply to the heart and reduces blood pressure.

There has been more than a little controversy about the safety of these drugs. Some studies suggest that heart patients run a greater risk of death with calcium channel blockers than with the placebos tested. Some calcium channel blockers have been tested as treatments for tinnitus.

In 1985, the calcium channel blocker nimodipine (brand name: Nimotop) was tested in Germany in an open tinnitus study. Thirty tinnitus patients received the drug (three 30-mg tablets per day) for 12 weeks. The results were interesting. Six out of the 30 reported complete tinnitus remission, two had 70% to 80% improvement, and two had slight improvement. But without a double-blind placebo control to measure the placebo effect, we need to wait for more study. Jastreboff et al. used nimodipine in an animal study in 1991 and found that it reversed the effects of quinine in rats. They presumed that the quinine-induced tinnitus was reversed too. There appears to be something about this class of drug that positively affects the perception of tinnitus. The question of its safety could well be limiting the research community's interest in subjecting patients to it.

There is an unusual contraindication with calcium channel blockers: They cannot be taken with grapefruit juice. Some component in grapefruit juice prevents the liver from clearing certain drugs from the body, and calcium channel blockers are some of these drugs.

Q **When I recently stopped taking prednisone, I noticed tinnitus for the first time. Is it possible that coming off this drug caused the tinnitus? I also have some hearing difficulty.**

A Prednisone is a corticosteroid, a hormone that our bodies naturally produce in the adrenal glands. It is possible that the prednisone was reducing the tinnitus and that coming off the prednisone caused you to notice the tinnitus. Here are two things you can try:

1. With your doctor's permission, go back on the prednisone to see if the tinnitus goes away.
2. Have your hearing and tinnitus tested. If the tinnitus is sufficiently low pitched and the hearing loss warrants it, try hearing aids. They can relieve some forms of tinnitus.

Q **I wondered if a drug company has thought about making drugs available for tinnitus through a skin patch, maybe something we could put right on or near our tinnitus ears.**

A At least one company is already testing such a drug delivery system for the treatment of tinnitus. The company, EpiCept, specializes in the development of topically delivered prescription pain products. According to EpiCept's medical director, Earle Lockhart, M.D., the company is developing a topical anesthetic drug system, a transdermal (through-the-skin) product called LidoPain TV, designed for tinnitus and vertigo relief. He could not divulge which anesthetic drug was being considered, but we think that the name of the product somehow gives it away. Lockhart adds that they are at least a year away from seeing any results from the testing. (Contact EpiCept at 270 Sylvan Ave., Englewood Cliffs, New Jersey 07632, 201-894-8980, Fax: 201-837-0200, mail@epicept.com, www.epicept.com.)

Q In the book *Life Extension,* the drug hydergine was cited as being able to improve hearing loss and relieve tinnitus. Is this drug being used today for this purpose?

A Hydergine was originally developed as an antihypertensive medication. It is still used for that purpose today, although newer drugs are more effective. It is also occasionally used to treat Alzheimer's disease. The claim that hydergine was responsible for improved hearing does raise some questions, since inner ear hearing loss is nearly impossible to remedy. Note that the reference in the book is based on testimonials, not tests.

A study of hydergine (though not a double-blind study) was conducted in Spain in 1990 on 17 patients with tinnitus, vertigo, and hyperacusis. Each patient was given 4.5 mg of hydergine daily for 90 days, and they were evaluated with audiometric tests and subjective evaluation tests throughout. The results: 93.7% reported relief from vertigo, 57.1% reported tinnitus improvement, and 20% reported hyperacusis improvement.

Q I've read about the drug Vastarel and its positive effect on tinnitus. The report indicated that Vastarel was 50% more effective than the placebo. This would seem to make it worthy of consideration. Has the study been repeated?

A Yes, the study was repeated in France by researchers Bebear, Lacomme, and Morgon and involved 315 tinnitus patients. (Interestingly, only 5% of these patients had normal hearing.) Vastarel, or trimetazidine, was used in a double-blind, placebo-controlled study to measure its effect on perceived tinnitus loudness. Forty percent of the trimetazidine group reported a 40% decrease in loudness compared to a 16.9% decrease in loudness in the placebo group. The best results were obtained with trimetazidine for patients whose tinnitus was of recent onset (less than 6 months).

Q Are any of the pharmaceutical companies working on finding a drug for the treatment of tinnitus? If so, which companies, and how far along are they? I wrote to one company but got no answer. Perhaps you have greater clout.

A We doubt the clout part. We recently learned that Pfizer Pharmaceuticals, one of the largest drug manufacturing companies in the world, is investigating drugs for tinnitus relief, so we wrote to the researcher in charge of the study. Like you, we received no answer.

The development of a new drug takes an extremely long time. The drug has to be run through the rigors of double-blind, placebo-controlled testing and often involves thousands of test subjects. Once efficacy has been demonstrated, the drug still has to be cleared through the U.S. Food and Drug Administration, a process that alone can take as long as a year.

It is quite possible that Pfizer will come up with an effective drug for tinnitus or that a researcher will stumble onto an existing drug that works for the majority of people and has little or no side effects. Obviously, no one knows when this discovery will be made, but it is very exciting that work is underway.

Q **I am totally deaf, so any form of sound therapy is not an option for me. What drugs can I try? Is there any way to know which drug would be right for me?**

A Dozens of drugs have been studied and are currently being used to relieve tinnitus. People vary so much in their responses to medications that it is impossible to know ahead of time what one patient's reaction to a medication will be. We never know with certainty if a medication will relieve the tinnitus or worsen it or if the drug side effects will be so severe that they will prevent a full trial of the drug. However, discuss these medications with your doctor: Xanax, Tegretol, caroverine, furosemide, Vastarel, lamotrigine, misoprostol, nortriptyline, and vinpocetine. All have given some patients some degree of tinnitus relief. Not all are available in the United States at this time.

If you have *any* hearing available at all, you might investigate implantable hearing aids. This new technology has already afforded incredible hearing restoration to some profoundly deaf patients.

If you are truly without usable hearing in either ear and at least one of your auditory nerves is intact, you could be a candidate for a cochlear implant. These surgically implanted devices have successfully brought back useful intelligible sounds to many patients. And for many of these patients the intrusive tinnitus diminished as well. (Note that only one cochlear implant is currently allowed per person.) Xanax or another drug treatment might be useful to you also. Speak with your ENT about these possibilities.

Q **I have been using Catapres to control my high blood pressure, which it does do. One day I got so desperate about my tinnitus that I put the Catapres patches on my mastoid bones. And they worked for the tinnitus, although they made my mouth dry and caused me some dizziness. Have you ever heard of using this drug for tinnitus?**

A We haven't. Because Catapres (clonidine) is an antihypertensive medication, it is possible that your reduced blood pressure caused the tinnitus to be reduced. This needs to be studied.

A Closer Look at Drug Studies

Hundreds of tinnitus-related drug research studies have been conducted over the last several decades. The body of research on these drugs, although extensive, has not produced a clear front runner. When Robert Dobie, M.D., reviewed the way that many of these research projects were designed, he noted that the studies were for the most part flawed. Some patient groups were too small, he noted. This could very well have excluded enough people with a certain kind of tinnitus who would have derived benefit from a tested drug. For example, it is possible that certain classes of drugs work better on certain subgroups of tinnitus patients. What if antidepressants were the drugs of choice for ototoxicity-induced tinnitus and no otoxicity-induced tinnitus patients were in the antidepressant study?

Dobie noticed another problem. Most of the drugs that produced significant tinnitus benefit when they were first studied failed to produce significant benefit in follow-up studies. He suggests that the fault could lie with the testers and not with the drugs.

Drug studies in general have another problem: the high rate of undesirable side effects that people experience from the drugs. Here is an example. A study of 20 patients yielded 5 patients who experienced tinnitus relief with a specific drug. But 100 patients had to take the drug first in order to find the 20 who could tolerate the drug's negative side effects long enough to participate in the study. During the study, 7 patients out of the 20 dropped out because they could not tolerate the side effects after all. Of the remaining 13 patients, 5 experienced tinnitus relief with the drug.

If you look at the study results narrowly, you will see that 5 out of 20 experienced relief with the drug. If you step back and look at the study results fully, you will see that 5 out of 100 patients experienced relief with the drug. You will also see that 87 out of a 100 experienced intolerable side effects from the drug. When a drug for a non-life-threatening condition causes intolerable side effects in 87 out of 100 patients, it will not likely meet with wide clinical acceptance, nor might it be tested again.

Sometimes the outcome of success in these studies is based on measuring predrug and postdrug tinnitus loudness levels, but not on predrug and postdrug assessment of how the tinnitus has affected the patient's life. (We already know that tinnitus loudness and tinnitus severity do not necessarily correlate.)

When researchers get very similar positive responses from both the placebo takers and the active drug takers, the drug is unfortunately considered to be of no benefit. But when we look closer at these studies, we see that the patients involved in the studies generally received care and attention from doctors for their tinnitus, something that in all likelihood had not happened before. This attention and caring could have been the cause of some of the relief. It is probably wise to look again at the positive responses in these placebo situations and try to understand the psychological benefit of counseling to the tinnitus patient. It might also be wise to look again at the drugs that generated relief even if their placebo counterparts also generated relief.

Another drug that is delivered through the skin has been tried anecdotally for tinnitus. Patches of scopolamine (an antivertigo medicine) have been placed on the mastoid bones of tinnitus ears. Anecdotally, a few patients have reported that these patches produced some tinnitus reduction.

Q Several years ago I served as a subject in a study in which I was injected with lidocaine intravenously. This treatment caused my tinnitus to completely disappear but only for 30 minutes. I understand that lidocaine is not a practical treatment for tinnitus because of the limited length of time that the relief lasts. Have any other drugs like lidocaine been tested?

A Yes, several other drugs have been tested. Tocainide is an oral analog of lidocaine, but it has not been found to be very effective in relieving tinnitus compared to its IV counterpart. Lidocaine is a sodium channel blocker, but other sodium channel blockers such as phenytoin have failed to provide much tinnitus relief.

Tinnitus researchers Simpson, Gilbert, and Davies decided to study lamotrigine, a new antiepileptic drug, because it has several pharmacological characteristics similar to lidocaine. Both lidocaine and lamotrigine are sodium blockers and both cross the blood–brain barrier. And because lamotrigine can be given orally and has few side effects, it was selected for a double-blind, placebo-controlled crossover study as a potential tinnitus relief agent. Thirty-one randomly selected tinnitus patients were given the drug for 8 weeks and then a placebo for 8 weeks. Twelve of the 31 patients reported a preference for the lamotrigine for their tinnitus, but there was also a fairly large number of patients who preferred the placebo. It seems that this medication needs additional study.

Q I've noticed comments in *Tinnitus Today* that suggest a relationship between pain and tinnitus. I have direct evidence of such a relationship. I have otalgia (ear pain) and tinnitus that started 8 years ago. The cause of my otalgia has not been discovered, but Demerol relieves the pain. It also reduces and sometimes eliminates my tinnitus. Should I be concerned about continuing to take this drug?

A Demerol (meperidine hydrochloride) is a narcotic drug and must be taken prudently and with medical guidance. Demerol can produce drug dependency and has the potential of being abused. Other adverse reactions are possible, such as lightheadedness, dizziness, sedation, and nausea. It is important that you stay in steady contact with your doctor so that he or she can monitor your progress on this medication.

Q I know that I have to take a very strong antibiotic that is known to be toxic to the ears. Is there any way I can protect my hearing before I take the drug so it won't be damaged?

A Experiments have been done, with animals only at this point, in which the cochlea was pretreated with *growth factor hormones* and in some cases growth factor hormones combined with insulin. Researchers hoped that the hair cells would be protected from damage from the ototoxic antibiotics that were about to be administered. In preliminary tests, this pretreatment prevented a noticeable loss of hair cells that would otherwise have occurred from exposure to ear-damaging antibiotics like neomycin.

Q I've read that the prostaglandins in our bodies are somehow positively involved in tinnitus. If so, can they be used as a treatment?

A Anti-inflammatory drugs are known to reduce prostaglandins, which are a group of fatty acids in our cells. It is also known that the ototoxic effect of aminoglycosides (a group of very powerful antibiotics including gentamicin and streptomycin) is due at least in part to their effect on prostaglandins. Both groups of drugs are known to cause tinnitus. So it is possible that tinnitus results when the prostaglandins are disrupted.

In a blinded study conducted at the House Ear Institute in Los Angeles, 24 patients with severe tinnitus were divided into two equal groups. One group was given a placebo and the other was given misoprostol, a synthetic prostaglandin. Patients started taking 200 micrograms (mcg) per day and worked up to 800 mcg per day. After 1 month, 3 (25%) of the 12 misoprostol patients reported a reduction in their tinnitus. None of the placebo subjects reported tinnitus improvement. The 12 placebo patients were then given misoprostol. Of these, five (42%) reported tinnitus reduction. In addition to a reduction of tinnitus severity, the positive responders from both groups also reported improvement in sleep patterns and the ability to concentrate. A total of 8 of 24 (33%) reported positive effects from this medication.

The results of this study are interesting in terms of the causes of the tinnitus. Of the 24 misoprostol patients in the study, 12 had suffered noise trauma (and 5 had relief), 5 suffered surgical damage (and 2 had relief), 3 were Ménière's patients (and none had relief), 1 had sudden onset (and had relief), and 2 had congenital hearing disorders (and neither had relief).

The outcome of this study supports the notion that prostaglandins might play a role, and maybe a significant role, in the reduction of tinnitus. It remains to be seen if increased dosages or a different prostaglandin would be more effective.

Q Are you aware of any research on tinnitus and Dilantin?

A Dilantin (phenytoin), Mysoline (primidone), and Tegratol (carbamazepine) are antiepileptic or anticonvulsant medications that have all been used as tinnitus relief agents.

Some years ago, scientists in New Zealand were treating epileptic patients with these medications when one of the patients reported that the treatment had stopped her tinnitus. The researchers immediately began treating tinnitus patients with these same drugs, but the success was only moderate. It is likely that the patients who had been helped with these drugs were those whose tinnitus perception area in the brain coincided with the seizure area in the brain. *Brain mapping* might actually provide a cure, or at least important clues on our way to a cure, for some forms of tinnitus.

Q   **Is vinpocetine as good for tinnitus as is suggested by a report from Interlab, its distributor? Has the drug been tested anywhere? How can I get vinpocetine and how much of it should I take?**

A   A study was conducted in Poland comparing the effectiveness of intravenous vinpocetine (10 mg) with another IV drug, Sermion (4 mg). According to this study, patients whose hearing loss and tinnitus were caused by exposure to excessive noise had a better chance of improvement if they sought treatment within a week of the acoustic trauma. The study further suggests that Sermion (nicergoline) was more effective than the vinpocetine in alleviating tinnitus. Sermion is a drug that is being studied (outside the United States) for its apparent use in increasing cerebral blood flow.

Nevertheless, we have heard from several people who have gotten tinnitus relief from the use of vinpocetine. But anecdotal information is all we have. We would like to see researchers conduct an open trial in which everyone in the study is given the drug and the effects are measured specific to tinnitus. If an open study produces positive results in high enough numbers, researchers could conduct a double-blind, placebo-controlled study on the drug.

If you do not want to wait for the results from such studies, you can purchase vinpocetine through General Nutrition Centers (GNC) in the United States. We found it online at www.drugstore.com, 60 tablets for $9.99, 5 mg per tablet. GNC's product combines vinpocetine with green tea extract, which has caffeine in it. We also found caffeine-free vinpocetine on the Internet from Life Extension Foundation (www.lef.org, 877-900-9073), 100 tablets for $13.50, 5 mg per tablet. Or you can contact Interlab in England to request an order form (www.unividual.com, BCM Box 5890, London WC1N 3XX, England). Vinpocetine, or Cavinton, is an over-the-counter drug in England. If you want to purchase vinpocetine from Interlab, note that you will need to send Australian currency to a Swedish address to get the product!

Vinpocetine is a synthetic derivative of vincamine, which is derived from *Vinca minor*, commonly known as periwinkle. One distributor of vinpocetine says it has wide-ranging effects and is used to improve memory, menopausal symptoms, macular degeneration, and tinnitus. Both Life Extension Foundation and Interlab suggest that for the first month patients should take two tablets three times a day for a daily total of 30 mg. After that, the recommended daily maintenance dose is one tablet three times per day for a daily total of 15 mg. GNC suggests a maximum intake of two tablets per day for a daily total of 10 mg.

Since the 1980s, researchers around the world have been evaluating this mild-mannered drug as an ulcer medication, a cerebral circulation enhancer, a space motion sickness stabilizer, and a treatment for both liver disease and Alzheimer's disease. Amazingly, the drug was moderately effective for several of the maladies for which it was tested, and in all cases no negative side effects were observed. Many of the studies were double blinded and several were conducted in the United States. We think it's time to retest the drug for tinnitus.

Q **Has anyone discovered a pill that could duplicate the tinnitus relief effect of lidocaine?**

A No one has yet discovered an oral drug that is equivalent to lidocaine in its tinnitus-reducing capability. In a study of 26 tinnitus patients at Oregon Hearing Research Center, 23 (88%) patients obtained complete tinnitus relief with IV injections of lidocaine (a topical anesthetic often used in dental procedures). Unfortunately, the relief lasted only about 30 minutes, indicating that lidocaine is not a practical therapy for tinnitus.

Tocainide has been used as an oral analog of lidocaine. But compared to lidocaine, its success rate for tinnitus relief is small and its side effects are many. Tocainide users report a very high incidence of dizziness, headaches, nausea, and skin rashes. In a study of 32 tinnitus patients who took 200 to 600 mg of tocainide hydrochloride daily, one had complete relief of tinnitus and two had partial relief.

Scientists at the University of São Paulo Medical School in Brazil recently experimented with an oral analog of lidocaine for the reduction of tinnitus. To select test subjects, the researchers gave 3-minute intravenous infusions of lidocaine to a group of 50 tinnitus patients. Thirty-eight (76%) of these patients experienced total or partial tinnitus relief as a result, with a more noticeable positive response in people with bilateral (two-sided) tinnitus.

The researchers then began administering daily doses of the anticonvulsant carbamazapine (Tegretol) to this positive-lidocaine group. The beginning daily dose was 50 mg per day and increased up to 600 mg per day. At the conclusion of the study, 18% indicated an abolition of their tinnitus, 32% indicated marked relief, 26% indicated partial relief, 22% indicated that their tinnitus was unchanged, and 2% indicated a worsening of their tinnitus.

In an isolated case, a Mayo Clinic patient was given an intravenous nerve block, which contained lidocaine and bupivacaine, for reasons unrelated to tinnitus. Following the procedure, he reported complications from the nerve block (like continued numbness). He also happened to mention that his longstanding and severe tinnitus was gone. One month later, his tinnitus still had not returned.

Note that neither the carbamazepine nor any of the IV lidocaine tests were conducted as double-blind placebo studies. Nevertheless, these experiments demonstrate that the chemistry of pain-relief substances can have positive effects on tinnitus.

Drug therapy holds a great deal of promise for the future of tinnitus relief. We are already familiar with the positive effects that some benzodiazepine drugs like Xanax and Klonopin, antidepressant drugs like nortriptyline, and intravenous anesthetics like lidocaine have on tinnitus. There are many other drugs within these classes of drugs that can be tested and many other classes of drugs to test. When we consider that 23 of 26 patients had their tinnitus disappear for 30 minutes when they were given intravenous lidocaine, drug therapy of *some* kind seems plausible for the relief of tinnitus.

Resources

American Heart Association Internet site: Calcium channel blockers, www.americanheart.org/Heart_and_Stroke_A_Z_Guide/calccb.html.

Attias, J., Weisz, G., Almog, S., Shahar, A., Wiener, M., Joachims, Z., Netzer, A., Ising, H., Rebentisch, E., and Guenther, T. Oral magnesium intake reduces permanent hearing loss induced by noise exposure, *Am. J. Otolaryngol.*, Jan.–Feb. 1994; 15(1):26–32.

Bebear, J. P., Lacomme, Y., and Morgon, A. A two-month multicenter double-blind, placebo-controlled study of trimetazidine in tinnitus, *Tinnitus 91— Proceedings of the Fourth International Tinnitus Seminar*, Aran, J.-M., and Dauman, R., eds., Kugler Publications, New York, 1991.

Blayney, A. W., Phillips, M. S., Guy, A. M., and Colman, B. H. A sequential double blind cross-over trial of tocainide hydrochloride in tinnitus, *Clin. Otolaryngol.*, Apr. 1985; 10(2):97–101.

Breggin, P. R. *Brain-disabling Treatments in Psychiatry: Drugs, Electroshock and the Role of the FDA*, Springer Publishing Company, New York, 1997.

Briner, W., House, J., and O'Leary, M. Synthetic prostaglandin E1 misoprostol as a treatment for tinnitus, *Arch. Otolaryngol. Head Neck Surg.*, June 1993; 119(6):652–4.

Denk, D. M., Heinzl, H., Franz, P., and Ehrenberger, K. Caroverine in tinnitus treatment. A placebo-controlled blind study, *Acta Otolaryngol. (Stockh)*, Nov. 1997; 117(6):825–30.

Dobie, R. A review of randomized clinical trials in tinnitus, *Laryngoscope*, Aug. 1999; 109(8):1202–11.

Guth, P. S., Risey, J., and Amedee, R. *Tinnitus: Treatment and Relief*, Vernon, J., ed., Allyn and Bacon, Boston, 1998, pp. 52–59.

Jastreboff, P. J., Brennan, J. F., and Sasaki, C. T. Quinine-induced tinnitus in rats. *Arch. Otolaryngol. Head Neck Surg.*, Oct. 1991; 117(10):1162–6.

Jimenez-Cervantes, Nicolas J., and Amoros Rodriguez, L. M. Hydergine in pathology of the inner ear, *An. Otorrinolaringol. Ibero Am.* 1990; 17(1):85–98.

Johnson, R. M., Brummett, R., and Schleuning A. Use of alprazolam for relief of tinnitus. A double-blind study, *Arch. Otolaryngol. Head Neck Surg.*, Aug. 1993; 119(8):842–5.

Konopka, W., Zalewski, P., Olszewski, J., Olszewska-Ziaber, A., and Pietkiewicz, P. Treatment results of acoustic trauma, *Otolaryngol. Pol.*, 1997; 51 Suppl 25:281–4.

Low, W., Dazert, S., Baird, A., and Ryan, A. F. Basic fibroblast growth factor (FGF-2) protects rat cochlear hair cells in organotypical culture from aminoglycoside injury, *J. Cell Physiol.*, June 1996; 167(3):443–50.

Morgenstern, C., Laskawi, R., and Juhn, S. K. The effect of alpha receptor-blocking agents on inner ear function, *Arch. Otorhinolaryngol.*, 1982; 234(3):313–20.

Sanchez, T. G., Balbani, A. P., Bittar, R. S., Bento, R. F., and Camara, J. Lidocaine test in patients with tinnitus: Rationale of accomplishment and relation to the treatment with carbamazepine, *Auris Nasus Larynx*, Oct. 1999; 26(4): 411–7.

Shambaugh, G. E. Jr. Zinc: The neglected nutrient, *Am. J. Otol.*, Mar. 1989; 10(2): 156–60.

Simpson, J. J., Gilbert, A. M., and Davies, W. E. *Proceedings of the Sixth International Tinnitus Seminar*, Hazell, J., ed., Tinnitus and Hyperacusis Centre, London, 1999.

Theopold, H. M. Nimodipine (Bay e 9736) a new therapy concept in diseases of the inner ear?, *Laryngol. Rhinol. Otol.* (Stuttg), Dec. 1985; 64(12):609–13.

Weinmeister, K. P. Prolonged suppression of tinnitus after peripheral nerve block using bupivacaine and lidocaine, *Reg. Anesth. Pain Med.*, Jan.–Feb. 2000; 25(1):67–8.

17

The Eardrum and Ear Cleaning

Q When ears are cleaned with a syringe, can anything be pushed back beyond the eardrum?

A The eardrum provides a physical separation between the outer ear and the middle ear space. Under most conditions, cleaning the ears with a syringe would not drive anything beyond the eardrum. On the other hand, if the eardrum is already perforated, then syringing the external ear can cause infection and debris accumulation in the middle ear space. Excessive pressure from the syringing process can even cause an eardrum to rupture. Always treat the ears gently.

Q My doctor prescribed Cerumenex to rid my ears of wax and gave me these directions: Insert the drops in one ear at a time and leave in for 20 minutes. Then place the tip of the syringe bulb deep in the canal and vigorously flush the ear canal ten times with warm water. The manufacturer's instructions suggested a gentle flushing, but unfortunately I did not see the manufacturer's instruction until I had already flushed vigorously. The tinnitus, which I've had for 50 years, got much louder immediately after this ear cleaning. Could the vigorous flushing have caused the increase of the tinnitus?

A Yes. Many tinnitus patients have reported that the noise produced by having their ears syringed made their tinnitus worse. Two patients reported that their tinnitus was produced, not just exacerbated, when a bulb aspirator was used to clean their ears. This procedure removes earwax and debris very effectively and for that reason health-care professionals like to use it. Clearly, excessive earwax needs to be removed, but vigorous flushing and aspiration are not the methods for tinnitus and hyperacusis patients to choose.

Alternatively, the ear can be vacuum cleaned and, yes, it is as noisy as it sounds. Ear vacuuming does not always remove the debris completely. The safest method of ear cleaning is also the quietest: manual wax removal. It does take more time and for that reason some professionals prefer not to use it.

If your physician provides you with solutions to soften earwax, ask that he or she check your eardrums for perforations first. Do not put fluid in the ear if your eardrum is perforated.

Your increased tinnitus loudness is quite possibly temporary. Look for it to return to its normal level within a few weeks. The recovery process can involve some reversals, so don't be discouraged by periodic flare-ups of the tinnitus.

Q **I went to my family doctor to have the excess wax removed from my ears. During the irrigation process to remove the wax, I heard a loud explosion, felt intense ear pain, and experienced ear bleeding. I was rushed to an ENT physician and treated with medication. The outcome of this experience is a severe case of tinnitus. Is it too late to do anything since the tinnitus has already started?**

A It appears that you experienced a rupture of the tympanic membrane, or eardrum. When it has properly healed, the tinnitus could either be greatly reduced or go away entirely. A ruptured eardrum can take 2 weeks to 2 months to repair. It is highly variable from ear to ear. If the rupture of the eardrum also induced some hearing loss, your hearing will likely return as the eardrum heals. If your eardrum has not repaired itself after 2 months, the intervention of an ENT surgeon might be indicated. The eardrum can be surgically repaired, often with a skin graft. Depending on the severity of your present tinnitus, it might be desirable to use masking as a temporary relief procedure until healing is complete. (The eardrum is a two-layered membrane. If it tears and then heals, only one layer repairs. The eardrum scar will remain a point of weakness.)

[The following is an exchange of questions and answers with one patient that took place over several months.]

Q: Why is it that moderate sounds produce pain in my ear?
A: Are you using the word *pain* to emphasize the discomfort you feel or do you mean real physical pain?

Q: I mean real physical pain, in the extreme.
A: Is the pain restricted to the ear or could it actually be facial pain that is then referred to the ear? We

(continued)

sometimes see the reverse situation where ear pain is referred to the facial region.

Q: I'm not sure. All I can say is that the pain feels like it is in the ear and loud sound produces it. For example, the sound of clanging dishes in my restaurant has all but driven me out of business. Why is this happening?

A: Let's assume that the pain is in the middle ear and that it is produced by sound. The most likely candidate as the source of the pain is the tympanic membrane (or eardrum). Middle ear infections can cause pressure against the eardrum that can in turn produce severe pain.

Q: If the eardrum is the cause of my problem, what can be done about it? Do I have to avoid all exposure to moderate and loud sounds?

A: No. We first have to determine if the eardrum is the likely cause. Go to an otologist and request that your eardrum be locally anesthetized. The usual procedure for anesthetization is to inject the ear canal in three different spots. However, this procedure is very painful. Instead, request that your eardrum be anesthetized painlessly by iontophoresis.

Q: I will certainly do this. But what is iontophoresis?

A: Iontophoresis is the technique of driving chemicals through the skin by electrical stimulation. One direct current electrode is placed in an anesthetic solution, such as lidocaine, and then placed in your ear canal. The other electrode is placed on your upper arm to complete the circuit. The positive direct current will repel (or send) the positive ions of the solution through the eardrum and thus anesthetize it. While your eardrum is anesthetized, return to your restaurant and determine if the clanging of the dishes produces pain for you. You will have about 2 hours of anesthesia.

Q: I did it!! And I did not experience any pain as long as the anesthesia was effective. After about 3 hours, I once again experienced pain from loud sounds. Does this prove that my eardrum is responsible for the pain? I imagine that I cannot have constant anesthesia in my eardrum.

A: The anesthesia demonstration clearly points to your eardrum as the cause of the pain, although we do not know why it reacts to sound in this manner. Strange as this might sound, your solution might be to get a new grafted eardrum. Ask your otologist if this procedure can be done for you.

[Three months later, the patient reported that he had a new eardrum and that he no longer experienced pain when in the presence of loud sounds. Hearing tests revealed that he had lost very little hearing due to the transplant. He also reported that, thankfully, he did not have to sell his restaurant.]

The procedure of iontophoresis has been used to deliver lignocaine (lidocaine) directly into the middle ear in an attempt to alleviate tinnitus. The

(continued)

study was done in Czechoslovakia in 1990 and used a Sanomatic device to deliver the drug by iontophoresis. The researchers claim that one-third of the patients studied had relief from their tinnitus with this procedure. The remaining two-thirds experienced no relief. A Dutch study that tried the same treatment with 49 patients reported that no one in the study experienced tinnitus relief. We don't know if every aspect of these two experiments was the same.

We know that the high vascularity of the eardrum carries the lidocaine away from the eardrum quickly. To combat that, an additional blood-vessel-constricting drug like epinephrine must be used along with the lidocaine. We have experimented to determine the correct ratio of drugs needed to accomplish eardrum anesthetization and learned that the epinephrine-to-lidocaine ratio needs to be 1 part to 1000 parts, instead of the usual 1 part to 100,000 parts.

Q I produce a *lot* of earwax. I've noticed it especially this last year. I wonder if this overproduction has anything to do with my tinnitus, which has gotten louder in the last year.

A People produce different amounts of wax, although older people seem to generate more earwax than do younger people. If you produce a lot of earwax, have your ears cleaned twice a year. As a point of information, some people produce clear wax and others produce colored wax. There is no significance to the distinction. Remember that wax is a good thing. It keeps debris and insects out of the ear.

A patient who had severely reduced hearing (40 to 50 dB) went to see an ENT physician. The doctor found a plug of wax in the patient's ear that was so deep and thick that when it was removed his hearing was restored. More than that, the plug of wax actually prevented his hearing from being damaged in his noisy work environment.

If your earwax is impacted and pressing on your eardrum, it could be making your tinnitus appear louder, and it might be making your hearing appear worse. See your doctor. And ask for the wax to be removed manually.

Resources

Laffree, J. B., Vermeij, P., and Hulshof, J. H. The effect of iontophoresis of lignocaine in the treatment of tinnitus, *Clin. Otolaryngol.*, Oct., 1989; 14(5):401–4.

Schonweiler, R. Therapy of severe tinnitus. A report of experiences, *Laryngol. Rhinol. Otol.*, (Stuttg), Dec. 1987; 66(12):643–7.

Sejna, I., and Marik, E. Treatment of tinnitus by Neolidocatone administered by iontophoresis into the middle ear, *Cesk. Otolaryngol.*, Aug. 1990; 39(4):221–4.

18

Electrical Stimulation

Q I've heard that electricity has been used to relieve tinnitus. How has this been done?

A Scientists have been putting electrical wires into deaf and tinnitus ears to try to reverse the conditions practically from the moment electricity was harnessed. It is hard to know what prompted Alessandro Volta, the man who invented the battery in 1801, to put probes from a direct current (DC) battery into his own ear canals. But he did it and the result was a shock to the head and, by his account, a "disagreeable bubbling noise" in the ears.

From that point forward, scientists have been scrambling to find just the right electrical current and the site to stimulate with it to relieve the already present disagreeable noises of tinnitus. Many of these scientists have gotten extremely close to a solution with their electrical stimulation experiments.

In 1802, one year after Volta invented the battery, the German physician C. J. C. Grapengiesser placed an electrode in the ear canal of a tinnitus patient and applied direct current to see what would happen. Grapengiesser discovered that positive-only direct current stopped tinnitus and that negative-only direct current caused auditory sensations.

In 1842, the French scientist Jobert de Lamballe used needles with DC electricity running through them (a process he called acupuncture) to stimulate the middle ear promontory as well as the eustachian tube. He claimed good results for tinnitus alleviation.

In 1855, another French scientist, G. B. A. Duchenne de Boulogne, used Faraday's newly invented induction coil that produced alternating current (AC) in experiments with tinnitus patients. Duchenne de Boulogne inserted electrodes in tinnitus ears that were half-filled with water and then ran alternating current through the electrodes. He claimed it cured tinnitus for eight out of ten patients.

In 1901, Victor von Urbantschitsch in Austria used both AC and DC electrical stimulation, but with some variations for treating tinnitus patients.

Also see Chapter 9, Cochlear Implants: Surgical Implants That Restore Hearing.

In 1960, U.S. researchers D. S. Hatton, S. D. Erulkar, and P. E. Rosenberg were studying the effects of electrical stimulation on the vestibular functioning of 33 patients. They noticed that 15 out of the 33 patients experienced a complete elimination of their tinnitus while the electrical stimulation occurred. The researchers ran additional tests and found that, when electrodes were placed on the cheekbones of patients with bilateral tinnitus, the tinnitus was eliminated by the positive (anodal) electrode and worsened by the negative (cathodal) electrode.

In 1968, W. House and D. Brackmann reintroduced electrical stimulation to the promontory of the middle ear. They found that half of those tested experienced tinnitus relief while the electrical current was flowing.

In 1977, John Graham and Jonathan Hazell reported that nine patients received tinnitus relief by electrical stimulation through a transtympanic needle to the middle ear promontory.

In 1978, J.-M. Aran and colleagues placed electrodes on the round window of the inner ear. A small hole was drilled in the bony wall of the ear canal, and the electrode lead was held in place there with a drop of acrylic glue. The researchers were able to suppress tinnitus in five of six patients when the ipsilateral ears (the ones with tinnitus) were stimulated, when positive electrical current was used, and only as long as the electrical current was flowing. Stimulating the non-tinnitus ear did not help the tinnitus ear.

In 1979, Portmann et al. were studying the possibility of electrically inducing hearing in people who were profoundly deaf. During the course of that experiment, they noticed that the tinnitus in 15 profoundly deaf ears was often eliminated when the cochleas were electrically stimulated. The tinnitus suppression lasted only as long as the electricity was flowing.

Also in 1979, the French research team of C. H. Chouard, B. Meyer, and D. Maridat studied 64 tinnitus patients and the effects of a variety of electrical currents (direct current, alternating current, and biphasic pulses, that is, two alternating current waves slightly out of phase with each other) on a variety of locations (behind the ear lobe, on the round window, etc.). Tinnitus ears as well as non-tinnitus ears were tested. Patients were able to try any configuration of electrical current and site until they experienced tinnitus relief. Thirty of the 64 patients experienced tinnitus suppression that lasted from days to weeks. Biphasic pulses were the most successful, and it did not matter in which part of the ear the biphasic electrodes were placed.

In 1984, John House reported on the effects of 64 cochlear implants. (Cochlear implants are surgically imbedded electrical devices that restore hearing in totally deaf ears.) All 64 ears had had tinnitus before surgery. Thirty-four implant patients reported some tinnitus improvement after the surgery. One year later, all 34 remained improved. Five of the original 64 implanted patients reported a worsening of their tinnitus.

In the 1980s, electrical engineer V. Rowland devised a machine that produced an alternating current with an altered negative pulse that was much safer to use than conventional alternating current. We already knew that the anodal electrical stimulus (positive pulse) reduced tinnitus but caused hearing damage. What we needed to find was an electrical waveform that could reduce tinnitus and not produce hearing damage.

In 1984, we conducted an open study at the Oregon Hearing Research Center using this altered waveform of electrical stimulation with five tinnitus patients. An electrical probe emitting the newly named *pulse of Rowland* was applied to various parts of the ear. Patients controlled the intensity of the probe. It was first applied to the pinna with no effect on the tinnitus. It was then applied to the ear canal and then the tympanic membrane with no effect. Then the eardrum was lifted up and folded back and the electrode was applied to the promontory in the middle ear space, again with no effect on the tinnitus. The last effort was successful. When the electrode was placed on the round window of the cochlea, three of the five patients had complete cessation of the tinnitus, one had partial cessation, and one had no response. Grapengiesser had observed that the tinnitus immediately returned when the electrical current was turned off, but we did not find that. Of the three patients who had complete tinnitus suppression, two had relief for several hours and one had relief for several days after the electrical stimulation was removed.

In 1985, Vernon and Fenwick used carbon-impregnated electrodes in front and behind 23 tinnitus ears. If a patient had bilateral tinnitus, the ear with the more severe tinnitus was selected for study. When a placebo trial was conducted with inactive electrodes placed in front of the ears, none of the 23 subjects reported any tinnitus relief. (To test patients with placebo electrodes, researchers told the patients that they probably would not feel the electrical stimulation because of its high-frequency nature.) When the inactive electrode was placed behind the ears, one subject had a positive response. When active electrodes were placed in front of the ears, 5 of the 23 reported 40% or more tinnitus relief. When active electrodes were placed behind the ears, nine patients gave positive responses to the electrical stimulation. Five different waveforms were tried; asymmetrical balanced biphasic pulses worked the best.

Figures 18.1 through 18.5 show the waveforms produced by the five indicated pulses.

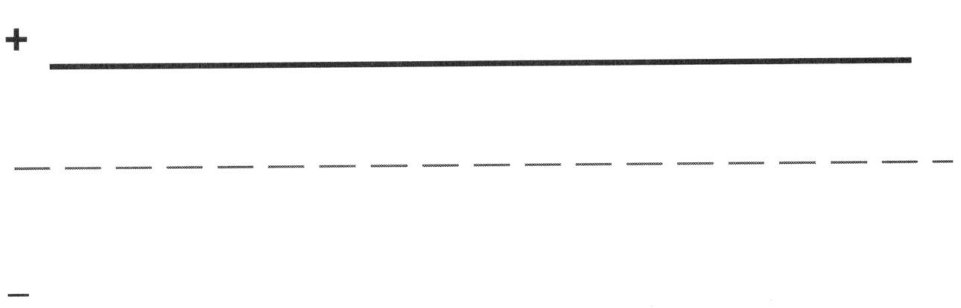

FIGURE 18.1 *Direct current (DC).*

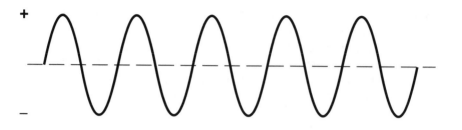

FIGURE 18.2   *Alternating current (AC).*

FIGURE 18.3   *Anodal monophasic pulse.*

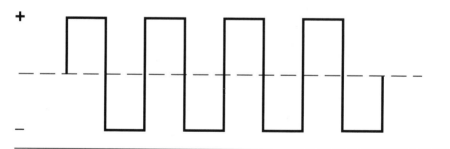

FIGURE 18.4   *Balanced biphasic pulse.*

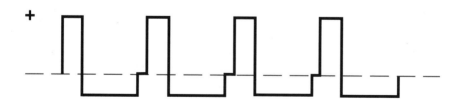

FIGURE 18.5   *Asymmetrical balanced biphasic pulse—the "Pulse of Rowland"*

In 1985, Abraham Shulman and Jergen Tonndorf noticed that some patients had tinnitus relief when their hearing was tested with electrical high-frequency audiometry. This observation led them to develop the Audiomax Tinnitus Suppressor, a device that required the patient to wear a headset with electrodes resting on the mastoid bones. According to Shulman, 13 out of 21 patients who wore the devices for 2 weeks had tinnitus suppression. Two follow-up studies evaluated the Audiomax in double-blind, placebo-controlled crossover conditions. The results: One patient (20%) out of five reported tinnitus relief. In another study, five (16.6%) patients out of thirty reported relief while using the device. Interestingly, three out of the five patients in the latter study experienced tinnitus relief with the placebo (inactive) device.

In 1989, Norwegian researchers Kaade, Hognestad, and Havstad studied the effects that transcutaneous nerve stimulation (TNS) might have on tinnitus. (TNS is controlled, low-voltage electrical stimulation administered through electrodes placed on the skin.) Of the 29 tinnitus patients treated with TNS for 45 minutes, 9 reported a reduction in tinnitus. Low-frequency tinnitus (125 to 500 Hz) was the most responsive to the treatment. Four of the nine patients were not able to sustain the positive effect with continued use. But five of the nine continued to use the TNS treatment successfully for several years.

In 1993, Japanese researchers applied electrical stimulation to 68 cochlear round windows in 62 tinnitus patients. The electrical stimulation caused tinnitus reduction in 46 of the 68 ears. Twenty of the 62 patients reported tinnitus reduction lasting from several hours to one week following the electrical stimulation.

More investigation in this area is needed and is rather exciting to consider. We believe that the proper arrangement of electrical stimulation will one day bring effective and sustained relief from tinnitus.

Resources _____

Kaada, B., Hognestad, S., and Havstad, J. Transcutaneous nerve stimulation (TNS) in tinnitus, *Scand. Audiol.*, 1989; 18(4):211–7.

Okusa. M., Shiraishi, T., Kubo, T., and Matsunaga, T. Tinnitus suppression by electrical promontory stimulation in sensorineural deaf patients, *Acta Otolaryngol. Suppl.* (Stockh), 1993; 501:54–8.

Portmann, M., Cazals, Y., Negrevergne, M., and Aran, J. M. Temporary tinnitus suppression in man through electrical stimulation of the cochlea, *Acta Otolaryngol.* (Stockh), Mar.–Apr. 1979; 87(3–4):294–9.

Tabachnick, B. From Volta's battery to cochlear implants—A chronicle of electrical stimulation, *Tinnitus Today*, June 1995; 20(2):7–12.

Vernon, J. A., and Fenwick, J. A. Attempts to suppress tinnitus with transcutaneous electrical stimulation, *Otolaryngol. Head Neck Surg.*, June 1985; 93(3):385–89.

19

Exercise

Q I find that my morning exercise makes my tinnitus worse, although, by the evening, the noise has settled back down again. Before I had tinnitus, I enjoyed exercising and really appreciated how it helped reduce my level of stress. But now exercise seems to make my tinnitus louder. So I'm torn—I want to exercise, but I'm concerned that the increase in my tinnitus will become permanent if I continue. Do you have any suggestions?

A When something exacerbates tinnitus, whether it is a food or a drug or exposure to noise, continued exposure to it or use of it should be stopped so that the tinnitus increase does not become permanent. But in the case of exercise this is not true. When tinnitus increases because of exercise, it is almost always temporary. (The exceptions involve very strenuous or very high impact, jostling activities.) You could easily argue that the benefit you derive from exercise justifies this temporary increase. But that is a determination only you can make.

Some people who found that their tinnitus was louder as a result of exercising reported that the exercise stopped affecting the tinnitus after they pushed through the first few weeks. Also, they began to feel better in general as a result of the exercise that they were getting.

In 1995, the American Tinnitus Association surveyed its support network volunteers and asked them what they did to relax. The lengthy list of their responses includes deep breathing, swimming, meditation, walking, woodcarving, prayer, oil painting, yoga, bike riding, and other physical activities. You might need to try a different form of exercise or do the kind you like and combine it with another form of stress reduction like T'ai Chi or yoga. Know that your tinnitus will reduce back to its original level a few hours after exercising.

Q I believe that my tinnitus was caused by the excessively loud noise in my aerobics class. I still do aerobics, although I now wear earplugs. If it was the noise level, why am I the only one who was affected by it?

A You are definitely not the only one. Many aerobics enthusiasts have reported not just tinnitus, but also vertigo, hearing loss, and ear fullness as the result of their aerobics activities. While the sound level of the music in aerobics studios can be painfully loud and even ear damaging, there could be another cause of the aerobics ear injuries.

Weintraub, a researcher in New York, studied 30 women (12 aerobics instructors and 18 longtime aeorobics enthusiasts) who complained of ear-related trauma after aerobics activities. Twenty of the 30 had tinnitus, 24 of the 30 had dizziness and balance problems, and 18 of the 30 reported new sensitivity to barometric pressure changes, for example while flying or scuba diving. With testing, Weintraub concluded that the repetitive jarring of this high-impact activity in conjunction with exposure to high noise levels appears to cause damage to cochlear hair cells in the organ of Corti and to the vestibular hair cells in the otoliths of the semicircular canals.

More recently, an aerobics enthusiast with tinnitus asked the owner of the health club that she attends to turn down the volume in the aerobics classroom. The owner refused to do so, citing that health clubs are recreational sites and therefore exempt from noise regulation guidelines. She didn't care. "This is a health club," she said, "and I want healthy ears." She contacted a state legislator and together they drafted a bill that would require health club owners in her state to post the decibel levels of aerobics classes and to supply earplugs for anyone in the classes who wanted them. Unfortunately, the bill was tabled. Fortunately, she is indefatigable about this topic and is currently refining the bill and lobbying to give the recreation noise issue the attention it deserves.

No, you are not alone!

Resource _____

Weintraub, M. I., Vestibulopathy induced by high impact aerobics. A new syndrome: Discussion of 30 cases, *J. Sports Med. Phys. Fitness,* Mar. 1994; 34(1):56–63.

Flying

Q I am wondering if flying is advisable for those of us with tinnitus. And when I fly, is it better for me to leave my hearing aids in or to take them out?

A Unless you have eustachian tube problems, flying should not be a problem. To make sure that your ears are not subjected to big pressure changes while you fly, you can remove your hearing aids and insert earplugs for the flight.

Many people, with and without tinnitus, experience ear discomfort while they fly, most often during descent of the plane. In theory, the air pressure inside commercial aircraft cabins is at the same level at all times (about 6000 feet). But in reality it is not always the same. As a plane descends for landing, the air pressure inside the plane increases. The increasing air pressure forces its way back into the eustachian tubes and through the middle ear to the eardrums, and this can cause troublesome ear pain and ear popping. Changes in air pressure also occur as the plane climbs. During takeoff, the air pressure in the cabin drops. This forces the air pressure inside the middle ear to drop as the air inside the middle ear escapes through the eustachian tubes. The eustachian tubes seem better able to handle air pressure leaving them than air pressure coming back up into them. This is probably why landings are especially hard on the ears.

Before you get on the plane, insert foam earplugs. Make sure that they are deeply seated and comfortable too. Leave them in until the plane has leveled off at its cruising altitude. (The pilot usually announces this.) Right before the plane begins its descent, put the earplugs back in. (You might have to time this if the pilot does not announce it first.) Or you can leave the earplugs in for the whole flight. After you are back inside the airport terminal, slowly remove the earplugs. Many people who had trouble with their

Also see Chapter 35, Noise Cancellation.

ears when they flew have found that this earplug routine eliminates airplane ear pain altogether.

Q Airplanes are so noisy, inside and out. Consequently, I have been avoiding them. But I have to fly to my daughter's wedding in a few months. What can I do to keep the noise from affecting my tinnitus?

A The noise level inside airplanes varies from one airplane design to the next. If a jet has its engines mounted on the wings, then the noisiest seats are either those over the wings (which are also near the air-conditioning and air-pressurization systems) or those toward the rear of the plane. The quietest seats are the ones closest to the front of the plane. One tinnitus patient took a sound-level meter onto a flight and determined that the aisle seats were slightly quieter than window seats. Airplanes with tail-mounted jet engines (like 727s and DC-10s) generally have the highest inside-noise levels of commercial aircraft.

Foam earplugs with a high noise reduction rating (NRR), like the Howard Leight Max-33s, are comfortable and can help cut the noise quite a bit. EarPlanes® are flexible molded earplugs designed for wear while flying. They let the air pressure on the plane escape out the middle ear and filter back into the middle ear very slowly. Because the EarPlanes are a fixed shape, we suggest that you try them on before your flight to see if they fit. (Your right ear canal is not necessarily the same size as your left ear canal.)

If the noise is especially bothersome to you, you could add protective earmuffs over the earplugs. With all the headsets being worn on the plane, few people would notice anything out of the ordinary.

Q The descent in commercial aircraft produces pain in my ears. Is this due to my tinnitus? Also, could the noise of a turboprop plane be the cause of the problem?

A The pain in the ears upon descent in aircraft is most likely due to pressure changes. During descent, if the pressure equalization is not correctly controlled, you could experience major pressure changes that could cause pain in the ears. It really has nothing to do with your tinnitus.

As for the noise of the turboprop, earplugs might provide sufficient protection, but you may also want to try active noise cancellation. Earplugs provide greater passive protection from high-pitched sounds than from low-pitched sounds. Active noise cancellation devices, on the other hand, provide more complete noise cancellation of low-frequency sounds like the rumble heard on planes. For about $190 you can buy Noise Cancellation Technologies' ProActive® headset. It combines a computerized, cordless, low-frequency, sound-canceling device with earmuffs that reduce high-frequency sounds by 20 dB. Noise Cancellation Technologies' products are sold with a 2-week money-back guarantee.

The new Bose Acoustic Noise Cancelling® headset was designed for airline passengers who are sensitive to onboard noise. This headset cancels or reduces the very low-frequency airplane rumbling, while still allowing the passenger to listen to in-flight music and movies.

Q Ever since a flight from London to Ireland following a bout with an ear infection, I have had a pressure sensation, popping sounds, and ringing or buzzing in my ears. Did I permanently damage the eustachian tube in the ear?

A Unless there was an out-of-the-ordinary and sudden pressure change during the flight, there should be no permanent damage to your eustachian tube. When a person has a head cold, often the eustachian tube is swollen and blocked. In the future, if you have a sluggish eustachian tube brought on by congestion, use earplugs to help stabilize the middle ear pressure changes that occur during flight. (We originally learned this from a patient.) Foam or specially designed filtered earplugs are very effective in keeping the air pressure the same on both sides of the eardrum.

If a person flies with a head cold, the result could be a middle ear infection and/or transient tinnitus. If you must fly when you have a cold, ask your doctor to recommend a decongestant (like Sudafed) or nasal spray (like Afrin) to be taken or used 1 hour before takeoff and 1 hour before landing. The best solution—one that is probably easier said than done—is to postpone the trip until the infection has cleared up.

Q When I fly, my tinnitus gets louder, and my ears pop and hurt quite a bit. So far, the pain has always cleared up and the tinnitus has always returned to its usual level a few hours after I land. Is there anything I can do to unplug my ears while I'm still on the plane?

A The popping and crackling we hear when we swallow or yawn is the sound of the eustachian tube opening and closing. It is nature's way of equalizing the pressure in the middle ear space with the pressure outside the ear. There are several things you can do to help the process along. During those critical times when the altitude of the plane is changing, you can chew gum, swallow by sipping on fluids, yawn or open the mouth as wide as is comfortable, or swallow and pinch the nose at the same time. All these motions have the same triggering effect on the muscles that open the eustachian tubes. The Valsalva maneuver (pinch nose, close mouth, and gently blow out through the nose, using only force from your throat and cheeks) will also open the eustachian tube and keep it open during descent.

Also, stay awake during takeoff and landing. When we sleep, we do not always swallow enough to keep the eustachian tubes open sufficiently to handle the changing air pressure.

Resources

American Academy of Otolaryngology, *Ears, Altitude, and Airplane Travel,* the Academy, Alexandria, VA, 2000.

Clarke, M. Ear care in the air, *Travel Holiday,* Mar. 1996; p. 22.

Brown, T. P. Middle ear symptoms while flying: Ways to prevent a severe outcome, *Audecibel,* Mar. 1995; pp. 1–13.

Hazell, J. W. P. Flying and the ear, *British Tinnitus Association Newsletter,* 1983; 19:2–3.

Schwade, S., Read this before you fly, *Prevention,* June 1996; pp. 103–109.

21

Head Trauma

Q My tinnitus started 10 years ago as a consequence of my fondness for hard rock music. Gradually, I adjusted to the tinnitus to the point where it was not bothersome. Recently, at a basketball game, a ball hit me directly on my tinnitus ear and caused a significant increase in my tinnitus. Since I now have to play a very loud masking sound to mask my tinnitus, I wonder if the loud masking sound is going to damage my hearing. Is this increase in my tinnitus permanent?

A The increase in your tinnitus could be temporary, and it can take many weeks or even months for the tinnitus to return to its normal level. Have your ear examined by an otolaryngologist to see if the blow to your head caused a rupture of the tympanic membrane (eardrum). If your hearing has decreased as a result of eardrum damage, this could be one cause of the tinnitus increase. An eardrum can heal itself or be surgically repaired. For the time being, avoid loud masking.

You can use sound to *partially* mask the tinnitus. Any background sound, a fan or even your masker set not too loud, can help reduce the contrast between the intrusive sound of the tinnitus and a quiet background environment.

Q My tinnitus began 2 years ago after I was beaten in an attack. I sustained several direct blows to my temple and jaw. The chronic head pain and the tinnitus are equally distressing to me. I've had an MRI scan, which did not show any obvious damage. I've tried masking, but the masker hurts my ear. Do you have any other suggestions?

A There are other scanning techniques to consider that might reveal the locus of the injury and lead to some help. Sataloff et al., at Thomas Jefferson University, studied patients with neurotologic complaints pertaining to inner ear and related nerve damage. The researchers used SPECT (single-photon-emission computed tomography), MRI (magnetic resonance imaging), CT scan (computerized tomography), and EEG (electroencephalogram) to evaluate these patients and found that abnormalities were identified far more frequently with SPECT scanning than with the other scanning techniques. Overall, 78% of SPECT scans revealed abnormalities, compared to the 43% rate of MRIs, 40% rate of CT scans, and 29% of EEGs. SPECT scans allow doctors to see physical and chemical changes in the brain tissue.

Post-head-trauma syndrome is often typified by a group of symptoms that include chronic head pain or headache, tinnitus, vertigo, and memory loss. A minute amount of nerve damage might cause these distressing symptoms. The fact that the damage is hard to detect can certainly make this syndrome difficult to treat. A blow to the head, depending on the severity and the circumstance, could also cause a rupture in one of the inner ear windows. Technological advances in cranial scanning science are helping us move closer to relief for hard-to-diagnose head injuries.

When we studied head injury patients at the Oregon Hearing Research Center, we learned that head-injury-induced tinnitus was significantly louder and had a higher severity rating than tinnitus produced by other causes. Interestingly, this particular group of patients did not require higher levels of masking to cover the tinnitus. Patients with head-injury-induced

A New Way to Image—the Multislice CT Scanner

Multislice CT scanning is a new, very high-speed X-ray-based technology. While lying down on a scanning table, the patient and the table move through the CT device—a spinning donut-shaped apparatus. The scanning time is dramatically brief. A multislice CT scanner can gather as much information in 68 seconds as a conventional CT scanner can gather in 20 minutes.

Here's how to picture it. Think of yourself as a loaf of bread. Each image of you that is produced by these scanners is a very thin slice out of the loaf. The thinner the slice (or image) is, the less that can be missed. Multislice scanners produce bone and soft tissue *slice images* as narrow as 0.5 mm. Also, test results are available instantaneously and can be pieced together by

computer to form three-dimensional images of the scanned body part. These images can then be rotated and viewed from any angle.

How much noise does the multislice scanner make? We can't report definitively because official decibel levels are not published. Unofficially, the noise level of General Electric's multislice CT scanner does not exceed 75 dB, says GE's Richard Nelson. (For most people, a 75-dB sound poses no threat to hearing.) Toshiba spokesperson John DeBoer says that their multislice device is "very, very quiet." General Electric, Toshiba, and Picker (now Marconi) all manufacture these breathtakingly quick diagnostic devices. Ask your physician if you can benefit from this type of diagnostic tool.

tinnitus more frequently experienced residual inhibition than patients whose tinnitus had other causes. While you investigate further diagnostic scanning techniques, you might consider using a tabletop masking device for your home environment and a masking Sound Pillow™ by Phoenix Productions to help you sleep at night.

Resources

Sataloff, R. T., Mandel, S., Muscal, E., Park, C. H., Rosen, D.C., Kim, S. M., and Spiegel, J. R. Single-photon-emission computed tomography (SPECT) in neurotologic assessment: A preliminary report, *Am. J. Otol.*, Nov. 1996; 17(6):909–16.

Sidi, J., and Tovi, F. Traumatic labyrinthine fistulas, *Isr. J. Med. Sci.*, Feb. 1979; 15(2):156–8.

Vernon, J. A., and Press, L. S. Characteristics of tinnitus induced by head injury, *Arch. Otolaryngol. Head Neck Surg.*, May 1994; 120(5):547–51.

22

Hearing Aids

Q Is my hearing aid dispenser just trying to sell me a $1000 hearing aid or are his claims of tinnitus relief and residual inhibition with the hearing aid correct?

A It all depends on the pitch of your tinnitus and the location of your hearing loss. For example, if you have a hearing loss in the relatively low frequencies and you also have relatively low-pitched tinnitus, then the hearing aid may do exactly what your hearing aid dispenser claims. On the other hand, if you have high-pitched tinnitus, it is less likely that the hearing aid will relieve the tinnitus. We have referred many tinnitus patients to hearing aid dispensers to be fit for tinnitus maskers only to have the dispensers insist on fitting hearing aids that ultimately were unhelpful for the tinnitus. It is possible that the dispenser was not familiar with masker technology and stayed with what was familiar.

You can tell almost immediately if a hearing aid will work to relieve your tinnitus. Put the device in your ear and listen for your tinnitus in that ear. Conduct this test in an area of normal environmental sounds and not in a sound-shielded room.

As for residual inhibition (the reduction of tinnitus for a period of time after removal of the hearing aid), that is not true. Residual inhibition occurs for 83% of those who find relief with tinnitus maskers. But it never occurs with the use of hearing aids, even when the hearing aids effectively mask the tinnitus.

We did a study of 592 tinnitus patients all of whom could be effectively masked by one or more of the three kinds of tinnitus masking devices. Hearing aids alone were effective for 16% of the cases, tinnitus maskers were effective for 21%, and tinnitus instruments (units that combine tinnitus maskers and high-frequency-emphasis hearing aids) were effective for 63%. Of these 592 patients, only those who used tinnitus maskers or tinnitus instruments experienced residual inhibition.

Q In 1996, I purchased a new digital hearing aid with automatic volume control that works very well. However, 6 months ago, I developed a new tinnitus sound that is a low-pitched beat or drum roll. Two months ago, I stopped wearing the hearing aid, and now the new tinnitus is gradually declining. Is this experience a usual occurrence?

A Historically, hearing aids do not negatively affect tinnitus, although it can happen. We suggest that you return the aids to your hearing aid dispenser for evaluation to ensure that the units are functioning properly and that they are properly adjusted. Is the volume set too high? Give it several more months to see if the new tinnitus sound goes away completely. It is not possible to determine if the new tinnitus was generated by the hearing aid or by some unrelated cause. But it is not likely that the two events are related, since you purchased the hearing aid 3 years ago and the new tinnitus appeared 6 months ago.

Q For the last 4 days my hearing aids have been in the shop for repairs. Coincidentally, over the last 4 days my tinnitus has gotten considerably louder. In fact, my ears are screaming! I don't think that the absence of the ambient masking sounds brought in by the hearing aids is the cause because my hearing loss is quite slight. Why do you think my tinnitus has gone up over the last few days?

A Many people with hearing loss, who do not wear the hearing aids they should, are stressed by the strain of staying in conversations they cannot fully hear. Even though your hearing loss is slight, you have come to depend on the hearing aids to understand speech. For some people, this can be very stressful. And stress can cause tinnitus to scream.

Here is another possibility: Your brain had gotten used to hearing things clearly with the hearing aids and, in their absence, it "turned up the gain" to hear anything it could. The loss of ambient sounds brought in by the hearing aids might also be part of it.

[When the patient put the repaired hearing aids back in, the tinnitus immediately returned to its previous non-intrusive level.]

Q After using a hearing aid for 2 weeks (I am a first-time user), my tinnitus seems to have increased. Could the amplification of my hearing actually have caused this?

A We have seen a few cases where the initial use of hearing aids exacerbated the tinnitus. In each case, the hearing aid fitting was the cause of the problem. There was too much occlusion, or blockage, of the ear canal by the hearing aid. This earplug-like blockage stopped much of the high-frequency sound from getting in. High-frequency sound will often soothe and somewhat mask tinnitus naturally. Also, be sure that you are not running up the volume of the hearing aid.

In cases like yours, we had the patients switch from in-the-ear hearing aids to behind-the-ear devices and the problem was solved. The tube fitting of the behind-the-ear hearing aids leaves the canal quite open.

Q What is hearing impairment? Is it the same thing as hearing loss?

A Hearing impairment has a variety of definitions. It usually refers to a condition wherein a person has difficulty understanding human speech. People can also have hearing loss that is only noticeable in the presence of background noise. Because they hear acceptably well the rest of the time, they do not believe that they have any hearing impairment and often blame the speakers for mumbling. (We might all know someone like that!) If you have difficulty understanding speech under most conditions or even if you just have difficulty understanding speech in the presence of background noise, have your hearing tested. Based on the results of the test, your hearing health will be explained to you and you will learn your level of hearing loss. Retain a copy of the test results for future reference.

Our range of speech spans from around 200 to 4000 Hz. We hear consonants in the higher frequencies and vowels in the lower frequencies. It is easy to see how some words can sound quite muddy to someone who has a hearing loss at 3000 Hz.

Q I know I need a hearing aid and yet I keep putting it off. The thought of having a hearing aid squeal in my ear sends chills down my spine. I'm sure that the squeal won't be good for my tinnitus either. How can I get around it?

A There are several reasons why a hearing aid will make a squealing sound.

1. It is not securely inserted in the ear canal.
2. The behind-the-ear tubing is cracked or has hardened.
3. The in-the-ear instrument or the behind-the-ear earmold no longer fits properly because the ear canal has changed shape with time. (And they all do.) A weight gain or a weight loss will affect the shape of your ear canal and therefore the fit of your hearing aid.
4. The volume of the hearing aid is too high. (The high amplification picks up the circuit noise and causes feedback.)
5. The plastic earmold has shrunk and is therefore ill-fitting.
6. The device is malfunctioning.

Maskers, tinnitus instruments, hearing aids, and sound generators are all designed to alert the wearer, usually with a beeping sound, when their batteries are running low. Audiologists recommend that people change the batteries in their hearing instruments on a regular calendar schedule, perhaps once every 2 weeks, before the warning beeps start. You would base your schedule on how often and how long you use the device.

A point of information and another good reason to change batteries often: As batteries begin to wear down, they first lose their ability to bring in high-frequency sounds (in the case of a hearing aid) or produce high-frequency sounds (in the case of a masker). This all happens before the device gives off its low-battery warning.

Q A hearing aid dispenser told me that he could relieve my tinnitus with the new in-the-canal hearing aid. Is he correct?

A As with most things concerning tinnitus, there is only one way to find out: Try it and see. As a general statement, 16% of tinnitus patients will experience tinnitus relief with hearing aids. But these data are based on studies with more conventional hearing aids and not with the newer in-the-canal (ITC) or completely-in-the-canal (CIC) hearing aids. We have heard from two patients who were fitted with ITC aids and found that the devices relieved their tinnitus.

Q How can I find out if hearing aids or masking devices can help my tinnitus without it costing me a great deal of money?

A All hearing instruments and tinnitus devices are returnable, and most of the costs are refundable. But return policies vary from manufacturer to manufacturer, from state to state, and from dispenser to dispenser. Some hearing aid manufacturers offer a 60-day money-back guarantee on their products. Other manufacturers have a 30-day refund policy. Thirty days is usually long enough to know if a device is comfortable enough to wear and helpful enough to keep.

Individual states also have their say over the sale of these products. In Oregon, for example, hearing aid dispensers are only required by law to refund 80% of the hearing aid price. The majority of local dispensers, however, refund 100% of the cost because it is good business to do so. Earmolds are another matter, some of which can cost $100 a pair. Obviously, earmolds cannot be returned. Nevertheless, hearing instrument dispensers set their own policies on earmold refunds. We talked to two local dispensers who refund 100% of the purchase price of returned hearing aids including the cost of the earmolds. Under any circumstance, expect to pay for the hearing aid dispenser's professional services.

Q What are the advantages of digital hearing aids over conventional aids? Do they have a noticeable benefit for tinnitus?

A Conventional analog hearing aids lack some of the flexibility and features found in the newer programmable and digital hearing aids. Also, analog hearing aids can only approximate the patient's threshold of hearing curve. Digital aids can exactly reproduce it. As of 1998, more than 60 programmable and 8 digital hearing aids were on the market. These new high-tech aids account for 40% of all hearing aid sales in the United States, even though when tested they did not appreciably increase speech recognition. People still prefer them and say that they provide a more comfortable sound and better amplification of quiet sounds. Digital hearing aids can help in noisy environments by limiting or compressing very high-decibel sounds down to quieter levels.

A few of the more sophisticated aids have another highly desirable feature. They specifically block out background noise. They accomplish this through the use of two microphones, one that is pointed back to pick up background noise and suppress it and another that is pointed forward to pick up conversation and enhance it. The cost of this new hearing aid technology can be prohibitive—$2000 or more per aid.

Q I have been told that the hearing in my left ear is so bad that there is no use trying a hearing aid on it. This is also the ear that has severe tinnitus. I wonder what can be done to relieve it.

A The first thing to do is to have your hearing tested to see how impaired it really is. One very hearing-impaired patient had a test that revealed a 75- to 80-dB hearing loss across all frequencies. The pitch of her tinnitus was matched at 2200 Hz. We decided to try a hearing aid on her even though the aid was not designed to correct for that much of a hearing loss. Her speech intelligibility did go down with the hearing aid. (She got distortion through it.) But, amazingly, it completely masked her tinnitus. The tinnitus relief was so desirable to her that she decided to simply turn the hearing aid off when she wanted to converse with people.

Q I have heard that it is now possible to have implanted hearing aids. Is this true? And if so, do these devices offer any special help for tinnitus?

A Yes, it is true. Implantable and semi-implantable hearing aids are being developed and tested, and a few are available now. This technology appears to deliver clearer and more natural sounding speech than conventional hearing aids, hence the excitement about it. The devices use either *piezoelectric crystal stimulators* or *electromagnets* to stimulate the inner ear.

These implantable devices are intended for individuals who have moderately severe to severe hearing loss and who cannot benefit from or tolerate conventional hearing aids. Other guidelines determine if someone is a candidate for an implant. Ask your doctor to discuss all the options with you. Some of these implantable devices correct for conductive hearing loss, others for sensorineural hearing loss, and some for both.

Here is a listing of some of the implantable devices:

- Entific Medical Systems continues the development of a semi-implanted bone conduction hearing aid called the BAHA® (bone-anchored hearing aid). The device consists of a small titanium fixture that is implanted in the mastoid bone behind the ear and a sound processor that attaches to it on the outside of the head. The element titanium was selected because it was found to actually integrate with living tissue. The implant therefore forms a bond with the bone at the molecular level.

- Implex has created the Totally Integrated Cochlear Amplifier (TICA)™. Its microphone is implanted under the skin in the ear canal, and the processor is implanted on one of the middle ear bones. The device uses piezoelectric technology and is powered by a rechargeable lithium battery. This implant has been tested in Europe and has demonstrated some success. It is now being studied in the United States. The FDA has not yet approved this device for sale.

- Symphonix Devices, Inc., in San Jose, California, has developed a semi-implantable device called the Vibrant Soundbridge™. (The company publicizes this product as a medical prosthesis, not a hearing aid. Their reasoning: Hearing aids make sounds louder. Their device converts sound energy into mechanical vibrations in the middle ear.) A transducer is surgically attached to the middle ear bones and is connected by a coil to a receiver implanted under the skin. The receiver gets its signals from the microphone that is on the outside of the head and held in place by a magnet. The implanted transducer vibrates the middle ear bones just as normal sounds would vibrate the bones. Amazingly, the implantation of this device is an outpatient procedure. The Vibrant Soundbridge has just been approved by the FDA.

- St. Croix Medical is testing a totally implantable hearing restoration system called the Envoy™. This device is designed with piezokinetic transducers that are implanted in the middle ear to pick up the vibrations from the malleus and transmit them to the stapes. This technology uses the eardrum as the microphone. The company is seeking otologists to perform animal or human research trials with this device. The Envoy has not yet been approved by the FDA for sale in the United States.

Even more innovative, the Implantable Device Laboratory at the University of Virginia is studying a round window implantable magnet. The magnet is attached to the round window membrane of the inner ear, and an electromagnet coil induces sound energy to it.

In early 2000, Jack Hough, M.D., at the University of Oklahoma, began clinical trials on an implantable hearing aid, the SOUNDTEC, Inc.™ DDHS (direct-drive hearing system). Twenty patients, each of whom had one ear implanted with the device, averaged 50% improvement in speech intelligibility in the implanted ears over what they had been able to achieve with conventional hearing aids. All 20 reported less distortion and no feedback, and all asked to have their other ears implanted as soon as possible.

Hough has now implanted 100 Soundtec hearing aids, which is the number of devices that must be implanted and analyzed before the FDA will approve (or disapprove) such a device. All 100 Soundtec patients reported increased intelligibility with these hearing aids over conventional aids.

This implantable device functions with a microphone worn behind the ear, much like a conventional hearing aid. The microphone sends the signals to an O-shaped magnet held in place in the ear canal. This magnet sends signals to another magnet that is implanted on the ossicular chain in the middle ear. So if vanity is the motivation behind the desire for an implantable hearing aid, you need to know that this device is far from invisible. It also has a rather high price tag at the moment. Implantation surgery plus one device costs approximately $10,000.

If these implantable devices continue to perform better than conventional hearing aids in bigger research trials and for all forms of hearing loss, they might be well worth the price. Until more data are available on these devices, conventional hearing aids are probably the way to go. Remember that if both ears are hearing impaired it is essential to have—and wear—two hearing aids.

We don't yet know whether these devices will offer any special help for tinnitus over and above the help that conventional hearing aids now offer. But implant technology is advancing quickly. We will soon find out.

Resources

Carmen, R., ed. *Hearing Loss & Hearing Aids—A Bridge to Healing,* Auricle Ink, Sedona, AZ, 1998.

Wayner, D. *Hear What You've Been Missing,* Chronimed Publishing, Minneapolis, MN, 1998.

Zenner, H. P., Leysieffer, H., Maassen, M., Lehner, R., Lenarz, T., Baumann, J., Keiner, S., Plinkert, P. K., McElveen, J. T., Jr. Human studies of a piezoelectric transducer and a microphone for a totally implantable electronic hearing device, *Am. J. Otol.,* Mar. 2000; 21(2):196–204.

23

Hearing Conservation

Q I am certain that I got tinnitus from doing construction work for many years. Why don't my co-workers have this same problem? We were all equally exposed to the noise and none of us wore ear protection.

A Individuals vary greatly in their reactions to noise. Some individuals have very tough ears and show little or no damage from excessive noise exposure. Other people have very tender ears and experience excessive damage from relatively minor noise exposure. And there are all grades of susceptibility in between. Everyone should use ear protection (earplugs, earmuffs, or both) when operating tabletop saws, routers, power lawn mowers, and leaf blowers and when attending indoor sports events and concerts of all kinds. Interior amplification at some of these indoor events has been measured at 120 dB.

Q How can I reach children with the message that noise exposure can damage their hearing? Does anyone know how many children already have tinnitus?

A A study in Sweden involved 964 seven-year-old children. Its goal was to determine the incidence of tinnitus in this youthful age group. The researchers took into account that there are difficulties involved in getting information from children. Children have a tendency to try to please the researchers by answering the way that they think the researchers want them to. Children might not always understand the questions they are asked. And sometimes a child will answer a question one way and then change his or her response when asked the question again. If the interviewers had any doubt about a child's positive answer or if a child answered yes to one tinnitus question and then no to another, the response was considered a no. Out of the 964 children, 120 (12%) stated yes, they experience tinnitus. Of the 120, only 12 had hearing loss.

You can reach children with this vital information by taking videos, posters, earplugs, and other teaching materials into elementary school classrooms and telling them about it yourself. The American Tinnitus Association developed a hearing conservation and tinnitus prevention program called *Hear for a Lifetime*. It is designed to teach second and third grade students that overexposure to loud noise can cause hearing loss and tinnitus. Students learn that they can avoid that misery if they start protecting their ears now. They also learn how to properly insert earplugs into their ears.

When we went into the classrooms with the program, we were surprised to learn how many children in a classroom had tinnitus (sometimes 2 out of class of 25). They did not call out and say so during the presentation. Instead, they waited until the presentation was over and then came up to us quietly and described the tinnitus that they hear. And they do hear it.

If you want to get involved in tinnitus prevention for school-age children, contact the ATA (800-634-8978). They will send you their *Hear for a Lifetime* school packet. Then you can make an appointment to visit the PTA at a local school to show them the materials. Many schools and districts around the country have adopted the program and are grateful when individuals from the community present it. The poster in and of itself can reach youngsters with the positive message, *"You have the power to hear for a lifetime. Turn it down. Walk away. Cover your ears."*

If only someone had told *us* when we were young.

Resource

Holgers, K.-M. Tinnitus in 7-year-old children, *Proceedings of the Sixth International Tinnitus Seminar,* Hazell, J., ed., Tinnitus and Hyperacusis Centre, London, 1999.

24

Hearing Loss

Q I was involved in military action many years ago in which a mortar shell exploded very near me. I wasn't hurt, but I could not hear for days after and my ears rang loudly. Gradually, the hearing returned and the ringing went away. Now, 30 years later, my ears are ringing again. I've examined my life-style, but can't find anything that might have started the ringing this time. I have not been exposed to loud sounds, and I am not taking any medications. Can you explain the return of the tinnitus?

A We hear this story often. You might have had some level of tinnitus all along, but your hearing was good enough for ambient environmental sounds to mask it. As you have grown older, your hearing might have declined to the point where your tinnitus has reappeared.

Consider this analogy. Tinnitus is a piling in the ocean. When the tide is in, we can see very little or maybe none of the piling. But when the tide goes out, we can see a great deal of the piling, even though it has not changed in length. As hearing goes up, tinnitus goes down; and as hearing goes down, tinnitus goes up, just like the piling and the tide. If you have noticed any difficulty in understanding speech when you are in a noisy situation or social gathering, it could be an indicator of hearing loss in the upper frequencies. The aging process alone can cause hearing loss that can lead to the perception of tinnitus that had been previously hidden.

Q My family berates me if I try to back out of attending weddings or other noisy functions. How can I convince them that tinnitus is a life-altering condition without hurting their feelings?

A Harry Truman often said, "You cannot make an omelet without breaking a few eggs." You might have to temporarily disregard what they feel and become more concerned with what they know. They need to be taught about what happens to you in noisy environments.

There are probably two reasons why attendance at these functions is undesirable to you. For one thing, the noise levels can exacerbate tinnitus, possibly in the extreme. Another problem might be a high-frequency hearing loss (90% of people with tinnitus have measurable hearing loss of some kind). High-frequency hearing loss can make speech difficult to understand when there is a lot of background noise.

With properly fitted hearing aids, you might solve the communication problem caused by hearing loss and possibly help your tinnitus at the same time. Newer hearing aids are built with compression technology. Compression hearing aids automatically give more amplification to softer sounds and less amplification to louder sounds. Contact the American Tinnitus Association for their brochure, "Understanding Tinnitus—Advice for Family and Friends." This material might help your loved ones understand how devastating tinnitus can be.

Q **Why do I have trouble understanding conversations in restaurants or at a party? I don't have a problem talking with people one on one. My tinnitus is loud, but it isn't loud enough to block out what people are saying.**

A Speech is generally composed of midrange frequencies, from about 200 to 4000 Hz. The background sounds at social gatherings are also predominantly composed of mid-range frequencies from about 200 to 4000 Hz. When the background sounds are loud, the part of the ear that deciphers mid-frequency speech becomes dominated by the loud mid-frequency background sounds. The ear compensates by shifting the function of speech deciphering to the high-frequency portion of the ear. So when a person has a high-frequency hearing loss and the speech deciphering has shifted to the high-frequency part of his or her ear because of background noise, speech comprehension can drop sharply away.

The cochlear hair cells that are responsible for the perception of high frequencies are the ones closest to the opening of the cochlea. If the ear is exposed to very loud noise, these high-frequency hair cells are the first to get hit with the blast of sound energy. Very often they are the first to be damaged. This might be why high-frequency loss is the most common hearing loss.

Q **I recently had surgery to relieve the vertigo from Ménière's disease. The surgery left me completely deaf in the operated ear, which is the ear with severe tinnitus. What can be done for me?**

A There are two problems. First, you could try a CROS hearing aid for the hearing loss. This is an arrangement of equipment with a microphone on the deaf ear that feeds into a hearing aid in the good ear. With this arrangement, you will be able to hear sounds on your deaf side because they will be piped over to your good side. You will no longer have to put people on your good side to hear them. And you will not be surprised by people and things that approach you on your deaf side. In time, you might even learn to correctly localize sound.

The CROS aid will not likely relieve your tinnitus. But as a related idea, it is sometimes possible to contralaterally mask the tinnitus. To do this you would put a masker in the good ear to help the tinnitus in the deaf ear. It can work! If the masker provides relief for you, you will probably sacrifice speech intelligibility when you use it. And when you wear the hearing aid for speech intelligibility, you will probably sacrifice tinnitus relief. At least there are options.

Q My doctor said that I have conductive hearing loss. He is optimistic that my hearing will return. What does *conductive* mean? And how can he be so sure that my hearing will come back?

A Conductive hearing loss is caused by something that has gone wrong in the middle ear, such as a fixation of the middle ear bones. It can also be caused by an outer ear problem, such as earwax, a foreign object resting against the eardrum or plugging up the ear canal or growths in the ear canal. Ear blockages and middle ear bone problems physically stop sound waves from being *conducted* to the inner ear. These problems can be remedied and the hearing loss restored. The tinnitus, if present, is usually alleviated when the outer or middle ear problem is resolved. This could be why your doctor was so optimistic. If your inner ear function was measured with bone conduction testing and the results were normal, that, too, could have accounted for the optimism.

There are two other kinds of hearing loss. *Sensorineural hearing loss* is the kind that is acquired from environmental events, such as the following:

- Extreme noise exposure that can damage the hair cells in the inner ear. Excessive noise exposure is the second most common cause of acquired sensory hearing loss.
- Ototoxic (poisonous to the ear) drugs that damage the structures of the cochlea and the semicircular canals. Some common drugs are particularly toxic to the ear, including certain antibiotics (like streptomycin and gentamicin), salicylates (the primary ingredient in aspirin), and quinine. The damage caused by these drugs often depends on the dose and can be permanent. Figures 24.1 and 24.2 are images of outer hair cells in the cochlea before and after drug damage. Excessive noise can cause similar destruction of the hair cells.
- Viruses such as measles, mumps, and the group of viruses that cause respiratory infections and damage to the cochlea.
- Presbycusis, the degenerative changes in the ear that are associated with the aging process. (This is the most common cause of sensory hearing loss in adults.) Thirty percent of those in the 65- to 70-year age category have to deal with the effects of presbycusis. The percentage increases to 40% of those over 75 years of age.

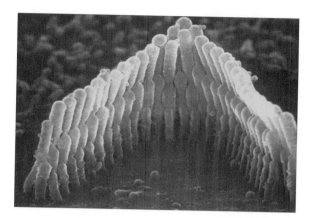

FIGURE 24.1 *Normal outer hair cell. Micrograph reprinted from J. O. Pickles, An Introduction to the Physiology of Hearing, 2nd ed., Academic Press, London, 1988 by permission of the publisher. Copyright © Academic Press, 1988.*

In *neural hearing loss,* the outer, middle, and inner ears are functioning normally, but there is an abnormality of the hearing nerve. The patient usually complains of unilateral (one-sided) hearing loss, tinnitus, and sometimes balance problems. The most common cause of neural hearing loss is the growth of tissue, or an acoustic neuroma, on the eighth cranial nerve. Other

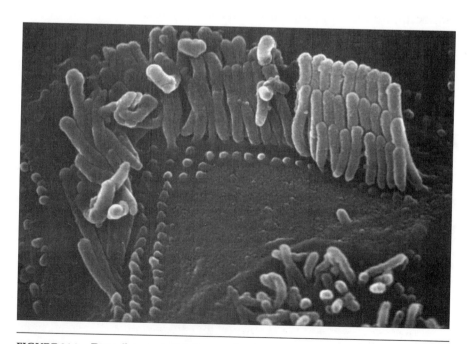

FIGURE 24.2 *Drug (kanamycin)-damaged outer hair cell. Micrograph courtesy of J. O. Pickles, copyright © J. O. Pickles, 2000.*

causes of neural hearing loss include conditions like multiple sclerosis and muscular dystrophy that cause the nerve coverings to degenerate.

Neural hearing losses typically do not respond well to hearing aids. In these cases, the route from the ear to the brain has been interrupted or the perceiving area in the brain has been impaired.

Q   **What is severe hearing impairment and how often does it occur? Is it the same as total deafness?**

A   You can have very severe hearing loss and not be totally deaf. For example, someone with a 70- to 80-dB hearing impairment might still be helped with some form of hearing prosthesis. You can never know in advance if an amplification device will or won't help. You have to give it a try.

According to Peter Steyger, Ph.D., professor at Oregon Health Sciences University, for people less than 20 years of age, 1 in 20 has a hearing impairment. For people aged 20 to 40, 1 in 10 has a hearing impairment. And for people 65 or older, 1 in 2 has a hearing impairment. Steyger, who is severely hearing impaired, made an interesting comment. He said, "The biggest problem for hard-of-hearing people is *denial*, both by the patients and by others. Once one gets past denial, the hard-of-hearing person can do anything."

Q   **Is tinnitus always associated with a hearing loss?**

A   This is very often the case. About 90% of tinnitus patients have some form of hearing loss. As a consequence, many hearing instrument dispensers believe that tinnitus patients simply need hearing aids to relieve their tinnitus. Unfortunately, this is not true. In one study, 192 tinnitus patients with hearing loss were told that their tinnitus would be relieved if they wore hearing aids. Of this group, only 7% found relief with hearing aids. Sixteen percent found tinnitus relief using tinnitus maskers. And 62% found relief with tinnitus instruments (a unit that combines a masker with a hearing aid). The rest could not be helped with the instrumentation that was tried. It is important to note that 85% of these patients were helped with some form of properly fitted instrumentation.

Resource

Carmen, R. *Hearing Loss & Hearing Aids—A Bridge to Healing,* Auricle Ink, Sedona, AZ, 1998.

25

Hearing Protection Devices

Q I am a young dentist. I've read that the high-speed drill I use can cause hearing loss and tinnitus. How can I protect my hearing while still being able to converse with my patients?

A Westone Laboratories produces custom-fitted filtered earplugs (called the Westone #49) that protect ears from loud noise and simultaneously allow conversation to get through. Etymotic Research makes two styles of custom-filtered earplugs (the ER-15 and ER-25) that are popular with musicians because the plugs are *flat attenuators*. Thin filters run through the earplug centers that work to reduce the volume of sound across all frequencies. Consequently, filtered earplug wearers notice that speech and other sounds appear normal though quieter. (Solid earplugs reduce high-frequency sounds predominantly.) When properly inserted, custom-filtered plugs can suppress an 80- to 90-dB drill noise down to 65 to 75 dB. The earplugs are molded to the exact shape of your ear canals.

Sound-dampening earmuffs (like Howard Leight's Thunder 29s) are more easily removed than earplugs. For this reason alone, they might be a good choice for you. They would allow for 20 dB or so of protection and then easy communication with your patients when the drilling is over.

Q Due to my tinnitus, I wear earplugs quite a lot. I find that I frequently push on them to adjust them. Could the buildup of moisture and wax and the continued pressure of the earplugs damage my ear canals?

A Many store-bought earplugs are solid foam or silicon plugs that do not let air into the canal. These solid plugs can cause soreness in the ear canal if they are overworn and if they are reworn without being washed with soap and water between wearings. In general, the ear canal will feel better if the earplug is seated correctly the first time and then left alone. If, however, the earplugs wiggle loose when you chew or talk, which they can do, take them out and reinsert them to give yourself the best hearing protection. Some foam earplugs (like Howard Leight and Aearo plugs) do allow air to move in and out of the ear canal space very slowly. As a last thought, you might want to consider spending less time in noisy environments, thereby lessening your need for earplugs.

A vented earplug (with a tiny tube running through the center) allows circulation of air in the ear canal, although it is usually a little less effective in noisy situations. Custom-molded earplugs are made specifically for your ear canal. Once in, they do not need to be adjusted. The drawbacks are that they can cost a bit of money ($50 to $75), and they will have to be remade every 2 to 3 years because ear canals change size and shape over time. Weight gain or weight loss will also affect ear canal dimensions.

Q   **Twenty-eight years ago, I worked in a newspaper pressroom where I was exposed to very loud sounds. Back then we didn't know to protect our ears. Now that I am retired, the main noise problem I face is mowing our large lawn. I have to use a riding—and very noisy—power mower to do it. If I use custom-molded earplugs *and* earmuffs, would I be protected? Or will my hearing still be damaged and my tinnitus exacerbated because of the sound vibrations through the body?**

A   Yes, sound waves are transmitted to the ear by bone conduction through bones in the head and by air conduction through the ear canal. However, the mechanical vibration from the mower is separate from the mower's sound vibration. The former is not damaging to the ear. People vary enormously in their susceptibility to noise exposure. Thus, the only way to determine if the earplugs and earmuffs will be adequate protection is to give them a test run.

Whether an earplug is custom molded, silicon, or foam, the absolute maximum protection that it can provide is 30 dB of sound blockage. If earmuffs have new and "springy" ear cups and are properly placed over the ears (and no stems from glasses are breaking the seal), the most protection that they can provide is 25 dB. However, the protection that earplugs and earmuffs provide when worn together is not 55 dB. The maximum sound attenuation that can be achieved by blocking the air pathway to the ear is about 36 dB.

Here is one other thought. Earplugs and earmuffs block the higher-frequency sounds better than they block low-frequency sounds. You might need protection from your mower's loud low-frequency noise. If so, an active noise cancellation device might help. Noise Cancellation Technologies and Bose Corporation make these computerized devices that are housed in standard protective earmuffs. The earmuffs themselves can block out 25 dB of higher-frequency noise. This just might solve the mower noise problem for you.

Q I am a family practitioner who sees more than my share of young adults, several of whom are musicians who complain of tinnitus. What can be done about musicians and the potential hearing damage to which they expose themselves?

A Many of the musicians who contact us because of their tinnitus are very reluctant to wear on-the-job ear protection. We know the dangers involved, but it is not hard to understand their position: Their ability to hear clearly is their livelihood. We routinely introduce them to musician's earplugs, by Etymotic Research, because these devices can provide adequate hearing protection (depending on just how loud their music environment is) and make it possible for the musicians to hear well enough to perform.

Unlike solid foam or silicon plugs that block mostly high-frequency noise, musician's earplugs have a built-in filtering system that allows all the frequencies through. The full range of music can still be heard—just 15 or so decibels quieter. Many people who have tried the musician's earplugs say that music sounds better with the plugs than without them.

Encourage your musician patients to have their hearing measured once a month. If there are changes in their hearing levels, the changes will be caught quickly. This frequent testing will also provide objective evidence of the effects of the loud music exposures.

26

How the Ear Works

Q If a hundred people were exposed to a tremendously loud sound, only a few would have hearing damage as a result of it. Are some people just immune to hearing damage from noise exposure?

A Immune, probably not. More muscular, maybe. When loud noise first enters the ear, the stapedius muscle (which is connected to the stapes in the middle ear) contracts and tilts the stapes. The tilted stapes stretches the annular ligament to which it is connected. This creates a more rigid seal to the oval window, a process that aggressively and naturally limits the amount of sound that gets into the inner ear. If the sound stimulation continues, however, the stapedius muscle relaxes and the protective reaction gradually diminishes.

Some stapedius muscles function better than other stapedius muscles. We don't know why this is so. And, unfortunately, there is no easy way to test which kind of stapedius muscle you have short of having your eardrum pulled back and the muscle's reaction physically observed. This muscle variation might explain why some people are more susceptible to noise damage than others.

Q I have read that a tiny microphone inserted into the ear canal can detect the tinnitus sounds we hear. Is that true? Are these emissions really the sounds of tinnitus?

A You have been reading about *otoacoustic emissions*, which were discovered by English engineer Colin Kemp. Otoacoustic emissions are extremely low-level sounds that are produced by the ear itself. An *evoked* otoacoustic emission is produced when a sound enters the ear canal, travels through the inner ear, comes out of the inner ear, and is reflected back through the eardrum into the ear canal. It is a kind of echo and can be detected by a microphone. The other kind of emission is a *spontaneous* otoacoustic emission, which is a detectable sound that the ear makes without the introduction of outside sound. When spontaneous emissions were first discovered, many scientists thought with great excitement that the source of tinnitus had been discovered. And what a wonderful thing that would have been. Unfortunately, spontaneous emissions do not correspond to tinnitus and are present in many ears without tinnitus.

Q I seem to be hearing tinnitus in my head, not in my ears. Do my ears still have something to do with it?

A Tinnitus is unquestionably a complex thing. It sounds high and shrill for some; low and rumbling for others. Some people have tinnitus in one ear and then have it "spread" to the other ear, without apparent injury to the second ear. Some people hear it in their ears while others hear it in their heads. This latter puzzle might be easily answered. It is often the case that "head" tinnitus is actually tinnitus in both ears of exact pitch, loudness, and phase. We discovered this possibility by introducing a single external tone to two ears. If the two tones were of exact pitch and loudness and were *in phase* (the curves of the sinusoidal waveforms were matched), the sound was heard in the head. When the loudness on one side was changed just a little bit, the perception of the sound moved a little closer to the louder ear. If the pitch was changed, it made the tones out of phase with each other and the sound perception immediately moved back to the ears.

Q What are hair cells? Are they really hairs that are altered by the aging process like the hairs on my head that turn gray and fall out?

A Hair cells are microscopic cells in the cochlea that line up in three V-shaped rows. These cells are responsible for the initiation of our hearing, and they are very different from the hairs on the head. They have been dubbed "hair cells" because of how they look under the microscope. Each of these cells has a tuft of projections at one end that looks like a bad haircut.

It is true that we lose these inner ear hair cells over time as we age, but this process is more the result of a lifetime of accumulated noise damage and possibly exposure to medications and other environmental toxins. Typically, we lose the high frequencies first, likely due to the fact that the high-frequency receptor cells of the ear are those first encountered as sounds enter the ear. The high-frequency receptor cells are located in the base of the cochlea, and the low-frequency receptor cells are located up in the apex of the cochlea. The auditory nerve that leads from the cochlea to the brain is also laid out that way: The higher-frequency transmitters are on the outside of the nerve, and the lower-frequency transmitters are in the core of the nerve fiber.

When the pressure of sound waves mechanically stimulates the outer hair cells, the outer hair cells send signals to the inner hair cells. The signals are exact copies of the sound energy waves that come into the ear. When the inner hair cells are activated, they release a chemical that causes changes in the electrical activity of the neurons to which they are connected. These neurons send the signals through the auditory nerve to the brain.

Q When I move my head either side to side or up and down, I hear a new sound added to my already existing tinnitus. Is it possible that the fluid level in one of my ears is low?

A If you had a low fluid level in the inner ear, you would probably have a serious balance problem and possibly no hearing at all. We naturally generate a continuous supply of endolymph and perilymph, which are the fluids of the inner ear. More likely the tinnitus effect is the result of neck muscle activity or a disturbance of the temporomandibular jaw joint.

Q Does something chemically happen to our bodies when we are exposed to constant noise?

A Investigators at the University of Florida studied the effects of *acoustic stress* (noise exposure over a long period of time) on the inner ear. They exposed rats to 85 dB of white noise for 4 hours a day for 3 consecutive days. After this experience, they measured the number of the glucocorticoid receptors (also called GR) in their inner ears. The researchers found a 27% decrease in GR in the inner ear's organ of Corti for the exposed ears as compared to non-exposed ears. Glucocorticoid is the recognized stress hormone that is normally released during periods of stress. The acoustical exposure somehow inhibited the production of this hormone.

The researchers conclude that there is a specific GR reaction in the inner ear as a response to acoustic stress. The researchers also believe that these receptors are related to Ménière's disease and, by association, to tinnitus, since tinnitus is a symptom of Ménière's. Dexamethasone, a synthetic glucocorticoid, has been used in the treatment of Ménière's disease, but has not yet been tried for tinnitus.

Q I have read that the bone around the ear is very hard and somewhat massive. Why do you think it's so big?

A The inner ear is encased in the temporal bone. The temporal bone is considered the hardest bone in the body, and it's a good thing too. The inner ear is an incredibly delicate structure that controls hearing and balance. The organ of Corti (named after Count Corti, an Italian nobleman with enough time on his hands to count hair cells) contains approximately 17,000 outer hair cells, 3700 inner hair cells, and 24,000 nerve fibers connecting it to the brain. Try to imagine 45,000 individual working parts in that very small space. Nature apparently invented miniature electronics long before we got around to it. Nature also put these miniature electronics in a safe case.

Resources

Brownell, W. E. How the ear works—nature's solutions for listening, *Volta Review*, 1999; 99(5):9–28.

Rarey, K. E., Gerhardt, K. J., Curtis, L. M., and ten Cate, W. J. Effect of stress on cochlear glucocorticoid protein: Acoustic stress, *Hear Res.*, Feb. 1995; 82(2): 135–8.

27

Hyperacusis: Supersensitivity to Sound

Q What is hyperacusis? And since I have tinnitus, do I also have hyperacusis?

A Hyperacusis is a supersensitivity to everyday sounds, technically a lack of loudness tolerance. Sounds that are perfectly acceptable to others can be miserably uncomfortable to hyperacusis patients. Refrigerator motors, normal conversation, even the sound of a dish placed on a table can be uncomfortably loud. About 90% of those who have hyperacusis also have tinnitus. Conversely, a very small number of those who have tinnitus have hyperacusis.

People with sound supersensitivity tend to overprotect their ears, which is understandable since everyday noises seem almost painful. But the result of overprotection is actually a worsening of the condition. Hyperacusis patients need to protect their ears from truly loud sounds. (We all do.) But they also need to therapeutically expose themselves to constant low-level sounds to overcome their sensitivity.

Consider joining the Hyperacusis Network, founded and run by Dan Malcore. Malcore writes and edits an exceptional monthly newsletter for hyperacusis patients.

Q Due to my hyperacusis, I can only tolerate TV by muting it and then listening to a small radio that receives the audio portion of the TV transmission. Why is it that the small radio can present the audio at an acceptable level, but the TV cannot?

A Hyperacusis is inversely related to the pitch of the sound. This means that, the higher the pitch is, the less the person with hyperacusis can tolerate

Also see Chapter 48, Tinnitus Testing, and Chapter 50, TRT: Tinnitus Retraining Therapy.

it. It is quite possible that the small radio does not reproduce the high pitches as well as the TV speakers do.

It is possible for you to reinstate your normal loudness tolerance with a two-part approach:

1. Do not overprotect your ears.
2. Listen to low-level broadband (or *pink*) noise for several hours every day at the loudest level that is comfortable.

While this is not an easy procedure, it can be extremely beneficial if you stick with it.

To start the process, make sure that you do not use ear protection for sounds that are less than 65 dB for a period of 1 month. You can buy a sound-level meter at Radio Shack for $35 to $55 to measure the sounds in your home and elsewhere. For the next month, do not use ear protection for sounds that are 70 dB or less. Since there is a big difference between 65 and 70 dB (70 dB is almost two times louder than 65 dB), you can increase your loudness exposure by 2 or 3 decibels from one month to the next. Progess made gradually is still progress. Eventually, you will reach a level of normal loudness tolerance.

Q My hyperacusis and tinnitus have grown increasingly severe over the past 15 years although my hearing is intact. My major problem is that exposure to almost any level of sound causes my tinnitus and hyperacusis to increase. All outside noises are intolerable to the extent that I cannot attend family affairs, including our daughter's wedding, or reunions or gatherings of any sort. Restaurants, shopping malls, ball games, and street traffic are all off-limits to me. A slammed door or a dropped plate is torture. What can I do? Is there any device that could protect me from loud and sudden sounds?

A James Nunley, an audio engineer at the Oregon Hearing Research Center, devised electronic earplugs for hyperacusis patients. These special devices compress, or actively reduce, loud sounds so that *all* loud sounds are immediately reduced to a level of no more than 60 to 65 dB. This means that you could go out without fear of being suddenly bombarded by unexpected sounds.

Nunley worked with a hyperacusis patient on the prototype of these Star 2000 sound attenuators/processors. By the patient's account, the Star 2000 has helped him reestablish a normal quality of life. He can now go to restaurants and shopping malls. Recently, he picked up his grandson who screamed in his ear. Previously, that one simple action would have laid him low for weeks. But this time it produced no problem at all. He says that he is no longer a prisoner in his own home or anywhere else.

The Star 2001 soft silicon electronic earplugs are now digital and custom made by hearing scientist Jim Fenwick. To order them, you will need to have earmolds made that are deep enough to reach the second bend in the ear canal. The electronics in these unvented devices effectively balances sound input with sound protection. This keeps them from overprotecting the hyperacusics' ears. Quite clever.

Micro-Tech Hearing Instruments also makes an electronic in-the-ear plug called the Refuge Hyperacusic™ designed for the needs of hyperacusis patients. The Refuge amplifies low-level sounds so that there is no overprotection, and it automatically adjusts down (or compresses) the volume of loud incoming sounds to your specific loudness tolerance. As of this writing, Micro-Tech still manufactures this well-made product. However, the company is currently deciding if they will continue to carry it.

Q **What is the difference between *white* noise and *pink* noise. Should I listen to just one kind of noise to help my hyperacusis or are they interchangeable?**

A There is a significant difference between pink noise and white noise. *White noise* contains all frequencies heard by the human ear: 20 through 20,000 Hz. *Pink noise* contains frequencies from 200 through 6000 Hz. Hyperacusis patients are instructed to listen to pink noise at the loudest level that is comfortable and slowly reestablish normal loudness tolerance for everyday ordinary sounds. The usual sounds in our environment are composed of frequencies from around 200 to 4000 Hz.

Many years ago, a patient at the OHRC Tinnitus Clinic was using white noise therapy for his hyperacusis. One day he questioned our use of white noise desensitization for his hyperacusis since he found the high-frequency portion of the white noise to be highly annoying. He believed that it was delaying his recovery process. The patient suggested that we use *pink noise* instead, since it contained the frequencies found in normal environmental sounds, but not the high frequencies that were so hard to listen to. We have been using pink noise (from the Moses/Lang CDs) ever since with much better success, primarily because patients actually listen to it. Allen Moses donated the CD machinery to the OHRC lab. And patient Tom Lang suggested the use of pink noise.

Tinnitus Retraining Therapy (TRT), developed by Pawel Jastreboff, Ph.D., Sc.D., utilizes devices similar to in-the-ear or behind-the-ear maskers as part of the protocol for tinnitus relief. TRT is a long-term program designed to retrain the brain to listen to the quieter sounds from the ear devices and to eventually habituate (no longer notice) the tinnitus. Jastreboff was initially surprised by the effect that this tinnitus treatment had on his patients who also had hyperacusis. The tinnitus was still taking 6 to 24 months to resolve, but the hyperacusis in many of these patients was improving in 3 to 6 months. As a result, he changed the name of his University of Maryland clinic from the Tinnitus Clinic to the Tinnitus and Hyperacusis Clinic. The TRT ear-level devices emit a lower range of broadband sounds in the 300- to

6000-Hz range, comparable to the Moses/Lang CDs and what our patient suggested long ago: pink noise.

Q Because of my tinnitus and hyperacusis, I cannot stand any noise. I turn the refrigerator off half the time. I cannot watch television or listen to the radio. In the summertime, the sound of lawn mowers or chain saws is intolerable. I am essentially a recluse. Nevertheless, I've purchased the Moses/Lang CD and want to give it a try. Is there a particular type or brand of CD player that would optimize the pink noise sound and maybe speed up the healing?

A It does not matter what brand of CD player is used. However, if you use one with headphones, you will have the freedom to move around while allowing the established loudness level for each listening period to remain constant. The headphones will block some ambient sounds, which is a slight drawback. If the pink noise is delivered over stationary speakers in a room, the loudness level will vary somewhat as your position changes relative to the speakers, but ambient sounds will be included, and this is a slight advantage.

The most important aspect of sound therapy for hyperacusis is to expose your ears to low-level sounds for several hours every day. Establish a listening period of at least 2 hours (longer if possible) each day during which you listen to the loudest sound that is comfortable. Never listen to sound at an uncomfortable level.

Each time you begin a listening period, you must reestablish a new listening level. To do this, adjust the loudness level from zero upward until you approach the level of discomfort, and then reduce the loudness slightly and use that level. The advice is similar for the TRT sound generators used for hyperacusis. Reset the level of sound every morning, find the quietest level that you can hear, then listen to this quiet broadband sound for 8 to 10 hours every day.

One main problem with this hyperacusis desensitization technique is that it takes a considerable amount of time, and patients are apt to become discouraged and quit. This routine has proved itself very successful for many patients with hyperacusis. With time, you can regain your normal loudness tolerance and lead a normal life once again.

Q My doctor said that I do not have hyperacusis but that I have recruitment instead. What is the difference between recruitment and hyperacusis?

A Hyperacusis is a collapse of loudness tolerance. For someone with hyperacusis, all sounds except the quietest of sounds are uncomfortably loud. Recruitment is the rapid growth of loudness of certain sounds that happen to be in the pitch region of the patient's hearing loss. (See Figure 27.1) The recruiting ear reaches the same loudness level as the normal ear, but it does so sometimes quite suddenly. This can have an interesting though negative

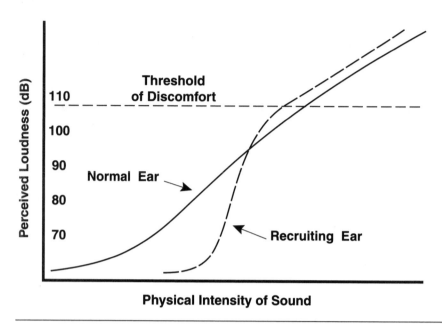

Physical Intensity of Sound

FIGURE 27.1 *The recruiting ear and the normal ear. The suddenness of the recruiting ear's awareness of sound causes the perception of loudness.*

effect on communication. Here is an example. A woman calls to her husband. He does not hear her, so she, assuming inattention, repeats the call. He still does not hear her, so she raises her voice for the third call, whereupon he answers, "You don't have to shout. I can hear you!"

The majority of hyperacusis cases are the result of exposure to extreme loud noise, either a one-time exposure or continuously over a long period of time. Patients with other conditions, such as Lyme's disease, chronic fatigue syndrome, Bell's palsy, head injury, and epilepsy, experience hyperacusis. Hyperacusis is also an associated symptom of autism. Children with autism often complain that everything is too loud.

Recruitment can follow ear surgery or ear-related illnesses. Or it can be the result of sensorineural hearing loss. Recruitment and hearing loss usually occur together.

In 1990, the American Tinnitus Association conducted a survey of its members (approximately 35,000 people) to determine how many hyperacusis patients experienced hearing loss. Of 104 patients who indicated that they had hyperacusis, 65 (62%) reported some degree of measured hearing loss. Did all the responders have true hyperacusis or did they have recruitment? We don't know. But the incidence of hearing loss was so pronounced that we must conclude that at least some hyperacusis patients have hearing impairment. When these patients were asked which condition, tinnitus or hyperacusis, was worse, 56% said that hyperacusis was worse, 26% said that they were equally bad, and 17% indicated that tinnitus was worse.

This survey helped us learn some demographics of people with sound sensitivity. Here are their responses:

Which ear has hyperacusis?
Both ears: 88%
Right ear only: 10%
Left ear only: 2%

What was the rate of onset?
Sudden: 50%
Gradual: 47%
Unsure: 3%

Were you experiencing stress at the onset of your hyperacusis?
Yes: 46%
No: 49%
Unsure: 5%

Is your hyperacusis the result of recreational noise exposure?
Yes: 72%
No: 28%

Does your hyperacusis affect your social recreation?
Yes: 90%
No: 10%

Has your hyperacusis caused you to change jobs?
Yes: 48%
No: 39%
Other: 13% (retired)

Do you have a feeling of fullness in your ear(s)?
Yes: 71%
No: 26%
Other: 3%

Does your hyperacusis fluctuate?
Yes: 70%
No: 26%
Unsure: 2%

Do you wear ear protection during all waking hours?
Yes: 93%
No: 7%

These data reveal that most (93%) of the hyperacusis patients who responded to the survey were thwarting their own recovery by overprotecting their ears. There is a serious need to get proper information into the hands of sound-sensitive patients.

Q **My father has hyperacusis, but without tinnitus. What treatment can he try for his hyperacusis?**

A He can try sound desensitization by wearing low-level, in-the-ear noise generators or by listening to a pink noise CD. Since most hyperacusis patients have tinnitus, it is possible that he might be confusing hyperacusis with recruitment. Hyperacusis patients find that almost all sounds are uncomfortably loud. Recruitment patients, on the other hand, find that only certain sounds are uncomfortably loud. Recruitment is also a frequent companion to sensorineural hearing loss, the kind of hearing loss that is often related to age. Have him get a hearing test and an additional test for recruitment. If he has recruitment, he might try hearing aids that can provide compression in the specific frequency ranges of his recruitment. These could make life much nicer for your father.

Q **Does tinnitus make a person perceive other sounds as being louder than normal?**

A No, the condition of hyperacusis can cause that perception. Hyperacusis (or supersensitivity to sound) is not necessarily related to tinnitus, and it is only occasionally present in tinnitus patients. When the two symptoms are present simultaneously, the hyperacusis is commonly judged to be the more severe condition. Usually, the person with tinnitus and hyperacusis is exceptionally sensitive to sound and begins to wear ear protection all the time. The all-the-time use of hearing protection is counterproductive to reversing hyperacusis. Doing so will make everyday sounds appear more uncomfortable. Ear protection should not be used for normal sounds.

Q **I read in the newspaper that a new type of surgery could stop seizures. The young child being discussed had been hyperactive and very sensitive to noise. The offending portion of the child's brain (it was found to be non-functioning) was surgically removed and, as a result, noise no longer disturbs him. Does the future hold such hope for hyperacusis patients?**

A Possibly, but it is complicated. Here is one explanation of why surgery for hyperacusis is a long shot. There are two general types of nerves in the body: afferent nerves and efferent nerves. Afferent nerves send the signals from the sensory organs such as the eyes and ears up to the brain, where they are interpreted (as sight, sound, etc.). The efferent nerves in the brain send signals out to the muscles and glands, causing their activation. Oddly enough, there is one bundle of efferent nerves that starts in the brain (in the olive of the brain, a part of the brainstem) and sends its signals to the inner ear. This bundle is known as the olivocochlear bundle. Since there are no muscles or glands in the inner ear, what is the function of this olivocochlear bundle of nerves? The best evidence indicates that activity in this bundle of nerves suppresses all incoming sounds. Presumably, it is the non-functioning or impaired function of the olivocochlear bundle that contributes to hyperacusis, the collapse of loudness tolerance.

Unfortunately, the olivocochlear bundle of nerves is entwined within the afferent auditory nerve (the eighth cranial nerve) so that the only way to surgically remove the olivocochlear bundle would be to cut the entire eighth nerve, resulting in total deafness. We realize that some patients with severe hyperacusis would select total deafness over their condition. It is very important for these patients to understand that the olivocochlear bundle can be retrained to function normally, which would relieve hyperacusis.

Here is another possibility for hyperacusis, although it is another long shot. Hyperactive and autistic children who also appear to be hyperacusic are being treated with secretin, a hormone that stimulates the pancreas. The excitement about this drug occurred when one autistic child responded remarkably well to a single dose of the drug. Following that, 56 autistic children were invited to participate in a double-blind, placebo-controlled study of the drug. Unfortunately, the children who were given secretin did not experience significant improvement. But the single dose given in this study might not have been enough to help. You can contact the Autism Research Institute (4182 Adams Avenue, San Diego, California 92116, 619-281-7165, Fax: 619-563-6840) for more information about secretin research. Incidentally, the majority of parents opted to continue the therapy for their children, so we can anticipate some longer-term results.

Resources

Sandler, A. D., Sutton, K. A., DeWeese, J., Girardi, M. A., Sheppard, V., and Bodfish, J. W. Lack of benefit of a single dose of synthetic human secretin in the treatment of autism and pervasive developmental disorder, *N. Engl. J. Med.*, Dec. 1999: 341(24):1801–6.

Tabachnick, B. Sound sensitivity, *Tinnitus Today*, Sept. 1998; 23(3):14–16.

28

Hypnosis

Q Do you think hypnosis could help my tinnitus? Will it put me in a trance?

A It was once thought that to be hypnotized was to be put into a trance, an altered state of consciousness, a deep sleep. (The word *hypnosis* was derived from *Hypnos,* the Greek god of sleep.) In this state, the hypnotized person, it was believed, would be vulnerable to any suggestion, embarrassing or otherwise, made by the hypnotist. Furthermore, the hypnotized person would not remember any event that took place while under the spell. In reality, it is not so dramatic, but it certainly is interesting.

Hypnosis is a procedure in which a practitioner (hypnotist) suggests changes in sensations, thoughts, feelings, perceptions, or behavior to the person being hypnotized. People who have been hypnotized liken the experience to that of being totally absorbed in a good book or a favorite piece of music, quite the opposite of being asleep. Hypnosis cannot force a person to do what he or she is not willing to do. The hypnotic state is not sleep. In fact, brain waves recorded during wakefulness are similar to brain waves recorded during hypnosis. And, as it turns out, some people are simply better hypnotic subjects than other people.

The medical uses of hypnosis are impressive. Some people have been able to successfully forego anesthesia for dental work, childbirth, and even surgery by using hypnotic suggestions. Hypnosis has also helped some cancer patients better tolerate the nausea associated with chemotherapy.

Psychotherapist Kevin Hogan, Ph.D., explains the uselessness of being told by one's doctor to go home and just ignore the tinnitus. "It is not possible to do," Hogan writes. For example, try to ignore an imagined picture you have in your mind of President Clinton. "Ignore it now. Ignore it. You see, you cannot ignore something you are trying to ignore." He believes strongly in the usefulness of hypnotherapy for tinnitus because it creates an external focus that redirects the patient's attention away from the noises within.

In one study, 41 tinnitus patients underwent three sessions of hypnotherapy specifically for their tinnitus. When they were evaluated 3 months later, 68% of the patients expressed some improvement in their tinnitus and 32% reported no improvement. Interestingly, about half of the group that did *not* benefit from hypnosis also had considerable hearing loss of 30 dB or more. Less than 15% of the improved group had similar hearing loss. The researchers safely concluded that hypnotherapy can be beneficial as a treatment for tinnitus, but that it is probably less useful for patients with significant hearing loss.

In a different study, the same researchers determined that three sessions with a trained hypnotherapist were more beneficial to a tinnitus patient than was one session with a trained counselor. Almost half (45.5%) of the hypnosis patients reported a general feeling of improvement compared to 14.3% of the counseling patients. The researchers don't know (nor do we know) if the positive hypnosis effect was due to the extra time the patients spent with their hypnotherapists. We also don't know why the effect of three hypnosis sessions was not compared with the effect of three counseling sessions.

Q **Do I need special training to do my own self-hypnosis? Do I have to see a hypnotherapist first? And can this really help my tinnitus?**

A Audiologist and hypnotherapist Diane Shultz, M.A., CCC-A, helps tinnitus patients both ways—with one-on-one hypnosis sessions, usually one per week for 6 or 8 weeks, and by teaching motivated patients to do it themselves. Shultz recorded the Quiet Mind self-hypnosis audiotapes specifically to help tinnitus and hyperacusis patients become self-hypnotists.

According to Shultz, hypnosis very much helps the healing process along for her tinnitus and hyperacusis patients. She also believes that anyone can benefit from hypnosis or the deep relaxation that it engenders. Patients report that they feel good after their sessions and that there is carryover beyond the sessions and into their daily lives. In her experience, left-brained people, like accountants and attorneys, have more difficulty and take more time getting to that relaxed state than do right-brained people. But they *can* get there.

Here is a simple "how-to" for self-hypnosis:

- Sit in a comfortable chair or lie down on a comfortable bed or sofa.
- Close your eyes and gradually relax each set of muscles, starting at the top of the head, moving to the face, neck, shoulders, arms, torso, legs, and feet. This is called progressive relaxation.
- Imagine that you are in a quiet, peaceful place—a forest, or near the ocean, or in a special restful room. Notice the colors and smells around you and "feel" the soft breeze against your face.

- Think of two or three positive affirmations like:
  My mind is quiet.
  All sounds are peaceful and relaxing.
  My body is relaxed yet refreshed.
  You can write down these affirmations ahead of time and repeat them several times before the self-hypnosis session to learn them.
- Repeat the affirmations several times quietly aloud or to yourself.
- Stretch, take a deep breath, and open your eyes. Move slowly for a minute or two.

You can make an audiotape of your hypnosis session in your own voice, talking yourself through the progressive relaxation, and so on, and then play it back for future self-hypnosis sessions. Shultz feels that 10 to 20 minutes is the ideal time length for a session. She also feels that tinnitus patients get the most help from self-hypnosis when it is done twice a day.

Q **This may sound like a strange question, but does hypnosis pose any danger to someone with tinnitus?**

A Hypnotherapy, either with a qualified hypnotherapist or done as self-hypnosis, probably relieves a great deal of stress and can be tried without concern of negative side effect.

There is an obvious exception. If tinnitus is a warning of something serious, for example a tumor, hypnosis would divert the patient's attention away from a warning that would need to be heeded. This is a potential problem with any therapy that trains patients to focus their attention away from their tinnitus. The prudent course of action is to see a medical doctor first, have whatever tests are recommended, and then, when all is clear, get hypnotized if you so desire.

Resources _____

Hogan, K. *Tinnitus: Turning the Volume Down*, Network 3000 Publishing Co., Eagan, MN, 1998.

Mason, J., and Rogerson, D. Client-centered hypnotherapy for tinnitus: Who is likely to benefit? *Am. J. Clin. Hypn.*, Apr. 1995; 37(4):294–9.

Mason, J. D., Rogerson, D. R., and Butler, J. D. Client centered hypnotherapy in the management of tinnitus—is it better than counselling? *J. Laryngol. Otol.*, Feb. 1996; 110(2):117–20.

Wade, C., and Travis, C. *Psychology*, Addison-Wesley Educational Publishers, Reading, MA, 1998.

29

Infection

Q I have poor hearing, one ear being worse than the other. Interestingly, when I have an ear infection in the better ear, my hearing improves and the tinnitus decreases. Why does my hearing improve with ear infections?

A You could have a disarticulation (or misalignment) of the middle ear bones that somehow is corrected by the fluids of infection. A bone conduction hearing test could detect this. If this is the case, then a middle ear prosthesis could be surgically implanted to restore your hearing in that ear. And if your hearing is fully or even partially restored, your tinnitus could be greatly reduced. Discuss this matter with an otolaryngologist.

Four other patients had the same experience with head colds and flu. One person reasoned that perhaps it was the increase in body temperature accompanying the cold or flu that reduced his tinnitus.

Another patient found that taking hot baths reduced his tinnitus not only while he was in the bath, but also for 45 to 60 minutes after the bath. It is true that an increased body temperature can increase the speed at which the nerves respond. But we don't know if this caused the tinnitus to go down. Perhaps the relaxation response from the hot bath helped to release tension in his neck and jaw, which led to his diminished tinnitus.

Yet another patient reported that during her flu attack she took Lorabid, a synthetic antibiotic drug used for moderate infections. Her tinnitus disappeared for the 6 days that she took the medication. All these experiences point to areas for scientific investigation.

Q There was a nasty epidemic in London last year during the time I was visiting. This resulted in my getting a middle ear infection followed by tinnitus. Could the infection have caused the tinnitus?

A Middle ear infection is the most common cause of earaches and tinnitus in children. Once the infection has cleared up, the pain usually goes away quickly. The tinnitus might not go away immediately, but generally it will abate. The typical tinnitus associated with middle ear infection is a very high-pitched tone. In the case of children, the pitch may be exceptionally high pitched due to their very high-pitched hearing ability. Once the infection is cleared, the tinnitus gradually goes away. But it can come again with another infection.

30

Insurance and Financial Assistance

Q I am 84 years old and living only on Social Security. My tinnitus seems to be getting worse by the month. Is there any hope for me?

A The increase in the loudness of your tinnitus could be due to a gradual decline in your hearing. If you are also experiencing difficulty understanding conversations, it is possible that a hearing aid would improve your hearing ability as well as your tinnitus. Hearing aids are expensive and, of course, this is a problem.

There are two organizations that might help you. The Starkey Hearing Foundation has been distributing hearing aids internationally for many years to people who cannot afford to pay for them. The organization Hear Now handles Starkey's U.S. hearing aid distribution also for those who cannot afford the devices and who do not qualify for governmental assistance to get them. They also make maskers and tinnitus instruments available to those in financial need. If you are interested in this program, call Hear Now (800-648-HEAR) for an application.

Some of the very high-powered behind-the-ear aids distributed by Hear Now are often ones that have been refurbished. However, any part of a device that goes into the ear is brand new. Hear Now will explain to you how to find a local affiliated audiologist. Joanita Stelter from Hear Now explains that they ask audiologists to not just fit the devices for patients, but to provide follow-up care too. According to Stelter, 3200 hearing health professionals in the United States generously provide this service.

Also, try contacting a local Lion's Club through your Chamber of Commerce or library. Or call Lion's Club International (630-571-5466, www10. lionsclubs.org/lion) and tell them of your financial situation and that you need a hearing aid. Community service organizations like the Lions and others, such as Sertoma (816-333-8300, www.sertoma.org), are dedicated to serving people around the world who have vision and hearing disorders. They might be happy to help. (Sertoma, incidentally, offers $1000 scholarships to hearing-impaired students entering 4-year colleges and $2500 scholarships to students going into graduate programs of audiology and speech, language, and hearing.)

Q **Because I have normal hearing, the Social Security Administration's disability division will not acknowledge the presence of my tinnitus. They claim that tinnitus is caused by and must be accompanied by hearing loss. Are they right?**

A In this case, they are not right. Out of 7000 patients at the Oregon Hearing Research Center's Tinnitus Clinic who had significantly severe tinnitus, fully 10% had normal hearing as determined by audiometric testing.

There are some predictable aspects to the Social Security Administration (SSA). Often the SSA will deny a claim when it is first filed. Those who are not discouraged by that first rejection can ask for a reconsideration of their claim. (This is done with paperwork. The person filing a claim is not present during either of these decision-making events.) If the claimant is again denied a claim, he or she can ask for a hearing and actually appear before a judge. Many negative decisions are reversed at this point in the appeals process. Even if the judge rules against the disabled person again, an appeal can be made and the case can move up to the federal district court.

One claimant in New York decided to fight the Social Security disability system that repeatedly denied his tinnitus claim because his hearing test was normal. He wrote, "When persons with the maddening maelstrom of tinnitus apply for Social Security disability, they are often rejected based on the result of their hearing test alone—because their hearing is okay. It's as if your toilet bowl is overflowing and an intervening governmental agency says you don't need a plumber because your water meter is okay!" This claimant eventually won his case in the federal district court of appeals. It is unknown how many people lose patience and heart during the appeals process and stop before all levels of appeal have been tried.

Q **Is it possible to have health insurance companies pay for tinnitus maskers? My audiologist prescribed the maskers.**

A Much depends on the kind of coverage your health insurance company offers. As a general rule, health insurance companies do not cover the cost of *prosthetic* devices, like hearing aids. It is very important that your insurance company know that the FDA classifies tinnitus maskers as *therapeutic* devices, not as prosthetic devices. Most insurance companies will pay for therapeutic devices. You might also point out that had you gone to a psychiatrist for treatment of your tinnitus the cost would have been many times the cost of maskers. Do not accept a rejection by your company until after you have approached them a minimum of three times.

31

Masking: Using External Sounds to Quiet Tinnitus

Q What is masking?

A Masking is the introduction of an external sound to a tinnitus ear with the intent of completely or partially covering (or masking) the internal tinnitus sound. Many people with tinnitus experience a perceived reduction of their tinnitus loudness in the presence of the masking sound. The masker sound—a "shhhh" sound, like static on an FM radio—is generally a broadband sound from 2000 to 8000 Hz.

Q What forms of masking are available? And how can an audiologist determine which is the best kind of masking for me?

A There are several different forms of masking. Ear-level masking can occur with an in-the-ear, behind-the-ear, or in-the-canal masker and also with a hearing aid or a tinnitus instrument (a device that combines a hearing aid with a masker). Environmental masking can occur with a tabletop sound-generating machine, an FM radio set between stations, a fan, an aquarium, a waterfall, the ocean, or any external sound source that provides a steady, monotonous, low-level noise that interferes with the perception of tinnitus.

When attempting to relieve tinnitus with masking devices, it is very important to know the pitch of the tinnitus and the degree and frequency location of hearing loss. Figures 31.1 through 31.4 show audiograms for a variety of hearing and tinnitus circumstances and give suggested therapies. Ideally, every tinnitus patient should have the opportunity to try every available sound device in an attempt to find the very best one or at least one that helps

Also see Chapter 40, Residual Inhibition: An Aftereffect of Masking, and Chapter 46, Tinnitus Instruments: Devices for Tinnitus Control.

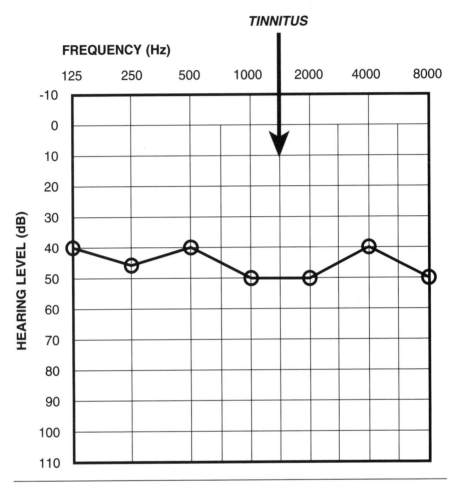

FIGURE 31.1 *Audiogram of low-frequency tinnitus and flat hearing loss. Suggested therapy: hearing aid.*

at all. A few clinics offer device sampling to their patients. In the absence of this, you and your clinician can use these audiogram charts to guide your decision.

But keep an open mind. Some patients experience tinnitus relief with sound levels nowhere near what should be working according to these charts. There are no absolute statements that can be made about masking and tinnitus relief. In the final analysis, you are the only one who can tell if what you are trying is helping.

Q My tinnitus was in my right ear, and when it was masked, it was substantially reduced. I was able to sleep without pills. I was in control of my

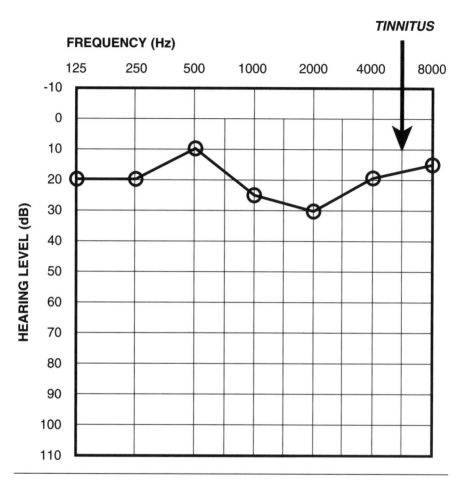

FIGURE 31.2 *Audiogram of high-frequency tinnitus and no hearing loss. Suggested therapy: High-frequency tinnitus masker.*

tinnitus and my life. Recently at a dinner party, my immediate table neighbor dropped a metal knife on her plate. It was like a gunshot! I awoke that night with increased tinnitus in my right ear and tinnitus in the left ear as well. I feel as if I'm back where I started and on an emotional roller coaster. The tinnitus seems to go from inside the head to outside the head. My physician has put me on Valium to help me sleep. Do you think there is any way to relieve my greatly increased tinnitus?

A First, it is very likely that your tinnitus will return to its original level. It could take weeks and possibly months, but the chances are good that it will come back down. Hearing damage that results from noise exposure is the product of the length of the exposure *and* of the loudness of the noise. The

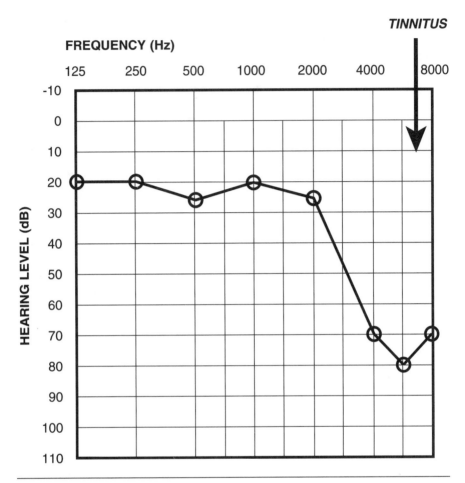

FIGURE 31.3 *Audiogram of high-frequency tinnitus and high-frequency hearing loss. Suggested therapy: tinnitus instrument.*

knife-on-the-plate sound to which you were exposed was fortunately very brief in length and of a relatively nondamaging intensity.

The fact that your tinnitus appears to be in the head might be due to balanced tinnitus signals coming from both ears, or possibly from both auditory pathways. Instead of using one masker, you might find that two maskers would bring the tinnitus under control.

Q I was fitted with an unusual tinnitus masker about 20 years ago. It did not produce a noise like most maskers. Instead, it produced a pure tone of 5600 Hz that exactly matched my tinnitus and that I have used with great success for all these years. Recently, the masker quit working and I had it

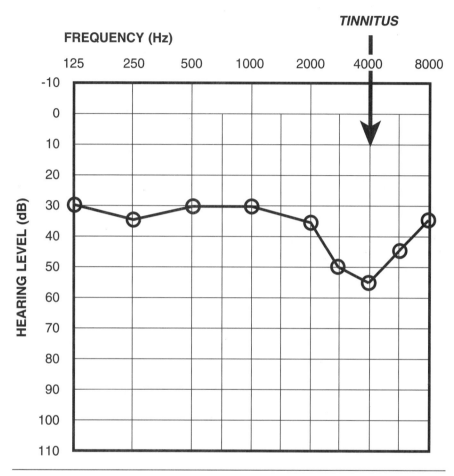

FIGURE 31.4 *Audiogram of 4000-Hz tinnitus and 4000-Hz "noise-notch" hearing loss. Suggested therapy: tinnitus instrument or high-frequency tinnitus masker.*

repaired. But when I got it back, it had been "fixed" so that it now produces a noise and not the 5600-Hz tone. Do you know of anyone who can provide me with a pure tone masker?

A   Twenty years ago, we tried the idea of pure tone masking on four patients. But when we got improved noise-type maskers, the other three patients switched to the newer maskers. We had forgotten all about you! The electronics in a hearing aid are said to last only about 5 years. You got a great deal more service than we would have expected. In any event, the technicians who made the original pure tone maskers have long since retired, but we do know one way to provide you with a pure tone masking sound.

We will have an audio engineer produce a digital CD of a 5600-Hz pure tone for you. You will need a portable CD player with earphones, which will undoubtedly be different from your in-the-ear masker of years past. You might feel a little odd going out wearing headphones. But so many people use them to listen to music that you will probably blend right in. More importantly, it might work.

[One week after receiving the CD, this patient reported that it was very helpful in relieving his tinnitus. He listened to it on an inconspicuous CD player with small earphones and had already gotten used to it. He thought that, in some ways, the pure tone CD was better than the in-the-ear device. It had a cleaner sound, and he felt that the volume level of masking that he needed with the CD was lower than the volume level he had needed with the masker. He was beginning to experience periods of residual inhibition lasting 30 minutes to several hours.

Four weeks later, the patient reported great improvement. He no longer used the masking CD during the day. Instead, he rigged the CD player as a bedside unit so that it provided pure tone masking sound all night long. Initially, he had trouble getting to sleep (and his wife didn't fare any better), but after four nights they were both used to it. When he woke up in the morning, his tinnitus was completely gone and it remained that way throughout the day.

Eight weeks later, he reported that the CD was not working as well for his tinnitus as it had been. It is possible that the pitch of his tinnitus has changed. We have asked him to have it retested, and we will have a new pure tone CD track made for him if it is warranted.]

Q I can hear people talk when I wear my hearing aids, but I can't understand what they are saying. As for my tinnitus, I was told that my hearing was so impaired that masking could not help me.

A Speech comprehension is a common complaint, especially among elderly patients with hearing losses. The act of understanding speech involves not only hearing the speech sounds, but also processing those sounds in the brain. The processing actually requires a certain amount of time to achieve. Apparently, as we age, our ability to process speech sounds (like many other things) simply slows down. And it doesn't have to slow down much for speech to become quite incomprehensible. David Lilly, Ph.D., conducted a speech comprehension study in which the time interval between utterances was increased by only 250 milliseconds. This delayed timing significantly improved speech comprehension for the elderly test subjects who were hearing impaired. Unfortunately, there is no wearable electronic device available that can slow down the presentation of words. It might be helpful for you to ask people to speak to you not louder but slower.

There are so many variables to consider regarding masking: the degree of your hearing loss, the tinnitus pitch, the type of tinnitus sound you hear, and the masking instrument used. We have never been able to judge in advance with total accuracy which device and setting will work. We encourage you to conduct a trial. And as is true for all therapies, success with masking is enhanced when it is administered by skilled and knowledgeable clinicians.

Q I've been wearing a masker and it has improved my tinnitus significantly. This new problem seems minor, but ever since I got the masker, people have been telling me that I talk too loud. Is there a connection and, if so, what can I do about it?

A Yes, there is a connection. You are "overtalking" the masking sound. (People often do this when they wear earplugs.) It seems like a minor problem, but we know it is not. When our ears are occluded, we tend to raise our voices. Make a conscious effort to speak more softly. Very often it is easier to speak more softly if we speak more slowly.

Q I am 84 years of age. Does my advanced age make it impossible to relieve my tinnitus?

A There is no reason why age alone would influence the choice of procedures used for tinnitus relief. At any age, it is safe to introduce a quiet, neutral external sound to the affected ear or ears with either in-the-ear, behind-the-ear, or tabletop sound-generating devices. If you are currently taking medications, your drug choices for tinnitus relief might be limited. Your doctor can help you to decide. If your manual dexterity is limited, you might find that it is easier to adjust a behind-the-ear device than an in-the-ear device. (The controls are a little bigger and easier to reach.) We encourage you to give a trial to any procedure that is recommended or approved by your primary care giver.

Q My maskers work very well to relieve my tinnitus. But when I'm wearing them I have trouble understanding conversation. Can this situation be corrected?

A It is true that masking can sometimes interfere with hearing, and it can do this in two different ways. First, some units block the ear canal so that speech signals have a reduced opportunity to reach the eardrum. Second, the masking sound itself might be interfering with your ability to pay attention to the conversation. However, because masking (and tinnitus) sounds are more commonly high-frequency sounds, it is not as likely that they will block speech sounds, which are made up primarily of lower-frequency sounds.

If you do not have a hearing loss, it could help your speech comprehension to use an open earmold or behind-the-ear configuration of tinnitus masker or the non-occluding Tranquil™ masking device made by General Hearing Instruments. These do not block the ear canal. Therefore, incoming speech and other sounds are not occluded. Another thing to try: use one masker instead of two.

If you also have some hearing loss, replace the tinnitus maskers with tinnitus instruments, combination units containing a tinnitus masker and a hearing aid. Adjust the hearing aid portion of the tinnitus instruments first and then adjust the masker. This way you will have compensated for the hearing loss and made it possible to use lower levels of masking to achieve tinnitus relief. And, obviously, the lower the volume of the masking sound is, the less sound there is to interfere with the speech sounds that you want to hear.

Q   I wear two tinnitus instruments through the day, which works well for me. However, each morning I wake up with an extremely loud and high-pitched tonal tinnitus. It takes at least half the day to calm it down with the tinnitus instruments. What could I try to bring the tinnitus into control faster in the morning? And what could I use to quiet the tinnitus at night?

A   Typical bedside maskers will probably not cover a high-pitched tonal tinnitus. Petroff Audio Technologies manufactures digitally mastered CDs that produce a variety of tinnitus-alleviating sounds, including a high-pitched band of sound with very little low-frequency sound in it. With digital technology, more precise choices of sounds can be produced. Consider using this at night with the volume of the CD adjusted to the lowest level that still provides tinnitus relief. Leave it that way through the night. Some people awaken with temporarily quieted tinnitus (residual inhibition), rather than louder tinnitus, when they use low-level, all-night-long sound stimulation. Residual inhibition might not occur right away, but give it time.

One patient reported that the Moses/Lang CD covers up his high-frequency tinnitus completely with track 7, a bandwidth of sound from 10,000 to 14,000 Hz. (This CD has seven masking tracks of varying bandwidths.) He even occasionally experiences a temporary cessation of tinnitus after the masking sound is removed. However, it is the low-frequency pink noise (200 to 6000 Hz) on track 1 that he finds to be much more pleasant, even though it does not completely mask his tinnitus.

As a matter of course, it is best to avoid extremely quiet environments, day or night.

Q   I've been prescribed a masker for my tinnitus. But I'm concerned about caring for it. (It seems like a lot of work.) How do I care for it and what maintenance will it require?

A   The circuitry of a masker is as delicate as that of a hearing aid. Therefore, these devices should be handled as carefully as hearing aids. If you have a behind-the-ear masker with an earmold, disconnect the earmold from the masker and wash the earmold once a week with warm water and gentle detergent. Let it dry thoroughly before reattaching it. Remember that our ear canals change shape as we age and even as we gain or lose weight. Have the earmold checked periodically to guarantee a continued good fit. When the behind-the-ear tubing starts to harden, replace it. The masker will work better that way.

Your audiologist will give you tools that are specially designed for removing earwax from hearing aids and maskers. Do this chore daily with the tools provided. To ensure healthy ear canals and masker longevity, put only clean and wax-free maskers in the ears.

It is also important to keep maskers away from moisture and humidity, which is not easy to do since we perspire. To help this along, you can buy a special drying kit that fits inside the overnight storage container. It does take a moderate amount of effort to tend to a masker. But if the masker helps the tinnitus, it is worth it.

Q I've tried the "faucet test" and my tinnitus can be heard above the sound of the water. Does that mean that masking is not a possibility for me?

A It might mean that your tinnitus is the kind that cannot be masked. Or it might mean that you have hearing loss in the high-frequency range to the degree that you are unable to appreciate the high-frequency portions of the water sounds that so often cover the sound of tinnitus. Tinnitus instruments might work for you since they contain both high-frequency-emphasis hearing aids and tinnitus maskers. Adjust the hearing aid portion first, and then add in just enough masking sound to cover up the tinnitus.

Q Isn't masking merely trading one sound for another? What good could that do? As an engineer I think I should be able to understand masking, but I don't.

A This comment is a common one. Tinnitus is an internal auditory effect. Masking, on the other hand, is an external auditory event, something that we are accustomed to. We have all spent a lifetime ignoring unimportant external sounds, like the hum of the refrigerator or the whir of an overhead fan. These sounds are constant, quiet, and generally boring, which is a rather accurate description of the sounds produced by maskers and noise generators. When the boring outside masker sound fully or even partially covers the inside tinnitus sound, we are able to ignore the outside sound along with the inside tinnitus sound because we have been ignoring boring sounds all our lives.

Second, the tinnitus sound is most commonly a high-pitched tone, whereas the masking sound is a band of noise, esthetically more pleasing by comparison and usually much more acceptable than a single tone. Another reason why masking sounds are often quite acceptable: the brain prefers hearing an outside sound rather than an internal sound.

Perhaps the greatest benefit of masker therapy is that, for many patients, it provides immediate relief from tinnitus, and the patient is always in control of when that relief will happen. The added benefit of residual inhibition, when it happens, can be a boon to the patient.

Q After I had ear surgery to enlarge my ear canals (tubes were inserted through both eardrums), I was left with severe high-frequency (7330 Hz) tinnitus and, I'm afraid, severe bouts of depression. I was fitted with bilateral hearing aids, but they have not helped my tinnitus. I do get some relief from a Walkman™. Why did the hearing aids fail to provide tinnitus relief?

A The fact that your tinnitus is at 7330 Hz means that it is well above any sounds that most hearing aids would amplify. (And there are very few environmental sounds in that frequency range *to* amplify.) Most patients with high-frequency tinnitus do not find relief with regular hearing aids. However, some do, which is why you did the right thing by trying.

You might need masking sounds in the 7000-Hz region to effect relief. Tinnitus instruments (combination high-frequency hearing aid and tinnitus masker units) could provide this needed condition for you. You might also consider using a tabletop bedside masker for sleeping. Marpac makes the Marsona® device with environmental sounds like waterfall, surf, rain, and wind. Although these are not very high-frequency sounds, they are often relaxing and distracting enough to aid sleep. A bedside CD player with Petroff's Dynamic Tinnitus Mitigation™ CDs or Personal Growth Technologies' Tinnitus Relief CDs could also help the sleep process. For your depression, which seems very much related to your having tinnitus, you could try a nontricyclic antidepressant like Wellbutrin or the herb St. John's wort. (Tricyclic antidepressants often worsen tinnitus.) Once your tinnitus is relieved, it is safe to assume that your depression will leave too.

Q I have noticed that I cannot hear my tinnitus when I'm standing near the refrigerator when the motor is running. The refrigerator motor is so low-pitched that I really don't hear it; I only feel it. Is it possible that sounds that are too low pitched or too high pitched to be heard by the human ear might produce "silent masking"?

A We tested a similar idea many years ago. We reasoned that if ultrasonic sound (which the human ear cannot hear) could mask tinnitus it would be the ideal condition for tinnitus relief. Several tinnitus patients were first tested to see which high-frequency region they could *not* hear. Then they were tested to see if masking in that frequency region could mask their tinnitus. As it turned out, if they could not hear the sound, their tinnitus could not be masked by sound in that frequency range. Recently, there was a new twist on this approach.

Hearing Innovations, Inc., developed the HiSonic® device, a high-frequency bone conduction hearing instrument for people who are profoundly hearing impaired. A modified version of the HiSonic was studied at the Oregon Hearing Research Center's Tinnitus Clinic to see if it could be used as a superhigh-frequency tinnitus masker. This modified device generates frequencies up to 36,000 Hz, way beyond what we are able to hear. Of the 20 tinnitus patients tested, 90% experienced some degree of masking, and 85% of them had a slightly longer duration of residual inhibition (although just minutes longer in most cases) than when conventional maskers were used. We don't know exactly what the HiSonic stimulates, since most of the profoundly deaf people who can hear with it have few if any functioning cochlear hair cells. Perhaps it stimulates the vestibular hair cells. Perhaps we need to investigate this further!

A Prisoner's Story

This is an extended account of an interaction with one tinnitus patient. There are many questions, answers, and comments, and it all got started in the following manner.

Q I am a prisoner in a federal prison, but my incarceration is not nearly as disturbing as my tinnitus. An explosion about 5 years ago initiated my tinnitus prior to my being an inmate. According to hearing tests conducted here, I have very little hearing loss and I certainly do not experience any hearing problems. The only problem with my ears is the ringing tinnitus that interrupts and prevents sleep. I am irritable, cannot concentrate well, and have difficulty maintaining attention long enough to do any prolonged reading. I probably will have to read your letter (if you answer this) a little at a time. My question is, can you help me with my tinnitus problem? The prison doctor says that there is no treatment for tinnitus and that I simply will have to learn to live with it. Is that true?

A Your doctor's statement is not true, although many doctors tell tinnitus patients the same thing. There

are treatments and medications that bring relief. One treatment, called masking, is readily available and effective for at least 65% of the people who try it. You can experience what masking is like by doing what is called the "faucet test." Stand near a sink with the water running full force. If the sound of the running water makes it impossible for you to hear your tinnitus, then it is likely that wearable tinnitus maskers will provide relief. Do the faucet test and write back with the results.

Q I did the faucet test and it works! In fact, it worked so well that I was reluctant to turn the water off, it felt so nice not to hear that [deleted word] tinnitus. Once you pointed it out, I also noticed that the shower noise had the same effect. But how do I arrange to have that water sound available all the time? I can't stand by the sink all day even though I'm tempted to try it. What do we do next?

A If you were a patient here in our clinic, we would fit you with a pair of tinnitus maskers. The masker looks exactly like a hearing aid and indeed is enclosed in

(continued)

A Prisoner's Story Continued

a hearing aid case. Do you have any vanity problem about wearing what appears to be a hearing aid?

Q I have absolutely no problem about wearing a set of devices that look like hearing aids. But given my circumstances, how can I get these maskers?

A We will send the tinnitus maskers to you, but first we need molds of your ear canals. Each earmold needs to have a hole in it so that tubing from the masker can be inserted into it. The tinnitus masker fits behind your ear and a tube extends from the masker to the earmold. This is how the masking sound is directed into your ear. Dental acrylic is one type of material that can be used to create the impressions of your ear. Can you arrange to have earmolds made? Each earmold needs to have a hole drilled through its center that is the length of your ear canal.

Q I am sorry about the delay in getting back to you. I had to escape from prison in order to have the earmolds made and then I had to escape (inscape?) back into prison. Please don't let any of the officials see this letter. I went to see the dentist who comes to the prison every year to treat prisoners. I showed him your letter and asked him if he would be willing to make earmolds for me. He agreed to try and was even able to drill the holes while the molds were in my ears. The sound of the drilling was a bit loud, but other than that there was no problem. I await the tinnitus maskers to see if these earmolds are adequate.

A Enclosed is a pair of Starkey maskers and two packages of extra batteries. You will see that there is a volume control on each masker. Put the maskers on and insert the tubing into your earmolds. Increase the volume of the masking sound until you cannot hear your tinnitus or until you feel that you are getting relief from your tinnitus. Once you have determined the loudness level that is appropriate for you, just leave the units set at that level all day. To turn the maskers off, simply open the battery compartment. And, speaking of batteries, as the batteries wear down the high frequencies of the masking sound are lost. It happens gradually at first, but a progressive loss of the remaining frequencies follows. If at any time you notice that the maskers are not providing tinnitus relief, even though you can still hear the masking sound or at least some part of the masking sound, change the batteries. The battery life depends on the extent to which you use the devices. In short order, you will learn when a battery change is needed. Give the maskers a try and write back if adjustments are needed.

Q No adjustment is needed, and the relief is wonderful. Now I wonder if I can use the maskers during sleep.

A Yes, you can use the maskers during sleep provided you can get to sleep with those units behind your ears!

Q I used several extra pillows and sort of encased my head so that I looked straight up while lying flat of my back. I got to sleep very easily and quickly. Lately, though, I have been wearing the maskers just during the day (every waking daytime hour) because I no longer need help getting to sleep. The relief is significant.

Recently I had to change batteries during the day, and when I took the maskers off I noticed that the tinnitus was gone. It stayed away for 10 to 15 minutes and then it came back. I am not at all sure that it came back to its usual loudness. Am I imagining things?

A You are experiencing residual inhibition, a phenomenon that occurs in 83% of the patients we have tested. Residual inhibition can increase in duration for some patients as they continue to use masking. Residual inhibition is an intrinsic part of masking, but we do not know how to extend it.

Q It is about 6 months since I last wrote. The purpose of this short note is to inform you that my residual inhibition has grown. There are times when I remove the maskers and my tinnitus does not return for half a day. Is that length of residual inhibition unusual? Unusual or not, let me tell you it is wonderful.

A We don't know how many people get extended residual inhibition like yours. But we know that it occurs. It might even continue to expand, so enjoy it.

Q A year has passed and much good has happened. I came up for parole 3 months ago. In the past, I was always refused parole on the grounds that I was far from a model prisoner. I am sure that much of my "unmodel" conduct was due to the tinnitus. But this time, I passed with flying colors. When the parole board asked what had so dramatically changed me, I said it was you. Of course, I went on to explain about the effects of tinnitus and about the relief through masking that I was able to get. Needless to say, I did not reveal my escaping escapades.

I now work in a prisoner rehabilitation program that helps newly released prisoners adjust to the conditions of normal life. I feel that I am especially helpful to these prisoners because of the difficulties I had adjusting to tinnitus. It is very nice to be on the outside and involved in a worthwhile activity. Please know that you have my undying gratitude.

That is the end of a story and the beginning of a life.

Q Sometimes the masking sound can become an irritant even though it is a preferred sound over my tinnitus sound. When this happens, I add in the environmental sounds from the Marsona TSC-350 sound generator. In effect, I "mask the masker." Why doesn't Starkey or some other hearing device company produce the same sounds in their wearable maskers?

A In some cases, very high-pitched tinnitus requires very high-pitched (and unacceptable) sound to mask it. Your invention of "masking the masker" is a great idea and possibly another way to assist others who have high-pitched tinnitus. Most people need to have their tinnitus frequency included in the masking sound to experience relief with it. Not surprisingly (since there is no one thing that works for everyone), some people have tinnitus that can be masked by any sound. Have your tinnitus evaluated to determine what works for you.

We have not heard from others who have experienced this. If more individuals report the same or similar results, we would take that information to Starkey Laboratories and General Hearing Instruments, both makers of tinnitus masking devices. Thank you for this comment and potentially significant observation.

Resources _____

Schleuning, A. J., Johnson, R. A. Use of masking for tinnitus, *Int. Tinnitus J.*, 1997; 3(1):25–29.

Vernon, J., Griest, S., Press, L. Attributes of tinnitus and the acceptance of masking, *Am. J. Otolaryngol.*, 1990; 11:44–50.

Wayner, D. *Hear What You've Been Missing*, Chronimed Publishing, Minneapolis, MN, 1998.

32

Ménière's Disease

Q Can you discuss the relationship between Ménière's disease and tinnitus? Also what is "burnt-out" Ménière's?

A Ménière's disease is a condition that commonly presents with four symptoms: vertigo, hearing loss, pressure in the ear, and tinnitus. Of the four symptoms, vertigo is the most troubling, so say Ménière's patients. In some cases, the condition is temporary and passes on its own. In other cases, all symptoms disappear over time except for the tinnitus. The low-frequency tinnitus associated with active Ménière's is usually easily masked. *Burnt-out Ménière's* is Ménière's that no longer has vertigo associated with it. The tinnitus that is left over in burnt-out Ménière's is often higher in pitch and tonal in quality.

Q I thought tinnitus was a ringing in the ears, but mine is a rumbling roar in one ear. I have also been having dizzy spells. Are the dizziness and the tinnitus related?

A Tinnitus is characterized by a variety of sounds—hissing, roaring, chirping, and ringing among them. A low-frequency roaring tinnitus that is accompanied by bouts of dizziness often points to the condition of Ménière's disease. If you have not already done so, it is a good idea to have a standard hearing test (pure tone audiogram) to see if you have a low-frequency hearing loss as well. It is a common symptom of Ménière's.

Dizziness and tinnitus are symptoms that individually or collectively can represent a serious health condition. It is best to see a physician to rule out other conditions. Special computerized balance tests can determine if your dizziness is the specific vestibular kind associated with Ménière's.

Also see Chapter 14, Drug Perfusion: In-the-ear Drug Treatment.

Q I have been diagnosed with Ménière's disease. Recently, I experienced a sudden increase in my tinnitus and at the same time an additional 30% loss in hearing. No one knows why this has happened. Is it possible that this was caused by the aspartic acid and phenylalanine in the vitamin supplement that I take?

A The increase in your tinnitus is probably due to your hearing loss, not to the vitamin supplements that you are taking. As hearing goes down, tinnitus almost always seems to increase. If you insert an earplug in your tinnitus ear, you will probably notice a marked increase in the loudness of your tinnitus in that ear. But in this case the tinnitus has not actually increased. Rather, your hearing ability has been decreased so that the distracting effects of ordinary environmental sounds are not effectively masking the tinnitus.

You can conduct your own experiment regarding the vitamin supplement. Stop taking it for a period of time, 2 to 3 weeks perhaps, to see if the tinnitus level drops. Obviously, if the cessation of the vitamin supplement coincides with a reduction of the tinnitus loudness, then you might have found your answer.

Most Ménière's-related tinnitus is in the low-frequency range and is easily masked. (Generally, the hearing loss associated with Ménière's is also in the low-frequency range.) If you want to get an idea about masking, stand near the kitchen sink with the water running full force. If the sound of the running water makes it difficult for you to hear your tinnitus, then it is possible that wearable tinnitus maskers or other low-frequency tabletop devices or masking CDs will provide tinnitus relief for you.

Q I know that there is a surgical procedure to relieve symptoms of Ménière's. Will the surgery relieve all the symptoms, including my tinnitus?

A Several surgical procedures, some more radical than others, are used to treat Ménière's disease. These procedures are aimed specifically at calming the vertigo associated with Ménière's.

One surgery involves the insertion of valves or shunts (a thin tubing) into the inner ear labyrinths to reduce the pressure of the swollen endolymphatic sacs, which are thought to be responsible for the condition. Sac decompression surgery aims for the same result and is often successful in reducing or eliminating vertigo. Many shunt patients experience only temporary relief from their dizziness and need the procedure repeated. Others find that the second shunt does not work and they need a different treatment altogether.

Certain drugs are administered to the inner ear by *perfusion*. In this surgical procedure, the eardrum is lifted and a microcatheter is inserted through the middle ear and into the round window niche. The drug (usually gentamicin) is delivered through the microcatheter. As it seeps through the round window, its target is the labyrinth that contains the damaged vestibular hair cells, the instigators of the vertigo. This perfusion procedure has been quite successful for vertigo control (65% to 95% of patients report relief), but the ototoxic gentamicin does take its toll on the cochlear hair cells. Somewhere between 10% and 65% of perfusion patients lose some hearing because of the gentamicin. A newer implanted catheter pump is helping to increase the incidence of vertigo relief. The pump narrows the aim and delivery of the drug. This advance in the procedure is expected to reduce the incidence of hearing loss as well. The tinnitus that accompanies Ménière's is sometimes reduced as a result of perfusion therapy, but it is a minimal outcome. Often tinnitus is unchanged by the procedure.

Some patients who do not respond to perfusion treatment consider a more extreme measure—the destruction of the inner ear labyrinth. The procedure is called a labyrinthectomy and is accomplished either by surgical excision or chemical destruction (or ablation) of the balance organ in the inner ear. With this procedure, all hearing is lost on the affected side.

Vestibular nerve sectioning (or severing) is a delicate and invasive surgical procedure that helps 90% of Ménière's patients with otherwise uncontrolled vertigo. Researchers Tewary, Riley, and Kerr from England studied 25 patients who had had their vestibular nerves sectioned. The auditory branches of their eighth nerves were spared to preserve hearing. Two years after surgery, these patients reported on average a 7-dB deterioration of hearing; after 10 years, a 15-dB loss; at 15 years, a 23-dB loss; and at 20 years, a 29-dB loss. Tinnitus became worse in five of these patients, which is understandable since a drop in hearing can lead to the perception of louder tinnitus.

Q I've long suspected that my sensitivity to some foods was in some way connected to the Ménière's-like symptoms I have (intermittent vertigo, hearing loss, tinnitus, and fullness in the ears). Could there be a connection?

A An allergic reaction is the body's chemical reaction to a food that has been eaten or a particle that has been inhaled. This chemical reaction causes many things to happen in the body, one of which is the deposit of microscopic debris in the endolymphatic sacs in the inner ear. If the debris somehow damages these sacs, Ménière's symptoms can be the result. Researchers at the House Ear Institute in Los Angeles evaluated 137 Ménière's patients who had been recommended for allergy treatment. Of the 137 patients, 113 followed through with allergy treatments of either desensitization or diet alterations and 24 did not. All 113 reported some improvement in their vertigo, tinnitus, and other Ménière's symptoms plus their allergy symptoms. Also, 61.4% of the patients who received allergy treatments also demonstrated stabilization or an improvement in their hearing. While the mechanism that links Ménière's with allergy is not thoroughly understood, the evidence clearly points to a connection.

Resources

DeCicco, M. J., Hoffer, M. E., Kopke, R. D., Wester, D., Allen, K. A., Gottshall, K., and O'Leary, M. J. Round-window microcatheter-administered microdose gentamicin: Results from treatment of tinnitus associated with Ménière's disease, *Int. Tinnitus J.*, 1998; 4(2):141–3.

Derebery, M. J. Allergic management of Ménière's disease: An outcome study, *Otolaryngol. Head Neck Surg.*, Feb. 2000; 122(2):174–82.

Haybach, P. J. *Ménière's Disease—What You Need to Know*, Vestibular Disorders Association, Portland, OR, 1998.

Tewary, A. K., Riley, N., and Kerr, A. G. Long-term results of vestibular nerve section, *J. Laryngol. Otol.*, Dec. 1998; 112(12):1150–3.

Vernon, J. Conservative Treatment of tinnitus in Ménière's disease, *Am. J. Otolaryngol.*, May 1988; 9(3).

Vernon, J., Johnson, R., and Schleuning, A. The characteristics and natural history of tinnitus in Ménière's disease, *Otolaryngol. Clin. North Am.*, Nov. 1980; 13(4):611–9.

33

MRI: Magnetic Resonance Imaging

Q My physician required that I have an MRI scan to check for a possible tumor on my eighth nerve. As it turned out, I did not have an eighth nerve tumor, but my tinnitus has been louder ever since that test. Why did the tinnitus become worse?

A If you were not fitted with earplugs when you had the MRI test, it is possible that the volume of noise inside the MRI machine increased the volume of your tinnitus. An MRI machine makes a loud knocking sound caused by the rapid changes in the magnetic field during the imaging process. The noise levels inside the MRI tube at the location of the patient's head run from 85 to 115 dB, depending on the test being performed. This is too much noise for too much time (an MRI scan can take 1 hour or more), whether or not you have tinnitus.

We have heard from nine patients whose tinnitus was exacerbated by MRIs and from two other patients who attribute the start of their tinnitus to MRI experiences. These patients were not advised by their doctors or by the MRI technicians to wear earplugs during the testing, nor were they told that the tests were going to be loud. Be advised here and now: *Always wear earplugs when having an MRI test.*

A new model of closed, high-field MRI, called the ExcelArt Pianissimo was released in early 2000 by Toshiba. Toshiba has redesigned the way the internal gradient coil is mounted (it is now baffled and enclosed in a vacuum), which reduces the noise output by 35 to 40 dB, so they say. This sound-baffling technology does not increase the length of time needed for MRI testing nor does it change the scanning process in any way. It just makes the procedure quieter for the patient. These MRI scanners, initially released in Japan, are now in a few American medical facilities. Contact Toshiba (800-421-1968, www.toshiba.com) for a quiet MRI near you.

165

Q Aside from the noise, are MRIs dangerous in any way?

A Magnetic resonance imaging technology was developed in the early 1970s, which has given scientists 30 years to look at its potential long-term effects on humans. None has been found. However, 30 years might not be long enough to completely assess the effects of this radio-frequency, magnet-based technology, since its widespread use has covered considerably less time. Incidentally, it was originally called NMRI, *nuclear* magnetic resonance imaging, referring descriptively to the behavior in the nuclei of atoms upon which all MRI science is based. The word *nuclear* was dropped from the title due to its negative connotation, especially during the 1970s. No radioactive materials are used in this scanning.

Some things *are* known. MRI scans can induce tissue heating, the long-term effects of which are not known. In some instances, an enhancing agent (gadolinium) is injected into the bloodstream to help brighten the image. This element is excreted through the kidneys in less than 2 hours, but again the long-term effects are not known.

Immediate danger can occur for patients with surgically implanted devices such as cardiac pacemakers, cerebral aneurysm clips, insulin pumps, cochlear implants, and magnetic implantable hearing aids. These implanted devices can be damaged by the electromagnetic pulses generated from MRIs and should not be scanned. Orthopedic implants such as prosthetic joints, plates, or screws can be scanned safely. Some prosthetic heart valves are safe to scan, but others are not. Discuss this ahead of time with the MRI staff and your doctor.

Q According to my doctor, I need to have an MRI test. But I've read that they are noisy and I am, I'm embarrassed to admit, claustrophobic. Is there an alternative test that I can have that won't send my tinnitus through the roof or have me in a narrow tube for an hour?

A Open MRI devices are now available and are considerably quieter (less than 85 dB at the head level) than the closed models. Thankfully, these open machines do not need the patient to slip headfirst into a tube, so the new technology brings more than one advantage.

MRI is an important way to view the structures of the brain and even to map functions in the brain. MRI uses radio waves, magnets, and computers to create views of the soft tissue of the body. These views are then recorded on film.

There are more differences between closed MRI and open MRI machines than the tube and the noise levels. A *superconducting* electromagnet is the strongest magnet used in MRI technology. For a patient to be successfully scanned in a closed MRI machine, he or she must be placed in the center of its magnetic field, hence the tube arrangement of the closed MRIs. The open MRIs use a weaker type of magnet, called *permanent* magnets, made of solid magnetic material. Permanent magnets generally create a less powerful magnetic field. Consequently, open MRI devices with permanent magnets have less image resolution capability and are not as useful as the closed types for detecting small abnormalities.

Patients are usually more comfortable being tested in an open MRI machine than in a closed MRI machine, so you are in good company. Ask your doctor if the image clarity from the open MRI will produce a satisfactory image for diagnosing your condition. Or, ask your doctor for medication to counteract the claustrophobia.

Considering the leaps that imaging science has taken in the last 10 years, we believe that safe, thorough, comfortable, and quiet scanning technology will be available for all of us in the near future.

Resources

Brick, S. H. *MRI: How It Works,* Internet, www.idsonline.com/gcm/mrwkspt. htm, 4-21-00.

Hornak, J. P. *The Basics of MRI,* Internet, www. cis.rit.edu/htbooks/mri, 1996–99.

34

Musical Tinnitus

Q I am 57 years old, have been wearing hearing aids for 19 years, and have had tinnitus for just over 1 year. At first it was disturbing, but now conversation, music, radio, television, and road noises largely mask it. For some reason it lessens in volume late at night, so getting to sleep and staying asleep are not problems. The nature of my tinnitus is not like anything I've read about in *Tinnitus Today*. I either hear specific songs that are from my memory or ones that I've recently heard on the radio. The songs usually change of their own accord. But if one song keeps repeating, I can change it by deliberately concentrating on another song. I feel much more fortunate than the multitude of tinnitus patients who hear high-pitched tones or other unpleasant sounds. But I still would like to know if there is an effective relief procedure for me. I'm hesitant to tell my doctor about it for fear of what he might think of me. Have you ever had such a report before?

A We have known two other patients who heard musical tinnitus. One patient was a very religious woman who heard hymns, and a very long list of them at that. She, like you, would get disturbed by her musical tinnitus only when one hymn repeated over and over again. The other patient heard classical music, which happened to be his favorite style of music. Since these two patients heard music that they liked to hear, their choice was to either try relief procedures or enjoy their tinnitus songs. When both of these patients were evaluated, they learned that their tinnitus was maskable with low-frequency sounds.

The classical music patient opted to use the Moses/Lang masking CD. There was an interesting outcome to his trial with it. After he listened to the masking CD many times, he found that if he concentrated he could conjure up the masking sound and mask his musical tinnitus whenever he wanted to.

Musical hallucinations, as they are called, are not common, but they have been reported and studied by researchers all over the world. A German research team identified 26 mentally sane people (they were careful to point out) who experienced musical hallucinations. The researchers personally observed six additional patients with musical tinnitus, including two people in the same family. English researchers report that musical tinnitus is more common in women and that its onset is often related to ear disorders and, not uncommonly, to deafness.

It seems like a good time for you to visit your doctor and have your hearing tested.

Resources

Berrios, G. E. Musical hallucinations: A statistical analysis of 46 cases, *Psychopathology*, 1991; 24(6):356–60.

Gordon, A. G. Do musical hallucinations always arise from the inner ear? *Med. Hypotheses*, Aug. 1997; 49(2):111–22.

Klostermann, W., Vieregge, P., and Kompf, D. Musical pseudo-hallucination in acquired hearing loss, *Fortschr. Neurol. Psychiatr.*, July 1992; 60(7):262–73.

35

Noise Cancellation

Q Is it possible to cancel tinnitus with active noise canceling devices?

A These devices cancel *external* sounds, such as the drone of an aircraft engine or other low-pitched environmental noises. They achieve this cancellation with a set of microphones in the earphones of a headset that pick up the external sounds. The external noise is fed into an electronic circuit that analyzes the sound wave, reverses it, and produces a completely opposite sound that is played back against the incoming sound. This produces an active cancellation of both sounds. Technically, the cancellation is a phase reversal. Currently, these devices are only effective for sounds below 1500 Hz. Bose Company has been working on noise cancellation technology for several years. They hope that eventually they will be able to cancel sounds up to 10,000 Hz.

But can tinnitus be cancelled with active noise cancellation devices? No, it cannot, because no actual sound wave is produced by the tinnitus. Tinnitus is a perception of sound in the brain, much like the phenomenon of phantom limb pain. Since there is no physical energy to electronically detect or play back against itself, tinnitus cannot be cancelled with this technology.

Even so, some years ago, we experimented with *phase reversal*, that is, using a tone that duplicated the patient's tinnitus. Thinking it might be possible to effect cancellation by reversing the phase of the presented tone, we slowly rotated the phase through 360 degrees in an effort to find some phase relationship that cancelled the tinnitus. Of the 35 patients tested, only 2 noticed a difference in their tinnitus. They thought that their tinnitus had developed a "roughness" at about 135 degrees of phase, although the tinnitus was still clearly present. There were no cases of tinnitus cancellation.

Also see Chapter 20, Flying.

Q I recently attended a stockcar race at Indianapolis where I used earmuffs and form-fitted earplugs. During the 3 hours of the event, I experienced no discomfort, but afterward my tinnitus was increased for a while. Am I flirting with permanently increased tinnitus?

A The chances are good that if you continue to attend auto races your tinnitus will permanently increase. You had a temporary increase the first time, but repeated performances could produce an undesirable tinnitus increase and perhaps some hearing loss too. There is one other thing to try. Active noise cancellation technology samples incoming low-frequency sound and then reverses the phase and plays it back against itself, which effectively eliminates the sound. The ProActive 3000 headset from Noise Cancellation Technologies, Inc., is sold with a 30-day money-back guarantee. Several people have used the ProActive device while flying and found it to be very effective for canceling out low-frequency rumbling sounds. The cordless earphone/earmuff also provides some passive protection from the higher-frequency sounds because it covers the ears snugly.

36

Noise in the Environment

Q If a sound is made very close to my ear, will that sort of thing damage the ear or make my tinnitus worse?

A The ear canal has *resonance.* This means that certain sounds, usually in the 3400- to 3900-Hz range, are amplified by the way they bounce off of the bends and curves of the ear canal. Some ear canals amplify some sound, by as much as 20 dB. This, in and of itself, is not damaging unless the sound is exceedingly loud. Remember that acoustic damage is a time-intensity function. The louder the sound is, the greater the damage. And the *longer* the sound is present, the greater the damage. Thus, protecting our ears involves reducing sound intensity *and* sound duration as much as possible. Unfortunately, the input–output function of the ear is not very democratic. If loud sound goes into the ear rapidly and badly damages hair cells, the healing and recovery process can take an incredibly long time.

The variety of shapes and lengths of ear canals (and they do vary enormously) directly affects the resonance of the ear canal. This might explain why some people sustain hearing damage at a loud concert and other people do not.

Q I am moderately hard of hearing in both ears and I have tinnitus in both ears too. I've read that loud noise will make my tinnitus worse, and so I use earplugs in places where noise levels are high, even though the noise doesn't sound loud to me. Is it true that my tinnitus or hearing can get worse if I'm exposed to a loud noise that I can't hear?

A Sound is energy. And it is still affecting your auditory system whether or not you can hear it. You are wise to continue protecting the hearing you have left when you are in very noisy conditions.

People with hearing loss often wonder how to tell when they are in the presence of overly loud sounds. One way is to ask people who you are with to tell you. You can also be certain that you are in an overly loud environment if you have to raise your voice to be heard.

Q **We have two small fans running all night long in our children's bedroom. We have found that the fan noise masks outside noises and prevents their sleep from being disturbed. But we are worried that the continuous noise from the fan might ultimately damage their hearing. Will it?**

A We applaud your concern for the hearing health of your children. Unless your fans are louder than 80 dB, it is doubtful that they could cause any hearing impairment. But let's not guess about the decibels. Purchase a sound-level meter and measure the actual sound intensity of the fan noise. Radio Shack (817-415-3200, www.radioshack.com) sells a small analog sound-level meter for $35. (The analog meter uses a needle to point to the decibel number. Their digital sound-level meter for $55 displays the decibel number. Both are amazingly accurate.) With such a sound-level meter, measure the sound intensity at the children's ear level. If the sound level is 85 dB or more, you might want to purchase quieter fans.

Q **I am in the market for a quiet vacuum cleaner. Is there some way to know which ones on the market are quietest? I don't want to make my tinnitus worse.**

A Many companies are responding to the public outcry for quiet appliances. In the July 1999 *Consumer Reports,* three compact canister models are given a "very good" quiet rating: (1) Sharp EC 7311, (2) Sanyo SC24, and (3) Bissell Butler 3580. Four full-sized canister vacuums with a "very good" rating are (1) Kenmore 28712, (2) Miele Red Star, (3) Panasonic MCV 9635, and (4) Eureka Home Cleaning System. In addition, four upright models were also given "very good" quiet ratings: (1) Kenmore #38512, (2) Sharp ECT 2860, (3) Windsor Sensation SX2, and (4) Eureka 5180AT. Since we don't know the actual loudness measures for these vacuum cleaners, we recommend that you wear some form of ear protection while operating them.

On the other end of the noise spectrum, the Bissell Upright Pure Air Delux got a "poor" rating, and the Dirt Devil 086910 got a "fair" rating.

If you wear hearing protection in a noisy environment and still find that your tinnitus temporarily increases, the hearing protection that you are using is not sufficient. You can wear earmuffs over your earplugs while you vacuum. Simultaneously, you can reduce the length of time that you are exposed to very loud noise by breaking up the vacuuming task into several shorter tasks. Acoustic damage is a time-intensity function. To really protect your ears, you need to reduce the sound intensity *and* the sound duration as much as possible.

37

Pulsatile Tinnitus

Q My pulsatile tinnitus came on suddenly. It is exactly in phase with my heartbeat. Is there anything that can be done for this form of tinnitus that I find so very disturbing?

A Your tinnitus is not the usual tinnitus, the kind without a known physical cause. It is probably an objective tinnitus too—that is, detectable by others. Pulsatile (pulsing) tinnitus is uncommon. In a survey of 2838 tinnitus patients, 97 (3.4%) had pulsatile tinnitus.

This kind of tinnitus can be a symptom of a vascular or cerebral spinal fluid problem. Changes in pressure in the cerebral fluid can cause it. The condition might be correctable with either surgery or medication, which in many cases will eliminate the tinnitus. It is imperative that you contact a physician and have the pulsatile tinnitus investigated. Do not cover it up with masking. It could be a warning sign of something serious.

On the other hand, in 1982, a pulsatile tinnitus patient consulted an otolaryngologist who informed her that her hearing condition would progress to deafness in 5 years if she did not have the operation that he recommended. (She had a very mild hearing loss in addition to her pulsatile tinnitus.) He offered her no other treatment choices for her tinnitus. She opted to not have the operation and instead started taking evening primrose oil (EPO), which she felt quieted her tinnitus. Sixteen years later, she reports that she has the same very mild hearing loss. When her pulsatile tinnitus periodically returned through the years, she treated it with EPO, which always relieved it.

Q I have learned that pulsatile tinnitus can be caused by obstructions in the blood vessels leading to the head. When I lay down, I find that the pulsing gets louder. And when I put pressure on my neck, the pulsatile tinnitus stops. If I continue to put pressure on my neck, will the decreased blood supply to my head be harmful?

Also see Chapter 45, Surgery.

174

A The sound that you hear is probably the result of a vascular condition, one that involves blood flow through the veins and arteries. It is easy to imagine that a kink in an artery could cause your pulsatile tinnitus to come and go depending on the condition of that kink. You have already determined that reclining increases your perception of tinnitus, so your position affects it too. If you are reclining at night and in a quiet room, the lack of background sound can increase your perception of the tinnitus even more. Extreme quiet will exaggerate the loudness of almost all tinnitus. For now, do what you can to bring in some low-level background sounds when you go to sleep.

Obviously, you cannot go around with constant pressure against your neck. Your ability to relieve your pulsatile tinnitus with neck pressure strongly suggests that some occlusion or blockage in the arteries leading to the head is producing your pulsatile tinnitus. In some cases, it is possible to have the vascular obstruction removed surgically and the pulsatile tinnitus eliminated in the process. Have a physician listen to your neck with a stethoscope to detect the audible pulsing tinnitus. If your tinnitus is in the high frequencies, the listener will need to have good high-frequency hearing in order to detect it. If others can hear your pulsatile tinnitus, then a surgical exploration of the neck region might lead to a cure for you.

In just such a surgery, an ENT surgeon explored a patient's opened neck area with a stethoscope and discovered that the patient's pulsatile tinnitus came from a kink in the carotid artery. The surgeon completely sectioned (or cut) the abnormal artery, which in this case was possible to do because the patient had two carotid arteries. The operation completely removed the patient's pulsatile tinnitus. (Note that this is a major procedure.)

Another patient with high-pitched pulsatile tinnitus discovered that he could eliminate his tinnitus by placing his chin firmly on his chest. In his case, the pulsatile tinnitus was also coming from a partial occlusion in the carotid artery. Somehow his neck flexion caused this blockage to be relieved.

Q **Niacin has provided substantial tinnitus relief for my pulsatile tinnitus. Can you explain this result?**

A Niacin is a dilator of peripheral blood vessels. Your pulsatile tinnitus is probably due to a restriction of a blood vessel in the head or neck region. It is quite possible that the niacin opened this blood vessel sufficiently to reduce the pulsing sound. It is important that you see a cardiologist who can determine whether tests or further treatment are indicated.

Q **I have pulsatile tinnitus that is exactly in phase with my heartbeat. I've found that exercise and eating raw vegetables has helped. But I wonder if my doctor could detect my condition.**

A Pulsatile tinnitus is almost always audible to others. With a thorough stethoscope examination of your ear canal, eardrum, neck, and other locations around the ear, your doctor might well be able to hear what you hear. Some kinds of pulsatile tinnitus even cause the eardrum to vibrate in the same rhythm as the tinnitus. This vibration can be recorded.

Q **How can the source of my pulsatile tinnitus be diagnosed?**

A Aristides Sismanis, M.D., a specialist in pulsatile tinnitus, suggests a variety of diagnostic tests for pulsatile tinnitus. First, an air and bone conduction hearing test is done for all pulsatile tinnitus patients. If it is determined that the patient has a hearing loss of 20 dB or more, then the audiogram needs to be repeated while the patient applies slight manual pressure to the jugular vein on the side of the neck corresponding to the pulsatile tinnitus. If the patient has a venous (or vein-related) type of pulsatile tinnitus, the results of the second audiogram are usually better with the manual pressure maneuver.

The physician selects other tests to perform based on the patient's medical history. The doctor also determines which additional tests to order based on the results of each test. For example, if a patient is a smoker who also has diabetes and hypertension, the physician might suspect carotid artery disease and order blood tests along with magnetic resonance angiography (MRA), magnetic resonance venography (MRV), and magnetic resonance imaging (MRI) tests. If these tests are normal and the patient's pulsatile tinnitus happens to be objective (able to be heard by others), then a carotid angiography test and possibly an ultrasound test would be ordered to help confirm a diagnosis. (An angiography test looks for abnormalities in the veins or arteries.)

The following are possible causes of pulsatile tinnitus:

- Atherosclerotic carotid artery disease
- Intracranial hypertension syndrome
- Arnold–Chiari malformations
- Cervical venous hum
- Glomus tumors (skull base lesions)
- Heart murmur
- Hypertension
- Increased intracranial hypertension
- Jugular bulb abnormalities
- Neurovascular compression of hearing nerves
- Patulous eustachian tube
- Persistent muscular contractions
- Sigmoid sinus abnormalities

Heart murmurs, benign intracranial hypertension, and hardening of the arteries (atherosclerosis) can be treated successfully with medicine or nonsurgical procedures. These often lead to a reduction or even elimination of pulsatile tinnitus.

Diagnosis is a complicated series of steps. It is best to contact a doctor who specializes in this field. Sismanis can be contacted at the Medical College of Virginia, P.O. Box 146, Richmond, Virginia 23298-0146, 804-828-3965.

Q **I am excessively worried about my pulsatile tinnitus. (I can hear it and my doctor can hear it.) I am concerned that it means I have a tumor or some very serious life-threatening vascular condition. What do you recommend?**

A The best thing about pulsatile tinnitus is that the cause can be identified in so many cases. Once the cause is identified, a specific treatment can be prescribed or a procedure performed and the tinnitus can be eliminated. Yes, it is true that some treatments for pulsatile tinnitus involve surgery, and for a lot of people that is a scary prospect.

Pulsatile tinnitus can accompany the condition of benign intracranial hypertension (BIH), an increased cranial pressure caused by fluid buildup in the brain tissue. For many BIH patients, the condition is managed nonsurgically by weight loss, use of diuretics, and in a few cases the use of oral cortisone. Sismanis notes that the majority of his BIH patients are young overweight females. Other conditions and factors can cause BIH, which in turn can cause tinnitus. They include the following:

- Menstrual irregularities
- Pregnancy
- Hypothyroidism
- Hyperthyroidism
- Vitamin A deficiency or excessive intake
- Vitamin D deficiency
- Oral contraceptive use
- Iron deficiency anemia
- Tetracycline use

See a neurologist and discuss the possibility of being tested for BIH, which is medically treatable. If BIH is not the source of pulsatile tinnitus, consult with a cardiologist. A vascular blockage, or impedance, can produce objective tinnitus in phase with the heartbeat.

Researchers at the São Paulo Medical School in Brazil investigated all forms of scanning to determine the best way to diagnose pulsatile tinnitus. In 1999, they studied 26 pulsatile tinnitus patients (21 females and 5 males). All patients were examined with magnetic resonance angiography (MRA) scans. The results of the MRA showed that 20 of the 26 (77%) had either alterations in the space within the arteries near the neck or alterations of the velocity of blood flow. Once the precise causes of pulsatile tinnitus were determined, the proper treatments were selected.

Resources _____

Risey, J., and Amedee, R. G. Pulsatile tinnitus, *Tinnitus Today,* Sept. 1998; 23(3).

Sanchez, T. G., Sennes, L. U., and Bento, R. F. What the MRA has been showing in pulsatile tinnitus, *Proceedings of the Sixth International Tinnitus Seminar,*

Hazell, J., ed., Tinnitus and Hyperacusis Centre, London, 1999.

Sismanis, A. Pulsatile tinnitus, *Tinnitus: Treatment and Relief,* Vernon, J., ed., Allyn and Bacon, Boston, 1998; pp. 28–33.

38

Recreational Substances

Q To what degree does alcohol make tinnitus worse?

A People respond to alcohol in such a variety of ways that we cannot give a single answer. Several tinnitus patients swear that one glass of wine greatly reduces their tinnitus. Others swear that alcohol in any form greatly exacerbates their tinnitus. Some people get relief only from red wine, while others notice their tinnitus increase only with red wine. One patient found that getting heavily intoxicated completely relieved his tinnitus. But the hangover the next morning was so bad and the accompanying tinnitus was so loud that the previous relief was not worth the price. You will have to experiment to determine your limitations.

Q What is the effect of marijuana on tinnitus? Does it relieve the tinnitus and would it have an effect on hearing loss too?

A Eleven tinnitus patients, all of whom admitted to the regular use of marijuana, were requested to abstain from the use of marijuana for 1 month. Four patients noted a significant reduction in the loudness of their tinnitus. Two others reported that their tinnitus had completely gone away. Three patients found they could not give up using marijuana and two patients failed to report, perhaps because they, too, could not give up the drug. One patient thought that marijuana had started his tinnitus, but the remaining ten patients had experienced tinnitus prior to using marijuana. While we cannot do a double-blind study on this illegal drug, we can conclude that marijuana can exacerbate tinnitus. Those who are concerned that the use of this drug is affecting their condition can test themselves by abstaining to see if this is so.

39

Research

Q I have seen several terms for different kinds of research studies, but I don't understand the differences. The terms are open study; double-blind, placebo-controlled study; and double-blind placebo crossover study. Can you explain these to me?

A Yes. In an *open* study, all patients take the active drug and both the patients and the doctors know that only the active drug is being used. Typically, an open study is used to determine whether or not a drug works. Open studies often precede more detailed studies.

In a *double-blind, placebo-controlled* study, approximately half the patients in the study are given the active drug and half are given a *placebo* or sugar pill. It is *double blind* when neither the patients nor the experimenters know which are receiving the active drug and which are receiving the placebo. The patient does not know initially that a placebo is being tested. The implication is that all patients in the study are getting the active drug.

When the study is completed, the code is broken and everyone finds out who took what. The results are then recorded. If the active drug does not do better than the placebo, the drug is considered of little or no value as a treatment.

In a *double-blind placebo crossover* study, half the patients are given the active drug and half are given the placebo and neither the experimenters nor the patients know who is getting which. At the halfway point in the experiment, the two groups of patients are typically reversed. Those who had received the placebo are given the active drug, and those who had received the active drug are given the placebo. Sometimes side effects reveal the presence of the active drug, which would defeat any meaningful crossover design. There have been situations in which one group of patients experiences significant and immediate relief in the early part of the study. When this occurs, researchers generally

Also see Chapter 7, The Brain's Involvement in Tinnitus.

break the code before the crossover point is reached so that they can give the effective (and obviously active) drug to the placebo group.

For tinnitus studies in particular, we believe that it is important to measure the loudness of the tinnitus before the study starts and again after it concludes. In a Xanax study, for example, the researchers measured the loudness of the patients' tinnitus before and after the treatment. The patients' subjective ratings about their tinnitus were also recorded. Having done this, the researchers were able to learn that, for those who experienced tinnitus relief with Xanax, the average measured tinnitus loudness was 7.5 dB SL before treatment and 2.3 dB SL after treatment. This is a significant difference. It is possibly a more objective measurement than the verbal reports.

How We Learn from a Double-blind, Placebo-controlled Study

If we were interested in determining whether or not aspirin relieved headaches, we would conduct some kind of test. The best possible test would be a double-blind, placebo-controlled study.

Aspirin Double-blind, Placebo-controlled Study

Our aspirin study will use two groups of patients. One group (the experimental group) will be given the real drug and the other group (the placebo group) will be given the placebo. In the simplest language, *placebo* means a fake medication.

Double-blind means that neither the experimenters nor the patients (also known as subjects) know who is getting the real drug and who is getting the placebo. The double-blinding of research has improved the reliability of studies. Some physicians who know that they are dispensing the real drug are subconsciously encouraging in their interactions with their patients. Some experimenters who know that they are dispensing the placebo drug are subconsciously discouraging in their interactions with their patients. Our experimenters will not know which medication they are dispensing.

When the patients finish the course of the drug or placebo, we will tally the results and use the results from the placebo group to evaluate the results from the experimental group. For example, if we find that headache relief was obtained in 40% of the experimental group and that headache relief was obtained in 35% of the placebo patients, we would not be very interested in recommending aspirin for headaches. In this case, most of the patients who improved were responding to the placebo effect, that is, the wellness that comes from believing that a drug will work. If we had not used a placebo in this experiment, we would have come to an erroneous conclusion that the drug is good for headaches.

On the other hand, if 95% of the subjects in the experimental group experience headache relief and 30% of the placebo group report the same relief, clearly we would recommend the real drug for the relief of headache. (For the record, aspirin has never been tested in a double-blind, placebo-controlled study!)

One final comment about the *placebo effect*. In most drug studies, the placebo effect can be as high as 35%. This means that 35% of the patients on the placebo got the same relief as did the patients on the active drug. In *tinnitus* studies in which a placebo is used, the positive placebo response is often not over 10%. Several double-blind, placebo-controlled studies, such as ones that tested for response to lidocaine, taurine, misoprostal, and a homeopathic medicine, resulted in a 0% placebo response from tinnitus patients and a significant response to the active treatment. This may mean that tinnitus patients are not as susceptible to suggestion as patients with other health problems.

Q **I read an article in *Science Reports* that discusses the process of blocking impulses in specific nerves that transmit sensations of pain. Can this same thing be done to the nerves that transmit tinnitus?**

A We do not yet know which nerve fibers are responsible for the sensation of a specific pain. Therefore, we do not know which nerve fibers need to be blocked in order to eliminate the pain. You can imagine the same problem with tinnitus. The auditory nerve that runs from the ear up into the brain is a literal bundle of fibers. Moreover, we do not even know if certain fibers are dedicated to the condition of tinnitus.

Some patients have had their auditory nerves surgically severed in a desperate effort to relieve their tinnitus. Many of these patients found that, in addition to total deafness on the severed side, their tinnitus was unaffected. Some patients found that their tinnitus was worsened, probably because of the loss of ambient sound that had naturally masked the tinnitus. For others, the tinnitus was at first relieved, but soon returned to the same severe level. Tinnitus clearly involves a great deal more than peripheral nerve fibers transmitting tinnitus signals to the brain.

Researchers have already identified some areas in the brain involved in the perception of tinnitus. Now we have to determine if any sacrifice in hearing or memory or any other function would be produced if these tinnitus-perceiving brain areas were removed or inactivated.

The main problem with tinnitus research is not the shortage of ideas; it is the lack of money to fund these ideas. If one-tenth of one percent of the U.S. budget for space exploration were devoted to tinnitus research, the problem of tinnitus would be solved in short order. Your interaction with national legislators on behalf of tinnitus could possibly lead to the funding changes we need. Go hound them!

Q **In a recent issue of *Science* magazine, I read about regeneration of inner ear hair cells in birds that could lead to the return of hearing in humans. Could this hair cell regeneration also lead to a cure for tinnitus?**

A As it turns out, birds have the natural capacity to regenerate their inner ear hair cells when those hair cells are damaged by excessive sound or by ototoxic substances. And when the hair cells regenerate, their hearing is restored. This is a very exciting research discovery. But what does it mean for the human ear? If damaged or dead hair cells in the human ear could be regenerated, tinnitus might be cured, hearing loss might be corrected, and hearing aid manufacturers might go out of business.

Unfortunately, the human ear does not have the capability of regenerating its own cochlear hair cells. Human cochlear cells are highly differentiated; that is, each cell has a very specific role. In birds, the cells are somewhat undifferentiated, so if one cell is damaged or destroyed, another nearby cell can take over a different role.

Thankfully, the mammalian ear is not completely helpless. It can regenerate *vestibular* hair cells, the ones that help us maintain our balance. As microscopic as our hair cells are, we have discovered something even tinier. There are *tip links* (see Figure 39.1 on page 184), wispy filaments that connect the stereocilia together. (Stereocilia are the tufts of "hair" on top of the hair cells.) These tip links regenerate within hours if they are damaged or destroyed by ototoxic drugs or excessive noise. This tip link damage-and-regeneration process might serve as one explanation for temporary hearing loss and temporary tinnitus.

Researcher Douglas Cotanche, at Children's Hospital in Boston, has been studying hair cell regeneration for more than a decade. Based on his current research, his speculations for the future include the possibility of transplanting human vestibular hair cells into the human cochlea, even though the outcome is unknown. Researchers are also giving thought to transplantation of nonhuman cochlear hair cells into the human cochlea. Cotanche and his team are now branching off into a new series of experiments aimed at the development of these biological cochlear implants. He believes that the breakthroughs to human hearing restoration are still several years away.

Auditory science is taking more new turns. Controversial as it is, embryonic stem cell research might well change the direction of this and other areas of research. Experimentally, embryonic stem cells can be induced to become different kinds of cells—possibly even hair cells.

According to the *Science* article, scientists at Baylor College of Medicine in Texas have identified the gene (at least in mice) that is responsible for the development of cochlear and vestibular inner ear hair cells. Mice that did not have this *math1* gene were born deaf and with a lack of balance. Researchers have not yet taken the next step to determine if a new math1 gene somehow introduced into a deaf mouse could restore hearing. But it is inevitable that scientists will attempt it, and probably soon.

Q I recently saw a program on the Genome Project. I took notes so that I could ask better questions of you. The Human Genome Project will be completed in the next 2 years and with that will come the elimination of entire classes of diseases, so they say. They claim that the Genome Project will be as revolutionary to the life sciences as the computer chip has been to the information age. They didn't mention tinnitus, but my question pertains to it. Will the Genome Project reveal the gene that will lead to the cure for tinnitus?

A The Genome Project holds great potential for human health. Scientists will soon identify all the chemical codes of human DNA and understand the

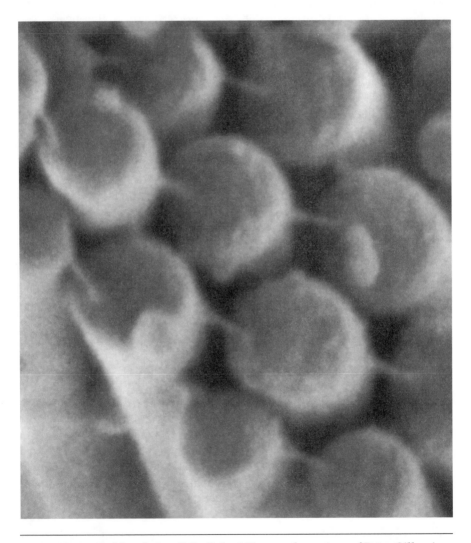

FIGURE 39.1   *Cochlear hair cell tip links. Micrograph courtesy of Peter Gillespie, Ph.D., copyright © P. Gillespie, 2000.*

function of every gene in our bodies. The ramifications of this identification process are staggering. In theory, once scientists learn all the components of our genetic blueprint, they will be able to design better drugs, predict a person's susceptibility to disease, and treat diseases with more precision. However, it will probably not produce an answer for tinnitus right away. Tinnitus is an acquired characteristic and, as such, it is not likely one with a gene related to it. On the other hand, there might be a gene that determines if your ears are prone or not prone to damage from the excessive noise or ototoxic drugs that can cause tinnitus.

Our bodies are made up of 50 trillion cells, and each cell contains all of our 100,000 genes. And yet each cell type only "reads" the instructions from specific genes within it. This is why a muscle cell is different from, say, a hair cell.

The basic idea behind treating disorders with gene therapy is to replace an abnormal gene in our cells with a normal gene. Once scientists learn which genes are responsible for which function, they face other challenges. They need to learn if some genes interact with other genes and if these interactions affect the way things work. And they need to find a way to deliver a normal gene to the part of the body that needs it. The Genome Project is a very exciting and breathtakingly complex program.

Q **Are any organizations funding research for the problem of tinnitus?**

A Yes, several agencies and dozens of medical facilities in the United States and around the world devote funds to tinnitus research. In 1998, the National Institutes of Health (NIH) awarded $1.5 million to tinnitus researchers Alan Lockwood, Richard Salvi, and Robert Burkard for their 5-year project to unravel the brain's involvement in the perception of tinnitus. This is the largest research grant for tinnitus funded to date. The Tinnitus Research Consortium, an independent organization of tinnitus researchers, was formed in 1998 by James Snow, M.D., former director of the National Institutes of Deafness and other Communication Disorders (NIDCD). Since 1979, the American Tinnitus Association has awarded $1.4 million for 53 individual tinnitus research seed grants. Seed grants are, by design, small grants to help researchers get ideas off the ground. If the ideas work, the researchers take their proven results to bigger funding bodies, like the NIH, and apply for the advanced research dollars. This is what Lockwood and Salvi did. Their original tinnitus/PET scan research was funded by an ATA seed grant. After it was a success on a small scale, the NIDCD funded the full project. So far, five additional ATA-funded studies have been further recognized and funded by the National Institutes of Health.

Research is the key, and research takes money. Support the American Tinnitus Association!

History of Tinnitus Research and Treatments

Tinnitus was part of the human experience long before boom boxes or electric guitars or, for that matter, before electricity had been harnessed in any way. A 3000-year-old document written on papyrus contains references to a treatment (an infusion of oil) for the "bewitched ear."

Contemporary tinnitus treatment can be followed with a little more precision. In 1802, C. J. C. Grapengeisser, a German doctor, experimented with the newly invented electric battery. He initially stimulated patients' ears with electricity in an attempt to cure their deafness. Despite the failure of this experiment, he still noticed that some variations of electrical stimulation suppressed tinnitus for short periods of time. (He also noted that some applications of electrical stimulation *caused* tinnitus.)

In 1883, Austrian doctor Victor von Urbantschitsch noted that tinnitus was reduced and sometimes eliminated for a minute or more when he exposed tinnitus ears to the sound of a tuning fork. Today this phenomenon is known as residual inhibition.

In the early 1900s, ENT physician A. J. Spaulding played his violin for his tinnitus patients. Some of them reported that the playing had a masking effect on their tinnitus. When he stopped playing, some of them remarked that the tinnitus had briefly abated.

In 1921, French doctor Jean-Marc-Gaspard Itard reported case studies in detail of patients with severe tinnitus. One such case involved a woman whose tinnitus was only tolerable when she was in a noisy environment. Itard suggested that she try listening to a crackling fire or to the sound of water dripping from one container to another. She finally experienced tinnitus relief when she moved into a water mill.

In 1947, M. Saltzman and M. S. Ersner experimented with hearing aids for tinnitus relief, having noticed that the ambient sounds brought in by the hearing aids helped to relieve tinnitus for some patients. The researchers also observed and noted that patients much more easily tolerated external sound than the internal sound of tinnitus.

In 1960, U.S. researchers D. S. Hatton, S. D. Erulkar, and P. E. Rosenberg administered direct-current electrical stimulation to patients as part of a vestibular test. Half the patients reported a complete elimination of their tinnitus as long as the electrical stimulation was present. Because the duration of tinnitus relief was short and the direct electrical current had damaged healthy tissue, Hatton decided that this therapy was not useful for tinnitus.

In the early 1960s, William House developed the technology of cochlear implants that surgically restored usable hearing in totally deaf ears. These innovative electrical devices offered the unanticipated relief of tinnitus for many patients.

In 1969, German scientist Harald Feldmann began to study the effects of narrow band and pure tone external masking sounds for tinnitus relief. He noted that some patients experienced total tinnitus relief with the external sounds. Others experienced partial relief (tinnitus fatigue) and were able to turn the masking sound down and still experience reduced tinnitus. Others experienced some relief, followed by a return of the tinnitus even with the masking signal present. Feldmann used audiometric testing equipment in a clinic setting to generate the masking signals. It did not occur to him, he later admitted, to use masking as a therapy for tinnitus. (Feldmann felt that the term *masking* was not accurate and preferred instead the term *inhibition*. However, by the time he had voiced his objection, the term masking had become too well established to change it. The phenomenon of residual inhibition was later named in his honor.)

In 1971, Jack Vernon studied his first tinnitus patient, Charles Unice. On a serendipitous outing, Unice's severe tinnitus was momentarily relieved while he stood in front of a cascading water fountain. Vernon observed this and devised a hearing aid-like device—a wearable masker—that emitted the same broadband frequencies produced by the cascading fountain. Vernon and audiologist Robert Johnson refined the masking protocol over the next two decades.

In 1981, French scientist J.-M. Aran studied the effects of surgical electrode implants on the inner ear round windows and promontories of tinnitus patients. When the round window electrodes were stimulated with positive direct current, the tinnitus was eliminated in 60% of the patients. When the promontory electrodes were stimulated with positive direct current, tinnitus was eliminated in 43% of the patients. The relief in all cases lasted only as long as the electricity was flowing to the electrodes and was experienced only in the electrically stimulated ears. Aran realized that this therapy destroyed cochlear hair cells and recommended its use only for patients who were deaf or who had no usable hearing.

In 1988, neuroscientist P. J. Jastreboff, along with J. F. Brennan and C. T. Sasaki, developed an animal model of tinnitus. Considered a medical breakthrough, this advance allowed researchers to measure tinnitus neurologically and chemically, as well as behaviorally. In 1993, Jastreboff introduced the concept of a neurophysiological model of tinnitus along with an auditory habituation treatment, later called tinnitus retraining therapy (TRT).

Interspersed throughout this long history are many trials of many different drugs for tinnitus alleviation.

To give you a better global and historical view of tinnitus research, we evaluated the documented tinnitus research projects that have been published in medical journals around the world. The results of our march through the National Library of Medicine's database produced some interesting results. For example, the trends in tinnitus research followed pace with the technology available at the time. One research project in 1969 proudly announced its high-tech data gathering techniques by including mention of computer punch cards in its title! We found it interesting that good and even great ideas for tinnitus relief were tried once or maybe twice, but not carried forward to practical clinical use. Hyperbaric oxygen therapy has been studied all over the world and over many decades, as has acupuncture, masking, most classes of drugs, and temporomandibular joint (TMJ) therapy which was incidentally the topic of the first published tinnitus-related paper (found in the *British Journal of Oral Surgery*) in 1964. In fact, it was the *only* published paper pertaining to tinnitus in 1964. It was also the first published

(continued)

paper pertaining to tinnitus in modern times.

Table 39.1 provides a synopsis of the trends of tinnitus research. These research studies were conducted in China, Italy, Russia, Japan, England, the Netherlands, France, the United States, and other countries, and the papers describing the research appeared in peer-reviewed medical journals. The topics listed are only highlights of each year's contributions, and all relate to tinnitus one way or another. Substances that were studied for tinnitus relief are listed in the right-hand column.

In addition to those in Table 39.1, an estimated 500 tinnitus studies were conducted and the findings presented at six international tinnitus seminars from 1977 through 1999.

Table 39.2 gives the number of tinnitus research studies by topic and Figure 39.2 shows these by year.

TABLE 39.1 *Tinnitus Research 1964–2000*

Year	No. of Studies	Study Topics	Substances Studied
1964	1	Temporomandibular joint disturbances	
1965	21	Salicylate toxicity, multiple sclerosis, palatal myoclonus	
1966	32	Excessive loud noise exposure, stapedectomy, eighth nerve surgery, eustachian tube, Ménière's disease, endolymphatic sacs, retrocochlear tumors	
1967	43	Objective tinnitus, ototoxicity of chemotherapy drugs, barotrauma, acoustic neuromas, pitch matching, radioisotope brain scanning	
1968	43	Paget's disease, glomus tumors, head injury, ototoxicity of antibiotics, contralateral masking, ultrasonic radiation of the round window	cinnarizine (Stugeron), uridine enzymes
1969	50	Labyrinthectomy, broad spectrum/narrow spectrum/pure tone masking, herpes, severing of the eighth nerve, whiplash and head trauma	propranodol, Aderazid, s-heparin
1970	41	Low-frequency tinnitus, premenstrual tension, Cogen's syndrome, insufficient cerebral circulation, presbycusis, IV furosemide (as cause), ear canal surgery	Duvadilan, ethacrynic acid, Instenon

(continued)

Year	No. of Studies	Study Topics	Substances Studied
1971	54	Subjective tinnitus measurement, long-term Ménière's disease, family with high-tone tinnitus, arterial aneurisms, pellagra	IV lidocaine, nucleic acid, Tryptanol
1972	47	Vein malformations, nystagmus, Lermoyez syndrome, high blood pressure and nosebleeds, nerve blocks, migraines, hearing survey of Israeli Defense Force inductees	propylthiouracil, Hydrosarpan 711
1973	61	Brain stem tumors, TMJ surgery, hypnotherapy, sudden deafness, hearing sensitivity in children, Waldenstrom's disease, perilymph fistulas	Dihydergot (dihydroergotamine), sulpirid
1974	46	Concussion, round window rupture, acupuncture, ototoxicity of indomethacin	
1975	45	Hearing restored with pressure chamber, spontaneous remission of objective tinnitus, pesticide poisoning	vincamine, betahistine hydrochloride (Serc), dimethyl sulfoxide
1976	61	Endolymphatic hydrops, acoustic trauma in the military, biofeedback, ototoxicity of tobramycin, neck extension injury	nicergoline, IV lidocaine
1977	53	Angiography for pulsatile tinnitus, cardiovascular disease, effects of aircraft noise, electrical stimulation of cochlea with electrode through eardrum	dextran
1978	70	Viral hepatitis, chemotherapy-caused tinnitus, Paget's disease, psychiatric aspects	sodium amylobarbitone, lidocaine, carbamazepine, tiapride
1979	55	Evoked response audiometry, pernicious anemia, multiple sclerosis, artificial cochlea, after-effects of earthquake	
1980	77	Behcet's disease, fluctuating tinnitus, masking and hearing aids, pure tone masking, hearing loss with recruitment, ABR and eighth nerve lesions, malaria	Urografin
1981	126	Electroacupuncture, epidemiology, children and tinnitus, sudden hearing loss, cochlear implants, anatomical correlates of tinnitus (central and peripheral), alcoholism, high-frequency hearing aids	mexiletine, Tegretol, protriptyline

(continued)

TABLE 39.1   *Tinnitus Research 1964–2000*, CONTINUED

Year	No. of Studies	Study Topics	Substances Studied
1982	62	High blood pressure, sensorineural tinnitus, disco music and auditory problems, biofeedback, intracranial pressure, temporal bone study, acupuncture	IV lidocaine double-blind study, alpha-receptor blockers
1983	105	Pure tone masking, loudness matching, relaxation–hypnotherapy, speech discrimination with masker use, musical hallucinations, electrical stimulation, residual inhibition, neurotology	doxepin, glutamic acid, and glutamic acid diethylester
1984	130	Acupuncture, otoacoustic emissions, stellate ganglion block for relief, computer-aided tinnitus characterization, multichannel cochlear prosthesis, adverse reaction to trizolam and flurazepam, relaxation and biofeedback, neurological implications, placebo effect, epidemiology	moxisylyte, trimetazidine (Vastarel), urea
1985	119	Electrical stimulation, hyperbaric oxygen, masking, diagnostic potential of CT scans, otosclerosis, peripheral versus central tinnitus through brainstem response evaluation, counseling, iontophoresis and local anesthetic, hearing aids	carbamazepine, nimodipine, aminooxyacetic acid
1986	120	Salicylate-induced changes in auditory pathway, masker preferences, pulsatile tinnitus, low-powered ultrasound as treatment, Chinese medicine connection between the kidney and ear, reassurance–relaxation–distraction, cognitive therapy	zinc, ginkgo, Dusodril, flunarizine, Dyazide, phenothiazines
1987	125	Electrotherapy, analogy between pain and tinnitus, gaze-evoked tinnitus, TENS stimulator, tinnitus without hearing loss, ear fullness, low-serum zinc (as cause), tinnitus in occupational settings, chemical labyrinthectomy, noise-induced tinnitus, amplified music, masking with sounds not covering tinnitus frequency	imipramine, nicotinamide
1988	86	MRI and CT scans, Walkman™ as masker, head trauma, Bell's palsy, aminoglycoside and chemotherapy ototoxicity, animal model for tinnitus, behavioral therapy, endolymphatic surgeries, computer tomography imaging, hypertension, tinnitus loudness pre- and post-masking	ginkgo, taurine, phenytoin

Year	No. of Studies	Study Topics	Substances Studied
1989	125	Auditory evoked potentials of brainstem, objectified tinnitus with neuromagnetic measurements, combined Chinese and Western medicine, depression, electrical stimulation, cochleovestibular neurectomy (severing of the eighth nerve), single-channel cochlear implant, arteriovenous fistula	nortriptyline, IV Xylocaine
1990	131	Self-hypnosis, loud music, HIV and tinnitus, dysfunction detected by MRI, hyperbaric oxygen, mechanisms of tinnitus generation and perception, scuba diving, endolymphatic sac decompression, otoacoustic emissions, transcranial Doppler ultrasonography, pitch matching	gentamicin, trimetazidine, Hydergine
1991	134	Habituation, Ménière's disease, angioplasty for pulsatile tinnitus relief, acupuncture, hypnosis, anxiety and depression, surgical complications of cochlear implants, acoustic neuroma, musical hallucinations, masker noise spectrum studies, ear canal magnets, cervical vertebrae treatment	azapropazone, flecainide acetate
1992	125	Craniomandibular disorders, TMJD with vertigo and tinnitus, involvement of auditory pathways, perforated eardrum, exercise, musical hallucinations, premenstrual exacerbation of Meniere's symptoms	aspirin as a palliative, antidepressants
1993	141	Neurophysiological approach to tinnitus, neural mechanisms, vitamin B_{12} deficiency, noise-induced hearing loss, sleep disturbance, MRA analysis of vascular lesions, jugular bulb diverticulum, cochlear tinnitus	soft laser with IV Tebonin, IV lidocaine, synthetic prostaglandin E1, furosemide, alprazolam (Xanax)
1994	147	Anemia and sudden hearing loss, low-frequency hums, carotid artery disease, MRI and MSA for pulsatile tinnitus, head injury, high-impact aerobics, suicide, coping with stress, animal model of tinnitus, preventing noise-induced hearing loss, benign positional vertigo, hypnosis, eighth nerve section, intracranial arteriovenous fistulas	taurolidin, calcium channel blockers

(continued)

TABLE 39.1 *Tinnitus Research 1964–2000,* CONTINUED

Year	No. of Studies	Study Topics	Substances Studied
1995	144	Lasers, hyperbaric oxygen, cognitive behavioral therapy, outer hair cell lesions, poor vibration of inner ear fluids (as cause), barometric changes, yoga, hyperacusis caused by 5-HT dysfunction	misoprostol, laser and *Ginkgo biloba*, piracetam, isosorbide (for Ménière's), alprazolam, glutamate receptors, L-Baclofen, D-Baclofen
1996	148	Intracranial hypertension, hypnotherapy versus counseling, temporal bone imaging, cerebello-pontine tumors, PET study, vascular decompression, high-volume music, acoustic neuromas, legal aspects, pulsatile tinnitus and congenital CNS malformation, auditory brainstem model of central tinnitus, low-threshold calcium spike bursts in thalamus, SPECT, hormone replacement therapy	inner ear perfusion of dexamethasone, clonazepam, diazepam
1997	198	Occupational noise-induced hearing loss in the music industry, white noise generators, air bags, partial and complete masking, allergy and Ménière's disease, tinnitus data registry, psychological profile, low-power laser, middle and inner ear implantable drug delivery system, transcutaneous nerve stimulation	baclofen, caroverine, ginkgo
1998	198	TRT, psychological distress, air bags, homeopathy, acupuncture, natural healing, jaw movement (as cause), low-frequency electromagnetic field, elevated blood fats, microvascular decompression, craniomandibular disorders, vascular loops, spontaneous otoacoustic emissions, gamma knife radiology for glomus tumors, middle ear myoclonus	sodium valproate, memantine, fluoxetine, melatonin, cyclandelate, glycopyrrolate (for Ménière's)

(continued)

Year	No. of Studies	Study Topics	Substances Studied
1999	205	Auditory cortex plasticity, Chinese acupuncture, acoustic neuromas, air bag impulse noise, back pain, lasers, eustachian tube, pregnancy, headaches, tinnitus classification, Oklahoma City bombing, hyperbaric oxygen, noise hazards to employees in discos, loudness match reliability, tinnitus evaluation with pulsed tones, Vontippel–Linday syndrome, Tolosa–Hunt syndrome, PET scans of cortical centers, hypersensitivity to sound, synaptic response patterns	
2000	(ongoing)	Physiological model of tinnitus, HIV, tinnitus retraining therapy, TMJ disorder, acupuncture	*Ginkgo biloba,* peripheral nerve block with bupivacaine

TABLE 39.2   *Number of Research Studies by Topic Pertaining to Tinnitus, 1964–2000*

Acoustic neuroma: 139	Masking: 179
Acupuncture: 34	Melatonin: 2
Air bags: 6	Ménière's disease: 441
Allergy: 32	Meningitis: 30
Biofeedback: 44	Musical hallucinations: 6
Calcium channel blockers: 19	Niacin: 2
Chinese medicine: 4	Noise induced: 173
Cochlear implant: 62	Nortriptyline: 9
Cognitive behavioral therapy: 9	Otosclerosis: 87
Eighth nerve section: 38	PET scan: 9
Electrical stimulation: 80	SPECT scan: 5
Ginkgo biloba: 12	Tegretol: 22
Head injury: 66	Tinnitus retraining therapy: 9
Homeopathy: 1	TMJD: 63
Hyperacusis: 38	Tumors: 488 (including acoustic
Hyperbaric oxygen: 24	neuromas)
Hypnosis: 13	Xanax: 3
Lasers: 16	Zinc: 8
Lidocaine: 120	

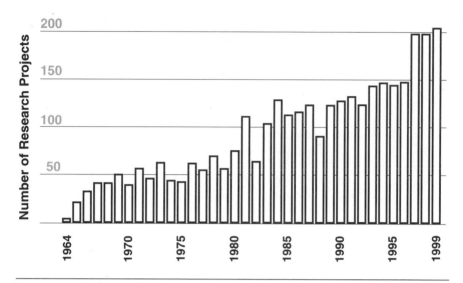

FIGURE 39.2   *Number of tinnitus research projects by year.*

Resources

Bermingham, N. A., Hassan, B. A., Price, S. D., Vollrath, M. A., Ben-Arie, N., Eatock, R. A., Bellen, H. J., Lysakowski, A., and Zoghbi, H. Y. Math1: An essential gene for the generation of inner ear hair cells, *Science,* June 11, 1999; 284(5421):1837–41.

Dooling, R. J., Ryals, B. M., and Manabe, K. Recovery of hearing and vocal behavior after hair-cell regeneration, *Proceedings of the National Academy of Science,* 94, 14206–10, 1997.

Hashino, E., and Salvi, R. Changing patterns of DNA replication in noise-damaged chick cochlea, *Journal of Cell Science,* 1993:105(1).

Jastreboff, P. J., Brennan, J. F., and Sasaki, C. T. An animal model for tinnitus, *Laryngoscope,* Mar. 1988; 98(3):280–6.

McFall, K. S. Turning science fiction into fact one gene at a time, *Oregon Health,* 2000; 2(2):21–23.

National Library of Medicine's Internet database, PubMed, www.ncbi.nlm.nih.gov: 80/entrez

Romand, R., and Chardin, S. Effects of growth factors on the hair cells after ototoxic treatment of the neonatal mammalian cochlea in vitro, *Brain Res.,* Apr. 1999; 17;825(1–2):46–58.

Sanchez, T. G., Monte Alegre, A. C., and Bento, R. F. Tinnitus effects on ABR thresholds, waves, and interpeak latencies, *Proceedings of the Sixth International Tinnitus Seminar,* Hazell, J., ed., London, 1999.

40

Residual Inhibition: An Aftereffect of Masking

Q I have often heard mention of residual inhibition. What is it, and is it the purpose of masking?

A Residual inhibition is the temporary suppression of the tinnitus after the masking sound has been turned off. Even though residual inhibition is not the purpose of masking, it could be viewed as a bonus when it occurs.

Residual inhibition comes in several forms. It can be a reduction of the tinnitus (partial residual inhibition), a total absence of the tinnitus (complete residual inhibition), or a combination of both, starting out as complete and then changing to partial. In general, it is of short duration.

The standard test for residual inhibition at Oregon Hearing Research Center's tinnitus clinic is to mask the tinnitus with a band of noise (2000 through 12,000 Hz) at the patient's minimum masking level plus 10 dB for 60 seconds and then to note the kind and duration of residual inhibition that results. A sampling of 1372 tinnitus patients from the Tinnitus Data Registry offered the following results:

- No residual inhibition: 240 (17.5%)
- Partial residual inhibition: 484 (35.3%)
- Complete residual inhibition: 9 (.7%)
- Complete and partial residual inhibition: 639 (46.5%)

These data reveal that 83% of the patients tested displayed some form of residual inhibition, with an average duration of 64 seconds. But don't let the results confuse you. Even though 60 seconds of masking produced an average of 64 seconds of residual inhibition, this does not mean that 1 hour of masking will produce slightly over 1 hour of residual inhibition. Indeed, 1 hour of masking will still only produce about 64 seconds of residual inhibition. As of now, we do not know how to extend the duration of residual inhibition.

Q Because of your instructions, I now wear protective earmuffs while driving my the tractor. The other day I plowed with the tractor for 8 hours almost nonstop. The sound of the tractor under the earmuffs was a low-pitched rumble. When I finally quit and took the earmuffs off, I expected to hear what I usually hear: my regular tinnitus. But this time I did not hear any tinnitus at all, and it took over a day for it to return! This has never happened before. Can you explain it?

A You had a rather extended case of residual inhibition, which is a temporary cessation or reduction of tinnitus following masking. There are two things about your experience that are most interesting:

1. The sound of the tractor was low pitched. Low-pitched sounds do not usually mask tinnitus or produce residual inhibition.
2. You experienced a very long period of residual inhibition.

Let's try to capitalize on this new experience of yours. Make two tape recordings of the tractor noise. Keep one tape and send the other to the Oregon Hearing Research Center for analysis. If you can establish residual inhibition with the tape, you will not have to drive the tractor every time you want tinnitus relief.

[This patient found that he could get fairly long periods of residual inhibition with the tape recording, although never as long as when he was actually riding the tractor. We sent him a variety of tapes with frequency spectrums that had been shifted all over the place. But his results with our tapes were never as good as those produced by his recorded tractor sounds.]

Q Are researchers studying residual inhibition as a way to possibly relieve or reduce tinnitus permanently?

A A residual inhibition study was recently conducted with a device called the HiSonic™ made by Hearing Innovations. The HiSonic is a superhigh-frequency bone conduction hearing instrument that amplifies sound from 20,000 to 36,000 Hz, frequencies all well above what human ears are theoretically equipped to detect. The HiSonic is worn like a headband, with a transducer disk at either the right or left side. The disk rests on the mastoid bone.

A modified version of this device was studied for its potential use as an ultrahigh-frequency masker. The 20,000+ Hz wave became a carrier wave for the "lower" high-frequency (6000 to 8000 Hz) masking signal. Twenty tinnitus patients were tested with both audible acoustical sound (2000 to 12,000 Hz) and the HiSonic sound (20,000 to 36,000 Hz). All patients had 60 seconds of sound exposure, after which the duration of their residual inhibition (RI) was measured. The results are shown in Table 40.1.

It is clear that the HiSonic produced residual inhibition in excess of that produced by acoustic stimulation, although there were individual cases for

TABLE 40.1

Patient No.	RI Duration with Acoustical (sec)	RI Duration with HiSonic (sec)
1	50	90
2	75	310
3	300	60
4	25	140
5	8	30
6	55	0
7	25	60
8	34	70
9	25	0
10	480	7200
11	15	30
12	35	90
13	No data	105
14	20	55
15	440	210
16	220	530
17	0	120
18	55	135
19	40	0
20	35	615
	Average = 101.95 sec	Average = 492.50 sec

which the acoustical stimulation was superior (patients 3, 6, 9, 15, and 19). We concluded that, although HiSonic bone conduction generally increased the duration of residual inhibition, it did not produce the extremely extended residual inhibition that we still seek. The HiSonic device was placed on the "sweet spot" directly behind the pinna on the mastoid bone. Perhaps variation in sweet spot selection would alter the residual inhibition results. (The device was able to help mask tinnitus for a different group of patients with much more severe hearing loss.)

Q **Is there some way to predict my ability to experience residual inhibition?**

A There is only one absolute requirement: You have to have tinnitus that can be at least partially relieved by a masking sound. Maskability does not guarantee that residual inhibition will result, but a full 83% of maskable patients can experience residual inhibition. We have learned that low-frequency masking in most cases does not produce residual inhibition. Also, hearing aids will not produce residual inhibition, even if the ambient sound that they bring in completely covers the tinnitus.

Q Is there a range of sound that triggers residual inhibition better than other sound ranges?

A Some time ago we tried various arrangements of masking to see if there was an optimal range that triggered the longest residual inhibition. And indeed there was. We found that *edge masking*, bands of noise located on either side of the tinnitus, produced the longest lasting residual inhibition. We also learned that we could produce longer residual inhibition when we applied masking tones, not bands of sound, that were slightly lower in frequency than the patient's tinnitus. For example, if the patient's tinnitus was a 5000-Hz tone, we would use a 4000-Hz or lower masking tone. It usually was not the patient's preferred masking sound. But the residual inhibition produced by this tonal masking usually extended beyond that which was produced by noise masking. Neither of these arrangements, edge masking or lower-frequency tonal masking, gave us the extended residual inhibition that we were seeking. Both arrangements added only seconds or, in a few cases, minutes to the average residual inhibition experience.

Years ago a residual inhibition study was conducted on tinnitus patients using *sweeping frequency* masking. The masking sound was a continually changing pitch from 2000 Hz up to 12,000 Hz and then back down to 2000 Hz, like playing up and down on a piano keyboard. This kind of sound produced rather long-lasting residual inhibition, but the study was discontinued when two patients had their tinnitus temporarily worsened by it. Still, this approach might bear more investigation.

Q I hear rather low-pitched, soft rumbling sounds when I wear earplugs and earmuffs to a football game. After each game, my tinnitus is totally quiet for several hours. In this scenario, I experience the rumbling sound for several hours and the resulting residual inhibition also lasts for several hours. Is the duration of the residual inhibition determined by the duration of the sound exposure?

A In the tests that we have conducted, the duration of the residual inhibition is not determined by the duration of the sound exposure. Anecdotally, however, several patients have experienced very prolonged residual inhibition after they have had a long ongoing experience with masking, say several years.

As a general rule, soft low-pitched sounds do not produce residual inhibition. Your tinnitus is a fortunate exception to the rule.

Q The periods of residual inhibition that I experience have lately been lasting several hours after I remove the maskers. Do other people also experience this?

A Many patients who have used tinnitus maskers for several years report the same kind of residual inhibition. In our continuing investigation to solve the mystery of this phenomenon, we studied 13 patients with pure tone tinnitus

Residual Inhibition Case History

Q I've had the tinnitus for over 60 years. (I got it from artillery fire during World War I.) The noises never leave me or let up. Everyone else says that there is nothing that can be done for it and you claim that you might be able to help. What is it that you do?

A What we do might seem unusual to you. We put sounds in your ears and use that sound to cover up your tinnitus.

Q One sound for another? What good would that do?

A Let's go through the testing and see if we can do any good for you. Remember that you decide if a treatment works. We don't.

At this point, we conducted a hearing test and the routine tinnitus tests: pitch matching, loudness matching, masking, and residual inhibition. The first four tests were not unusual in any way. But when we came to the residual inhibition test, the most unusual thing happened. Routine residual inhibition testing consists of ap-plying the masking stimulus, a noise from 2000 through 12,000 Hz at the minimum masking level plus 10 dB for 60 seconds. At the end of the 60 seconds it is customary for the tinnitus to be totally absent or greatly reduced for a minute or less.

The residual inhibition test was conducted for this patient and he reported, with some considerable surprise, that his tinnitus was totally gone for the first time in 60 years. We indicated that his tinnitus would return in a short time and we began to time him, waiting for the tinnitus to return. After 15 minutes, it had not returned. This was most unusual. After 2 hours it had not returned. This was very unusual. We sent him home and asked him to note the time of the return of his tinnitus and to inform us. It took 30 days for his tinnitus to return. He came to the clinic for his treatment every 30 days after that. "Zap me," he would say. For the rest of his life he lived in a peace he had not known in six decades.

This is a most unusual case of residual inhibition. Unfortunately, this case stands alone.

and looked at the following variety of masking arrangements and the impact that these variations had on residual inhibition. In each case, the masker was introduced at the patient's minimum masking level plus 10 dB for 60 seconds.

1. Masking with a tone half an octave below the pitch of the tinnitus produced 56 seconds of residual inhibition.
2. Masking with a tone that duplicated the pitch of the tinnitus produced 58 seconds of residual inhibition.
3. Masking with a narrow band of noise centered at the tinnitus frequency yielded 44 seconds of residual inhibition.
4. Masking with a tone half an octave above the pitch of the tinnitus produced 71 seconds of residual inhibition.
5. Masking with two tones placed on either side of the pitch of the tinnitus produced 74 seconds of residual inhibition.

Of the masking conditions that we investigated, we learned that using a bandwidth of noise produced the shortest length of residual inhibition and using a single tone or a pair of tones produced the longest length of residual inhibition. Ironically, patients who use masking to relieve tinnitus prefer the reverse: Tonal masking is generally uncomfortable and bandwidth sounds are favored.

Originally, it was a guess to study residual inhibition with a masking sound at 10 dB above the minimum masking level (MML). Years later we learned how good a guess it was. In the 1980s we decided to test to see if another arrangement would be better. We tested MML, MML + 5 dB, MML + 15 dB, MML + 20 dB, and MML + 25 dB. It turned out that MML + 10 dB produced the longest residual inhibition of them all.

Q **Is anyone studying the phenomenon of residual inhibition to figure out what factors produce it?**

A A team of scientists from the Department of Applied Psychology, University of Wales Institute of Science and Technology in Cardiff, Wales, studied residual inhibition and made some very interesting findings, some of them quite different from our findings. Studying 32 patients, the researchers measured the duration and magnitude of residual inhibition as a function of the masking composition (frequency, bandwidth, intensity, and duration). They found the following:

1. The masking frequency needed to produce the maximal residual inhibition was below that of the tinnitus frequency or pitch match.
2. In some subjects only a narrow band of noise produced residual inhibition.
3. Residual inhibition was proportional to the masker intensity. (The louder the masking stimulus was, the longer the residual inhibition lasted.) When the masking intensity was MML + 10 dB, the residual inhibition lasted an average of 35 seconds, after which the tinnitus returned to its normal level. When masking intensity was MML + 20 dB, the residual inhibition lasted an average of 106 seconds.

   [This is in contrast to our findings, which showed a decrease in residual inhibition when masking intensity was above MML + 10 dB.]

4. Little or no residual inhibition was produced by partial masking.
5. The duration of residual inhibition was linear. That is, the longer the subject was exposed to masking, the longer the residual inhibition lasted.

   [This is also different from our findings.]

6. A second masker presented during residual inhibition did not extend or intensify the residual inhibition.

7. Contralateral masking did not produce residual inhibition.
8. Masking sounds that produced residual inhibition also produced temporary hearing threshold shifts.
9. Masking at the minimum masking level (MML) caused no residual inhibition.

   [It is interesting to note that tinnitus patients are encouraged to use this level with wearable tinnitus maskers.]

10. Tinnitus patients with Ménière's did not display sufficient residual inhibition to be included in the study.
11. Subjects who had tinnitus located in the head tended to not display residual inhibition.

    [For purposes of this study, the researchers introduced the masking stimulus to one ear only. Tinnitus located in the head generally requires bilateral masking. This might have been the cause of their finding.]

Dr. Harald Feldmann, working in Germany in 1971, indicated that contralateral masking (masking on the opposite side of the tinnitus) produced more residual inhibition than did ipsilateral masking (masking on the same side as the tinnitus). This is contrary to the present findings and these differences remain unexplained. In a separate observation, several patients at the Portland Tinnitus Clinic experienced excessively long periods of residual inhibition (days or weeks) after years of tinnitus masking.

Resources

Meikle, M. B., Edlefsen, L. L., Lay, J. L. Suppression of tinnitus by bone conduction of ultrasound, *Assoc. Research Otolaryngol. Abstracts*, 1999;22:223.

Terry, A. M. P., Jones, D. M., Davis, B. R., and Slater, R. Parametric studies of tinnitus and residual inhibition, *Br. J. Audio.*, 1983; 17:245–256.

Sleep

Q Just as I doze off at night, my tinnitus wakes me up. I am edgy all the time. What can I do to get some sleep?

A Many people with tinnitus know instinctively—and correctly—that they would cope better with their tinnitus if they could just get a good night's sleep. The reverse is true too: If they did not have the tinnitus to cope with in the first place, they could get a good night's sleep. While this is not universally true (since millions of people who do *not* have tinnitus have sleep problems), the sleep-disturbed-by-tinnitus experience is wholly legitimate. Tinnitus can disrupt sleep, and disrupted sleep can worsen a person's perception of his or her tinnitus.

Sleep difficulties are associated with medical problems to be sure. They are also associated with psychological problems, a person's life-style, and poor sleep habits. We mention this for a reason. It is important to realize that there could be another factor, in addition to or maybe other than tinnitus, that is causing your sleep difficulty.

By making some life-style "housekeeping" changes, insomnia can be lessened regardless of its cause. If you have disrupted sleep, try the following:

- Ask your pharmacist if the medications that you are taking could be the cause of your sleep difficulty. (Insomnia is a side effect of many drugs.)
- Talk with a psychologist. Tinnitus might not be the only thing that is troubling you. It can be helpful to your sleep and to your tinnitus to try to resolve other problems (relationship, career, etc.). Anxiety and depression also contribute to sleep problems.
- Reduce or eliminate caffeine. It is a nervous system stimulant found in colas, coffee, teas, chocolate, and some medications. High doses of caffeine can cause anxiety and insomnia; even small amounts of caffeine cause some people to react to its stimulating effect.

- Reduce or eliminate alcohol. Excessive amounts of alcohol can cause sudden awakening and nightmares. Alcohol also suppresses the important rapid eye movement (REM) stage of sleep during which we do most of our dreaming.
- Design your bedroom for maximum sleep comfort. Keep the temperature between 60° and 65°F, not too hot or too cold. Use a foam egg crate mattress topper to make the mattress extra comfortable or replace a sagging mattress. Use sheets and bedding that are inviting and comfortable. Audiologist and sleep specialist Malvina Levy suggests that you "love your place of sleep."
- It is imperative that you put a source of non-distracting background sound in your sleeping space. An utterly silent environment makes tinnitus seem louder yet.

Q **I've read that melatonin can help with sleep. What is it? Is it available by prescription? Is it dangerous? As you might be able to tell, I'm nervous about taking sleeping pills.**

A It is wise to be cautious about any substance that makes you sleepy. Melatonin is a hormone that is naturally secreted into the body from the pineal gland deep in the brain. Interestingly, this secretion only happens during the dark hours. The pineal gland is able to detect external light changes by a complex connection to the eye. The melatonin secretion cycle keeps our internal clocks in phase with the cycles of light and dark.

Researcher Rosenberg et al. conducted a double-blind, placebo-controlled study on melatonin primarily to test its efficacy as a tinnitus treatment. In this study, the researchers initially found no difference between the effect of melatonin and the effect of the placebo on tinnitus per se. But when the researchers looked closer at the data, they found that 46.7% of the patients who had had difficulty sleeping because of their tinnitus reported overall tinnitus improvement with melatonin versus 20% who reported overall improvement with the placebo. Also, patients who had high scores on their pretrial Tinnitus Handicap Inventory showed a greater positive response to melatonin than to the placebo.

Researcher Bergstrom et al. wrote, "Unfortunately, this innocent [melatonin] molecule has been touted in recent books and many advertisements as an aphrodisiac, rejuvenator, protector against disease, and general wonder-worker." But how melatonin works as a supplement to our systems and what part of the nervous system it affects are still not really understood. Fortunately, research on it is continuing. Currently, melatonin can be purchased without a prescription at health food stores and over the Internet. It is being studied for its immunity-enhancing effect, its tumor-controlling effect, and its role in sleep.

Q   I am 70 years of age and would like to be able to enjoy the rest of my retirement, but tinnitus robs me of the joy of life. My tinnitus is especially bad when I lie down at night to go to sleep. When I am successful in getting to sleep, my tinnitus awakens me after an hour or so and then it's difficult getting back to sleep. Other than taking sleeping pills, is there an answer to my problem?

A   Many tinnitus patients have observed that their tinnitus worsens at night. One reason is clear: It is usually quiet at bedtime. Ambient daytime sounds were probably providing a partial masking effect and a distraction for your tinnitus.

You might be able to alter the situation. Try using a bedside masking unit or environmental sound machine, an FM radio "detuned" between stations, or a CD player with a relaxing CD selection set on replay. A masking sound in the bedroom will also form an acoustical fence around you. Outside noise disturbances (like barking and traffic noise) will be less likely to disrupt your sleep.

If your spouse is sensitive to noise disturbances at night, consider purchasing the very comfortable Sound Pillow by Phoenix Promotional Products. This standard-sized pillow has two wafer-thin speakers imbedded in it and a wire and stereo jack that extend from one of its side seams. The jack plugs directly into a radio, stereo, or CD player. You can try a variety of sounds, such as music, masking noise, or nature sounds, until you find one that works. When you lift your head off the pillow, the sound level decreases by about 20 dB. This keeps the sound in the pillow from disturbing your spouse.

Some people need several nights to adjust to nighttime masking; others adjust to it right away. We encourage you to give it a try.

Q   It is our plan to start a family, but I have been taking amitriptyline for depression that is probably due to my tinnitus. I have learned how to deal with my tinnitus, but the amitriptyline helps with sleeping. Since most drugs are not recommended during pregnancy, what can I do to help me sleep?

A   There are several non-medicinal ways to induce sleep. One is to introduce the sound of radio static. Simply detune the radio between stations on the FM band. The white noise of static contains all frequencies from 20 through 20,000 Hz.

Another solution is to use the sound produced by a bedside sound-making unit. Many companies make or distribute them, like Marpac and Sharper Image. The sounds produced by these devices are either like the "shhh" sound of FM static or environmental sounds like that of rain, waterfall, or the ocean's roar—all quite soothing. These devices allow you to adjust the bandwidths to your personal need. Petroff Audio Technologies and the Oregon Hearing Research Center produce CDs with similar sounds that you can use in a bedside CD player.

One woman in your situation set up an aquarium in the bedroom. The gurgling sound from the filtering water quieted her tinnitus and enabled her to sleep.

Q **My main problem with tinnitus is that it interferes with sleep. I can't remember the last time I had a solid night's sleep. Is sleeping medication the answer?**

A Many medications induce sleep, like the tranquilizers Valium and Librium. Most sleep-inducing medicines come with a price, which includes possible drug dependency, fragmented sleep, and daytime drowsiness. Some people also experience rebound insomnia—worse insomnia after using the drug than before using it. However, *some* sleep is better than *no* sleep. It might be helpful to look at your daily practices (foods eaten, medicines taken) and see if you can eliminate any practices that interfere with a good night's sleep.

Many over-the-counter drugs, like decongestants and cold medications, cause drowsiness for some people. But for other people these same drugs act as stimulants. Avoid taking them late in the day if you can. Also avoid alcohol and tobacco. Both cause sleep disturbances. Avoid consuming caffeine after lunch. Some foods, such as bananas, turkey, tuna, milk, whole grains, figs, dates, and nuts, are naturally rich in tryptophan, an amino acid that promotes sleep. You could eat these later in the evening. Other foods, such as bacon, sugar, spinach, tomatoes, potatoes, ham, cheese, and, yes, chocolate, contain tyramine, an amino acid that increases the release of a brain stimulant. Consider avoiding these foods late in the day. Consider also that as we age we are more easily aroused from sleep.

You could also try herbal remedies like valerian root and kava kava. We advise you to talk with a naturopathic physician before "prescribing" these herbs for yourself. A naturopath can help you find the right combination and dosage of herbs.

Zaleplon (brand name: Sonata) is a new sleep medication that was recently approved for use in the United States. What sets this non-benzodiazepine drug apart from other prescription sleep drugs is its short list of negative side effects. In 1999, Canadian researcher Elie et al. tested zaleplon in a 4-week-long, double-blind, placebo-controlled study. Patients who took 10 mg of the drug daily slept longer and better than those who took the placebo. After the drug trial, the zaleplon patients exhibited no evidence of rebound insomnia or withdrawal symptoms. According to the 2000 *PDR Companion Guide*, tinnitus is a side effect of this drug, but for less than 3% of those who take it.

Q In 1994, I became aware of a high-pitched ringing in my left ear. Within a year, the ringing was in both ears. I contacted an ENT, who told me that I would have to learn to live with it since no treatment was available. This was when my depression began and the ringing so overwhelmed me that I could no longer cope. I had a mental breakdown and contemplated suicide. Finally, my family physician diagnosed clinical depression and I was put on Xanax and Paxil. At this point, I began to feel able to cope with both the depression and the tinnitus. Some days are bad, about a 10 on a scale of 1 to 10, and other days are a 5 or even a 1. If I'm having a good day and I stay awake, the tinnitus remains low. If I go to sleep when the tinnitus is low, the tinnitus is bad when I wake up. Why does the tinnitus cycle through high and low periods? And after a period of low tinnitus, why does sleep reinstate the high tinnitus?

A It is very common for tinnitus to cycle through periods of highs and lows and for sleep to reinstate louder tinnitus. We simply do not know why. We are, however, fairly certain that the brain is the culprit. The brain goes through cycles during sleep, cycles that are marked by changes in chemical make up as well as electrical activity. We also know that some areas of the brain are more active during sleep than during wakeful periods. Fortunately, we now have research tools (PET scan, fMRI, and SPECT) that allow us to look at the brain as it functions during the tinnitus experience. Observing neural changes during sleep is just a research grant away.

Resources _____

Balch, J. F., and Balch, P. A. *Prescription for Nutritional Healing,* Avery Publishing, New York, 1997.

Bergstrom, W. H., and Hakanson, D. O. Melatonin: The dark force, *Adv. Pediatr.* 1998; 45:91–106.

Elie, R., Ruther, E., Farr, I., Emilien, G., and Salinas, E. Sleep latency is shortened during 4 weeks of treatment with zaleplon, a novel nonbenzodiazepine hypnotic. Zaleplon Clinical Study Group, *J. Clin. Psychiatry,* Aug. 1999; 60(8):536–44.

Levy, M. Sleep, *Tinnitus Today,* Dec. 1994; 19(4):12–14.

Rosenberg, S. I., Silverstein, H., Rowan, P. T., and Olds, M. J. Effect of melatonin on tinnitus, *Laryngoscope,* Mar. 1998; 108(3):305–10.

42

Sounds of Tinnitus

Q A friend of mine is seriously bothered by low-frequency tinnitus. I've noticed that her tinnitus severely interferes with her ability to understand conversations. Do you have any suggestion as to what might bring her relief?

A The vast majority of tinnitus patients have high-frequency tinnitus. Usually, they describe it as ringing if it is a single tone or hissing if it is a noise. In both cases the tinnitus is high pitched. In a survey of 2838 tinnitus patients, a hum was found in only 6% of the cases. Although this kind of tinnitus is relatively rare, it can often be treated successfully with a low-pitched masking noise. Marpac Corporation makes the tabletop Marsona Sound Conditioner that produces a variety of environmental sounds, including some that are relatively low pitched. The surf and waterfall settings peak at 484 Hz.

Additionally, if your friend has a hearing loss, hearing aids could be a solution. We routinely suggest hearing aids for tinnitus patients who have hearing loss *and* tinnitus below 4000 Hz. The rationale is that all environmental sounds such as speech and music are located below 4000 Hz. For example, no sound goes over the telephone above 3000 Hz. Low-pitched tinnitus is often maskable with hearing aids and the environmental sounds that they bring back in.

Q My tinnitus is a cricket sound. That's the only way to describe it. Is my case unusual? And does the fact that it sounds as it does preclude masking or any other treatment?

A Tinnitus is often described as sounding like crickets. A cricket sound is actually two simultaneous tones fairly close in frequency. For example, when we create a 2000-Hz tone in a laboratory and couple it with a 2040-Hz tone or couple a 4000-Hz tone with a 4060-Hz tone, the tone combinations duplicate most forms of cricket tinnitus. If the patient has hearing loss in the cricket-sound frequency region, hearing aids often provide relief for the cricket tinnitus. If the patient has normal hearing with cricket tinnitus, outside sounds can be introduced to relieve the tinnitus. We have heard from a few people who have actually purchased crickets, put them outside their bedroom windows, and enjoyed very restful cricket-masked sleep because of it.

When 1626 tinnitus patients at the Oregon Hearing Research Center were asked to describe the sound or sounds that most closely resembled their tinnitus, here is what they said, beginning with the most common sound (ringing) and ending with the least common sound (music). Note that many patients chose more than one sound.

Ringing: 924	Whistle: 97
Hissing: 317	Hum: 97
Clear tone: 281	Pulsating: 97
High-tension wire: 230	Ocean roar: 78
Buzzing: 195	Pounding: 18
More than one tone: 150	Clicking: 8
Sizzling: 123	Music: 6
Transformer noise: 116	Other: 207
Crickets or insects: 101	

Q If I hear tinnitus in my head, does that mean it is being generated in my head? Likewise, if I hear it in my ears, does that mean it is being generated in my ears? Also, is a ringing tinnitus caused by one thing and a hissing tinnitus caused by another thing?

A We have looked for a connection between the types of tinnitus sounds and the site of the tinnitus, but no connection was found. This does not mean that there isn't a connection. It just means that we are not yet smart enough to detect it. One conjecture is that tonal tinnitus could involve a restricted number of hair cells or auditory nerve fibers, like striking one or two notes on a piano; and hissing tinnitus could involve a broader range of hair cells or nerve fibers, like striking many notes on a piano simultaneously.

We have also learned that there is no connection between the sound itself (whether it is a ring or hiss or roar) and the cause of the tinnitus (noise exposure or ototoxicity or impacted earwax). Noise exposure can cause all sorts of tinnitus sounds, as can otosclerosis or impacted earwax. It would be so handy if the sound could tell us exactly where or what the problem is. It just doesn't work that way.

Q My tinnitus is the sound of dripping water, and I only hear it at night. I have found that when I put a swimmer's earplug in the affected ear the sound stops. Is the pressure of the earplug in the ear canal stopping the tinnitus?

A One guaranteed way to make tinnitus seem louder is to insert earplugs. Your opposite experience is quite unusual. It might be that you are experiencing what is termed *objective tinnitus*. Objective tinnitus is not a phantom sound experience, but rather a real sound being generated inside the ear. If it is a real sound that you hear, the earplug could be absorbing some of the sound or in some way changing the waveform of the sound. Even if the earplug cuts out just a few decibels, it could be making a very noticeable difference.

Try to locate an audiologist who has an Etymotic Insert Earphone or a similar device. These devices contain small, sensitive measuring microphones with which to listen to the ear. (Such systems are used for special tests that evaluate otoacoustic emissions in the ear.) This could help determine if you have a mechanical problem in your middle ear, such as a perilymphatic leak. If you do, it is possible to have the leak surgically repaired.

Q **Does everyone who has tinnitus have it to the same degree?**

A Everyone does not have tinnitus to the same degree. Not only are there different pitches, but there are different levels of loudness, different locations (bilateral, unilateral, or head), different sites of origin (either peripheral or central), different regularities (constant, fluctuating, and pulsatile), different sounds (like whistles, roaring, and crickets), and different combinations of sounds. An estimated 80% of those who have tinnitus have it to a mild degree and it is not a bother to them. We have observed that patients find pulsatile tinnitus to be more troubling than a steady tone of tinnitus.

One mild form of tinnitus, known as *spontaneous tinnitus*, is usually a high-pitched tone that lasts about 15 seconds and then fades away. Interestingly, if someone with "regular" nonstop tinnitus suddenly gets spontaneous tinnitus, the regular tinnitus disappears, usually for the duration of the spontaneous tinnitus experience. Sometimes the regular tinnitus stays away longer. This phenomenon suggests that there might be some kind of neurological event or condition that is capable of blocking the perception of regular tinnitus.

Tinnitus is subjective in more ways than one. For one thing, only those who have it hear it. For another, only the person who has it can decide how bothersome it is. Interestingly, the loudness of the tinnitus does not correspond directly to the degree of stress that it causes. So, two people with tinnitus of identical pitch and loudness would not necessarily rate their tinnitus as identical in severity. Our thresholds for pain—and noise—are quite individual.

43

Sudden Hearing Loss

Q One day a year ago, I heard a piercing tone in my right ear. By the next day, I was deaf in that ear. The deafness lasted for 2 days, but the high-pitched tone persists to this day. I've noticed that the tinnitus gets louder after I exercise. My hearing has been tested and is normal. Could my multiple sclerosis be the cause of the tinnitus and the 2-day episode of hearing loss?

A Multiple sclerosis (MS) is typified by inflammation and scarring of the protective covering of nerve cells in the brain and spinal cord. This inflammation and scarring ultimately lead to decreased nerve function. It is a rather mysterious disorder itself, and its origins are unknown. MS is associated with many symptoms, including fatigue, memory loss, numbness, tinnitus, and hearing impairment.

The description of your experience sounds more like what is known as sudden hearing loss (SHL), first reported in the medical literature in 1944, though no doubt around for a lot longer. Despite lots of research since that time, the problem of SHL remains a diagnostic and therapeutic puzzle. The vast majority of cases are *idiopathic*, meaning that the cause is unknown.

According to one research study, two-thirds of all SHL patients display spontaneous recovery. Another study conducted in Israel found that 71% of sudden hearing loss patients who also had tinnitus recovered their hearing, but only 39% who did not have tinnitus recovered their hearing. This may be one of the very few situations where the presence of tinnitus has positive implications. All researchers who have studied SHL indicate the importance of seeking medical assistance as early as possible. Most patients who recover their hearing do so in the first week. A study done at Stanford University indicated that only 5% of the patients who waited as long as 3 weeks to seek medical help recovered their hearing and had their tinnitus go away.

Another study conducted in London found that 77 out of 100 patients with sudden hearing loss had tinnitus. Of these 77 SHL/tinnitus patients, 53 had inner ear disorders. Of the 23 SHL patients without tinnitus, only 8 had inner ear disorders. The researcher concluded that not only was SHL associated with tinnitus in most cases, but that the SHL disorder was also found to be primarily due to inner ear problems as opposed to problems in the higher brain centers. Science is narrowing the problem down slowly.

If, speculatively, your sudden hearing loss and tinnitus are both caused by an inner ear disorder, why did your hearing recover, but your tinnitus persist? It is a very interesting question. One reported case of SHL accompanied by vertigo and visual problems actually helped doctors to identify the patient's multiple sclerosis. The patient was treated with steroids and her hearing, balance, and vision problems improved. Here is one other thing to consider. We have heard, anecdotally only, that the artificial sweetener *aspartame* (Nutrasweet) can cause tinnitus and other neurological symptoms that resemble those of multiple sclerosis.

Q **How common is it for tinnitus to be produced by sudden hearing loss?**

A When 873 tinnitus patients at the Oregon Hearing Research Center were surveyed about the cause of their tinnitus, 7 patients (0.8%) indicated sudden hearing loss as the cause.

Q **When I first experienced sudden hearing loss and roaring tinnitus in the right ear, my physician gave me a shot of cortisone. This seemed to be what restored my hearing and stopped the tinnitus. Could an allergy be the source of my tinnitus?**

A Your sudden hearing loss is probably not due to an allergy, but it is difficult to tell. Your physician, however, did exactly the right thing in giving you a shot of cortisone. The condition is often corrected if cortisone is administered within a few days of the onset of the sudden hearing loss. If there is a considerable time delay between the start of sudden hearing loss and the administration of steroid treatments, say 10 days or more, the therapeutic effect of the drug is most often lost. As widely used as this treatment is, there is only anecdotal data to support its use. Researchers still do not know what mechanism allows cortisone or other steroids to reverse sudden hearing loss.

Allergies can cause or exacerbate tinnitus, or so it seems. We have heard from patients who on their own discovered that they were allergic to certain foods or environmental agents, discoveries that ultimately led to varying amounts of tinnitus relief. One patient found he was allergic to wheat and that the elimination of wheat products from his diet completely relieved his severe tinnitus.

Q I have experienced sudden hearing loss—sudden deafness really—and I am devastated by it. I also hear tinnitus in both ears all the time. What can I do?

A Sudden hearing loss (SHL) is such a dramatic event that, in many cases, patients understandably overestimate the degree of the loss. Patients often declare that they have gone deaf in the affected ear when in actuality the hearing loss is at 40 dB. (You would have to have at least a 90-dB hearing loss to be considered deaf.) If you have a hearing loss in the 40- to 50-dB range, the chances are still excellent that your hearing will respond well to hearing aids. Since tinnitus associated with SHL is often relatively low pitched, hearing aids can help relieve the tinnitus too.

Sudden hearing loss can be reversed if treated soon after its onset. See a doctor or audiologist immediately for a complete hearing evaluation. Time is of the essence!

Resources _____

Michel, O., Jahns, T., Joost-Enneking, M., Neugebauer, P., Streppel, M., and Stennert, E. The Stennert antiphlogistic-rheologic infusion schema in treatment of cochleovestibular disorders, *HNO*, Mar 2000; 48(3):182–8.

Ozunlu, A., Mus, N., and Gulhan, M. Multiple sclerosis: a cause of sudden hearing loss, *Audiology*, Jan–Feb 1998; 37(1):52–8.

44

Support Groups

Q There is a tinnitus support group in my city, but I just don't know if it's worth the effort to go to it. Can they really do any good for people with tinnitus? I admit that I often feel depressed about the constant noises.

A Tinnitus clinic director, Robert Sandlin, Ph.D., supported and directed a tinnitus self-help group in San Diego for many years. During that time, he observed the behavior of dozens of people who attended the group meetings. One person in particular, a retired naval officer, caught Sandlin's attention. During his first several meetings, the fellow complained bitterly about his tinnitus and told everyone that nothing could be done. He also complained to others at the meeting that he was receiving very little benefit from attending. Still, he continued to go to the meetings.

The retired officer's attitude changed over several months, Sandlin noticed. Finally, at one meeting, the officer confessed that his negative feeling about interacting with others who had tinnitus was greatly reduced and possibly eliminated. He admitted to the whole group that, as a result of his attendance and interaction with them, he was able to cope much more effectively with his tinnitus. Sandlin reports that this experience was common among those who attended the group and stayed with it over time.

Of course, there is no way to follow the people who attend a self-help group meeting one time and do not return. Maybe the group was not what they needed. Or maybe it *was*. Some people go to tinnitus self-help meetings because they need reassurance that they are not alone, that they are not crazy, and that there are ways to cope with their tinnitus and feel better. They go to find a good local audiologist or doctor who has some savvy about tinnitus treatments, and they feel better when they learn that the American Tinnitus Association is funding research and publishing a magazine to keep patients informed about new tinnitus discoveries. When they learn these things, people are often more able to enjoy their lives despite the tinnitus. Many people stay with their support groups for years because of the friendships they have

213

developed and because they feel good helping other first-timers who show up needing encouragement.

You are fortunate that there is a group nearby for you to attend. Many tinnitus support groups bring in guest speakers—audiologists, biofeedback specialists, medical doctors, nutritionists, and others—who know about treating tinnitus patients. It might be worth the effort to go.

Q Lately my life has been very stressful. (I have a new job and have moved to a new state.) My tinnitus has been louder since the changes started. Do stress and tension have any effect on tinnitus? If so, I don't understand what stress has to do with the ears.

A There is no doubt that stress can exacerbate tinnitus. We have heard this from hundreds of patients and have seen it in research. In one study of 1097 tinnitus patients at the Oregon Hearing Research Center, 49.2% of patients reported that stress exacerbated their tinnitus. If tinnitus increases because of a stressful situation, most often the tinnitus returns to its previous level when the stressful situation is resolved.

Big, stressful life events, such as going through a divorce or losing a loved one, can cause sufficient chemical changes in the body to produce or alter tinnitus and other health problems too. Our immune system function, sexual function, cardiovascular function, and mental function are all affected by stress levels.

We cannot stop stressful things from happening to us, but we can keep our responses to the stressful situations under control. This is where many of us falter. And this is where many people benefit from professional counseling and learning practical coping skills. You might get helpful ideas from a local tinnitus support group. The American Tinnitus Association can tell you if there is one in your area.

45

Surgery

Q I'm totally deaf in my tinnitus ear. Should I have that auditory nerve cut to get rid of the tinnitus? There doesn't seem to be anything to lose.

A First, you need to determine whether you really are totally deaf in that ear. Standard hearing tests measure such a small part of the true range of our hearing—only what we can hear up to 8000 Hz. Newer audiometric equipment can test hearing up to 12,000 Hz.

Second, if you *are* totally deaf, you would qualify for a cochlear implant in that ear, which would give you hearing on that side again, as well as a significant chance of having the tinnitus relieved. If the hearing nerve is cut, a cochlear implant will not work. This technology needs to send its auditory signal through a functioning hearing nerve that connects to the brain.

It is very likely that the original damage to the auditory system occurred in the inner ear. But there is no way to know with certainty that the tinnitus is currently being produced in the inner ear. The perception of the continuous sound that you hear now is more likely being generated in the auditory cortex, the hearing part of the brain.

Some tinnitus patients have had the auditory nerves severed in their deaf ears. About half of these patients experienced increased tinnitus loudness. This unfortunate outcome suggests that these patients had some residual hearing in the so-called deaf ears and that it was enough to bring in some background sound to partially mask the tinnitus. There have been very few cases in which the nerve was sectioned and the tinnitus resolved. In some cases, the tinnitus does stop initially after surgery, but returns in 5 or 6 months.

A serious hearing loss is often mistaken for true deafness. This happens most often when patients have sudden hearing loss of 40 dB or so. They

Also see Chapter 7, The Brain's Involvement in Tinnitus; Chapter 9, Cochlear Implants: Surgical Implants that Restore Hearing; and Chapter 37, Pulsatile Tinnitus.

perceive that they are "totally" deaf because of the sudden difference in their hearing acuity. The opposite happens too. Patients whose hearing has declined gradually adjust to and even compensate for their hearing loss to the point where they deny that they need hearing aids.

Sectioning or cutting the auditory nerve is a very final act, one that should not be done unless all options are considered. And, even then, think again. It is always best to keep your hearing nerve intact.

Q I have heard about a microvascular operation performed in Pittsburgh that relieves tinnitus. Can you provide any information about this procedure?

A Some forms of incapacitating tinnitus can be relieved by a surgery called *microvascular decompression*. This operation for tinnitus was developed and is performed by Peter Jannetta, M. D., at the University of Pittsburgh Medical College (Department of Neurosurgery, 200 Lothrop Street, # B400, Pittsburgh, Pennsylvania 15219, 412-647-6778). The goal of this microvascular surgery is to move small blood vessels that are believed to be impinging on the hearing nerve. The hearing and balance nerves share space with many blood vessels between the skull and the brain. If, for some reason, the blood vessels press on the nerves, balance disorders, hearing loss, and tinnitus theoretically can result.

In several studies around the world, this specialized surgical procedure was performed on tinnitus patients who had severe tinnitus and had been screened with CT and MRI scans to verify the strong likelihood of cochlear nerve compression. One study in England followed nine patients for 5 years after their vascular decompression surgery. They reported that tinnitus was completely abolished in three patients (33%), very significantly improved in three patients (33%), significantly improved in one patient (11%), and unchanged in two patients (22%). Both of the unchanged patients had the surgery repeated, but the tinnitus remained unchanged. According to Jannetta, this surgical procedure is more successful for patients who have had tinnitus less than 2 years.

Another microvascular decompression study was conducted by Drs. Margareta and Aage Møller and J. P. Vasama. To qualify for the procedure, patients had to have severe tinnitus along with sensorineural hearing loss in the affected ear and/or changes in electrical responses from the eighth nerve. As a point of interest, 50% of these patients had tinnitus in only one ear.

The surgeons found vascular compression of the cochlear nerve in each of the 21 patients during the operations, although the surgeons did not know with complete surety beforehand that this would be the case. After the surgeries, two patients (10%) had total tinnitus relief, five (24%) had marked improvement, eight (38%) were slightly improved, four (18%) had no change in their tinnitus, and two patients (10%) reported a worsening of their tinnitus.

Researchers in Korea reported on the progress of 59 patients who had the Jannetta microvascular decompression surgery for their tinnitus. After surgery, 30 patients were either free of tinnitus or had a 75% improvement, 21 reported a 50% to 75% improvement, four reported 25% to 50% improvement, and four had either less than 25% improvement or reported no change.

This is serious surgery. Discuss it thoroughly with your doctor and read everything you can about it before you make a decision.

Q **Recently, I read a newspaper article about facial pain and facial spasms. The article referred to Japanese doctors who had performed surgery to relieve this condition. The article concluded by stating that the procedure could have some application for tinnitus. Do you know how?**

A The operation for facial pain was developed by Dr. Peter Jannetta at the University of Pittsburgh. It had been earlier discovered that the facial pain, or trigeminal neuralgia (also called *tic douloureux*), was caused by a blood vessel pressing on the facial nerve (the fifth cranial nerve). Jannetta perfected this microvascular decompression operation to move the blood vessel away from the nerve. Japanese doctors performed the same decompression surgery on 165 patients who suffered with facial pain, 12 of whom also had tinnitus on the same side as the facial pain. The doctors reasoned that the tinnitus was also due to a vascular compression of the eighth nerve and additionally performed decompression of this nerve in all 12 patients. Ten (83%) of the 12 patients reported that their tinnitus was resolved or markedly improved after the procedure.

Q **My ear problems began 6 years ago when an ear infection did not clear up with antibiotics or the insertion of tubes in the ears. A year ago I saw a new ear specialist, who discovered that I had a growth closing up my ear canal. The physician cleaned out the ear canal and did a skin graft. Once again the tissue is growing in this ear, and the other ear is closed off completely by the same sort of growth. My hearing is down and the tinnitus is worse than ever. What can I do?**

A You have a real and fortunately correctable physiological problem. Contact the physician who did the original ear canal surgery for a reevaluation. If the canal is filling in again, have the growth removed.

It is no wonder that your hearing is down. The growth in your ear canal is occluding, or blocking, sound waves from getting to the inner ear and then to the brain where they are interpreted as sound.

Remember that tinnitus is like a seesaw. When hearing goes down, tinnitus goes up. Our naturally good hearing disguises or drowns out the tinnitus sound. But when that hearing ability drops, tinnitus will seem louder. It really isn't louder. It is just less disguised.

Q My hearing has been greatly reduced. My doctor examined my ears and said I have otosclerosis. How does he know this for sure and does this mean I need surgery?

A The presence or absence of otosclerosis, a disease of the middle ear bones, can be determined by air conduction and bone conduction hearing tests. The middle ear bones, the three smallest bones in the body, are collectively called the ossicles. Individually, they are the malleus, incus, and stapes or, colloquially, the hammer, anvil, and stirrup. There are several varieties of otosclerosis. In one form, the joints of the bones lock up; in another, the footplate in the oval window is immobilzed.

The tests for otosclerosis are rather simple yet elegant, and they are excellent diagnostic measures of this condition. If the bone conduction tests show normal hearing and the air conduction tests show abnormal hearing, then the patient very likely needs to have the middle ear bones replaced to restore hearing.

A stapedectomy is the surgical removal of the diseased middle ear bones. When the bones are removed, prosthetic middle ear bones are implanted. (The prosthesis is actually a straight rod, which is a much more logical configuration of middle ear bones, like the ear bones of a bird.) The surgery is done directly through the ear canal.

Stapedectomies restore hearing to an excellent level in 91% of cases. If tinnitus is the direct result of this disease process, it, too, can resolve after this delicate surgery. Less than 1% of patients report postsurgical dizziness or partial hearing loss. One percent do lose hearing totally in the involved ear as a result of a stapedectomy. And although it rarely happens (0.3% of cases), tinnitus can be made worse by the surgery. If a stapedectomy is not successful and the procedure is repeated, there is a greater incidence of postsurgical vertigo, sensorineural hearing loss, and tinnitus. Clinicians report that it is most common for the tinnitus to be unaffected by this surgery. Laser technology is improving the safety of this surgery and the outcomes all around.

Q Is there anything I can do to keep my otosclerosis from getting worse so that I can avoid surgery?

A In 1991, a study was conducted in Italy to test sodium fluoride for such a purpose. The researchers selected 128 subjects who were relatives of people with otosclerosis. (There obviously is some hereditary component to the disorder.) Half the subjects were given 6 to 16 mg of sodium fluoride daily for 2 years (the size of the dose was age dependant). The other half of the subjects were not given the drug. All were followed and evaluated for 5 years. The researchers drew the conclusion that at the 2-year mark the drug had arrested the disease process of otosclerosis in 60% of the ears. At the 5-year mark, the drug had stopped the disease process for more than 50% of the ears. This interesting study has not been duplicated.

Q Does the stereotaxic laser surgery used to cure some forms of epilepsy actually kill a specific area of the brain? If so, could this same technology be used to kill the part of the brain that perceives tinnitus?

A When scientists are able to conclusively identify which part of the brain is generating tinnitus, we might be looking at laser surgery as a means to a cure. But a great deal of research will need to be done before brain surgery is performed for tinnitus, and several questions have to be answered first. What effect will the removal of the tinnitus-perceiving brain area have on other auditory functions? Once the tinnitus-perceiving area of the brain is removed, will another part of the brain take over the tinnitus function? We suspect that the latter will happen. The brain surgery for epilepsy was heralded as an immense success several years ago. Stereotaxic lasers were used to remove the offending area of the brain that caused the epileptic seizures. Over time, however, other areas of the brain took over this dubious role and the seizures for many have returned. Epilepsy patients still feel that a year or two of relief is a triumph. We know many people with tinnitus who would also consider a year of relief to be a success.

If we really wanted to speculate, we would say that implanted deep brain electrodes are more likely going to give continuous tinnitus relief than the removal of the offending area of the brain. This exciting research is underway.

Resources

Brookes, G. B. Vascular-decompression surgery for severe tinnitus, *Am. J. Otol.*, July 1996; 17(4):569–76.

Colletti, V., and Fiorino, F. G. Effect of sodium fluoride on early stages of otosclerosis., *Am. J. Otol.*, May 1991; 12(3):195–8.

Ko, Y., and Park, C. W. Microvascular decompression for tinnitus, *Stereotact. Funct. Neurosurg.*, 1997; 68(1–4, Pt 1):266–9.

McGee, T. M., Diaz-Ordaz, E. A., and Kartush, J. M., The role of KTP laser in revision stapedectomy, *Otolaryngol. Head Neck Surg.*, Nov. 1993; 109(5):839–43.

Møller, M. B., Møller, A. R., Jannetta, P. J., and Jho, H. D. Vascular decompression surgery for severe tinnitus: Selection criteria and results, *Laryngoscope*, Apr. 1993; 103(4, Pt 1):421–7.

Vasama, J. P., Møller, M. B., and Møller A. R. Microvascular decompression of the cochlear nerve in patients with severe tinnitus. Preoperative findings and operative outcome in 22 patients, *Neurol. Res.*, Apr. 1998; 20(3):242–8.

46

Tinnitus Instruments: Devices for Tinnitus Control

How the Tinnitus Instrument Was Invented

In 1955, a dentist purchased a then new high-speed dental drill. As an unfortunate consequence of using that drill in his profession, he developed bilateral tinnitus and significant high-frequency hearing loss. When his hearing and tinnitus were measured and tested, it was clear that he was a good candidate for hearing aids. His hearing loss, although primarily in the high frequencies, extended downward to 1500 Hz. His tinnitus was measured at 2800 Hz. Since environmental sounds are primarily below 4000 Hz and exactly what hearing aids bring in, it seemed likely that hearing aids would effectively cover his tinnitus. After he was fitted with two hearing aids, he reported that he was able to hear quite a bit better. He could hear bird song and enjoy music. But his renewed hearing had not touched his tinnitus. He returned regularly to the clinic to see if we could figure out other ways to help him.

During one of his regular visits, another patient marched into the clinic wearing her tinnitus maskers that she had somehow managed to insert in her ears backward so that the masking sound was spewing into the air. After her maskers were fitted in her ears properly and she left, the dentist asked if he could borrow one of the maskers overnight. (We said yes.) The next day he returned and announced that the tinnitus on one side was completely gone. He had tied his hearing aid and the masker together with a rubber band. He then affixed a Y-shaped tube to the two devices to direct the signal from each device into the one ear. Each device had independent volume controls. He experimented and discovered that the hearing aid needed to be adjusted first. By using this jury-rigged combination of hearing aid and masker, he found relief from his tinnitus for the first time. And the tinnitus instrument was born.

220

Years after this discovery, we retested the dentist's tinnitus pitch and discovered that it was 5600 Hz, not 2800 Hz as we had previously recorded. Years earlier, we did not know to test for octave confusion, or even know that there was such a thing. We finally understood why his hearing aids, which only brought in sounds up to 4000 Hz, did not relieve his tinnitus at 5600 Hz.

Many years later, we surveyed 592 tinnitus patients who were successfully using masking to relieve their tinnitus. We found that 16% were using hearing aids alone, 21% were using tinnitus maskers alone, and 63% were using tinnitus instruments. The tinnitus instrument had become the mainstay of the masking program, all due to that overnight invention by our dentist patient.

Q **I have had ear surgery whereby my ear canal was enlarged and grommets (or tubes) were inserted through both eardrums. I now have severe tinnitus as a result. So far, I've found that bilateral hearing aids are no help with my 7330-Hz tinnitus. I do get some relief from a Walkman™ and have now been fitted with bilateral tinnitus instruments by Starkey. Why didn't the hearing aids give me tinnitus relief?**

A At 7330 Hz, your tinnitus sits well above the sounds that most hearing aids can amplify. They are only designed to amplify up to 4000 Hz. Besides, there are very few 7330-Hz sounds in our everyday environment *to* amplify. (The highest note on an extended grand piano is just a little above 4000 Hz.) Masking is usually effective when the external sound that you introduce to the ear is around the same pitch as the internal tinnitus that you hear.

The hearing aids that are built into the Starkey tinnitus instruments are high-frequency-emphasis aids. This configuration of sound therapy (high-frequency-emphasis hearing aid with a high-frequency broadband masker) can successfully quiet high-frequency tinnitus.

Surgery on the ear canal or eardrum often causes a stenosis (or shrinking) of the canal. If you have custom earplugs made and then have surgery, bear in mind that the earplugs might no longer fit.

Q **Ever since I started wearing a hearing aid in my right ear, I hear tinnitus in my left ear. Why is that?**

A Your question suggests that you have had tinnitus in both ears all along, but that the right ear tinnitus was dominant. As a theory, when you got the hearing aid for the right ear, it produced enough masking on that side to leave you primarily aware of the tinnitus in the left ear. In many instances, when we put a tinnitus masker in the ear that a patient thought was the only tinnitus ear, the patient says, "You knocked the tinnitus over to my other ear!" If, in your case, there is a hearing loss in the left ear, try a hearing aid to see if it relieves the tinnitus. If the hearing aid does not relieve the tinnitus, try a tinnitus instrument, a combination unit that includes both a hearing aid and a masker.

Starkey Laboratories manufactures the high-frequency-emphasis tinnitus instruments that are in use today. (In fact, they were the first company to manufacture them.) General Hearing Instruments, makers of the Tranquil™ in-the-ear tinnitus sound generator, is completing its development of a new multichannel digital and programmable tinnitus instrument called the Jazz Harmony. The device will be able to amplify frequencies up to 8,000 Hz, as well as introduce a broadband frequency sound (for either masking or TRT use) from 200 to approximately 8000 Hz. The device will function as an adjustable masker/sound generator only, a hearing aid only, or a combination of the two. Tinnitus instrumentation is coming of age.

47

Tinnitus Miscellany

Q What is the correct way to pronounce the word *tinnitus*? My wife insists it is one way and I am certain I heard you say it the other way.

A In the United States, both pronunciations are correct. Amazingly, the pronunciation of the word *tinnitus* itself has been the center of mild dissension. The American Tinnitus Association places the accent over the second syllable and pronounces the second "i" like *eye* (tin *night* us). When the organization was first founded in 1972, they chose this pronunciation because this was how it was (and still is) listed in Dorland's Medical Dictionary. "Tin *night* us" is also the preferred pronunciation in the Oxford English Dictionary. Others place the accent on the first syllable, and pronounce all the vowels in the word like the "i" in "if" (*tin* i tis). This pronunciation is used in many European countries, though not all. In Germany, they say "tin i *toos*."

For some reason, it is a divisive issue. There are those who think that we need a single pronunciation in order to unite and inform the world about the urgency of the problem. Others feel that when research uncovers the cure it won't matter how the word is pronounced.

Q Is it true that many famous people have been afflicted with tinnitus?

A Yes, tinnitus knows no class dictinctions or boundaries in time. Here is a list of some notable historical figures who had tinnitus.

- Sappho, poetess from the sixth century B.C., wrote about her tinnitus in her poems.
- Aristotle wrote in *Problemata Physica* in the third century B.C., "Why is it that buzzing in the ears ceases if one makes a sound? Is it because a greater sound drives out the less?" (This could well be the first mention of tinnitus masking.)
- Martin Luther, in the 1500s, wrote "*Ist das du Teufel?*" ("Is that you devil?" as he described the sounds in his head), whereupon he threw

an inkwell at the wall of his study. The ink spots remain on the wall to this day.

- Michelangelo, in the 1500s, wrote "Bees buzz in one ear while the squeaky hinge is in the other."
- Francis Bacon, in the early 1600s, wrote about a violent sound he had heard with a Ménière's attack. By his description, it felt like something rupturing and sounded like "someone playing a lyre in my ears."
- Jean Jacques Rousseau, in the mid-1700s, wrote in his book *Confessions* about a "deep hollow buzzing, a murmur clearer than running water, a high-pitched ringing and a hammering." (This was a very complex case.)
- Francisco de Goya, in the early 1800s, talked about the incessant roaring in his head (he eventually became totally deaf) and depicted tinnitus anguish in his paintings.
- Beethoven, in the early 1800s, wrote "My ears continue to buzz and hum."
- Smetana, in the 1800s, reproduced the sound of his tinnitus as a piercing high-pitched tone in his symphony "Ma Vlast" (my life).
- Joseph Toynbee, the "father of otology," in the mid-1800s, tried to treat his own tinnitus by inhaling vapors through the eustachian tubes as suggested by the writings of Dr. Antoine Saissy. Saissy did not say which vapors to inhale. Toynbee unfortunately used chloroform and died as a result of the experiment.
- Vincent van Gogh, in the late 1800s, included references in his letters to his symptoms of episodic vertigo, imbalance, hearing symptoms, and ear noises.

Other more contemporary and notable people with tinnitus include Barbra Streisand, Steve Martin, Tony Randall, Jerry Stiller, Rosalynn Carter, William Shatner, Leonard Nimoy, and Pete Townsend.

Q **My husband has had a very bad case of tinnitus for over a year now. Since the tinnitus began, he has been totally uninterested in any physical relationship with me. My question is this: Can tinnitus really affect a person's libido?**

A Many patients, males and females alike, report that their tinnitus has driven all sexual interest out of them. So, yes, it is reasonable to assume that the problem with your husband is due to his tinnitus.

Although not specific to tinnitus, a study was recently conducted in Italy to measure sexual dysfunction in patients with multiple sclerosis (MS) and other chronic conditions. Of 97 patients with chronic conditions, 39.2% reported some sexual dysfunction versus 12.7% of the healthy control group and 73.1% of the MS patients. More males than females reported symptoms of sexual dysfunction, but both genders reported diminished libido. The researchers suggested that an actual physical condition might play a part in sexual dysfunction, but that the accompanying depression and anxiety were the more likely culprits.

We strongly urge you to initiate relief treatment for your husband. Once his tinnitus is relieved, it is very likely that he will become himself again.

Q **I get upset when I read newspaper reports about tinnitus patients and their complaints, especially their thoughts about suicide. Can you or the American Tinnitus Association do anything about these public media releases?**

A Media writers often attract the readers' attention with shocking opening lines or headlines. Since we live in a land of free speech, there is really nothing ATA or anyone can do to prevent such reports. Fortunately, most of the media articles on tinnitus outline useful treatments or focus on new research projects.

A study was done in England to determine what effect publicity about tinnitus had on tinnitus patients. Researchers questioned 316 tinnitus patients and found 279 (88%) who had recently read about tinnitus in a newspaper. Of these 279, 148 (55%) considered the information helpful, 88 (29%) found the information upsetting or worrisome, and 43 (16%) felt that the reports had both effects.

Patients who considered the information helpful appreciated reading that others had the same problem; that there were relief procedures, a support network, and continuing research; and that counseling was available on coping techniques and management. Those who became upset from the stories were disturbed by the inference that tinnitus was "all in the mind" and that there are no cures. They also became upset to read that tinnitus might indicate a very serious health problem and that it can become worse as people get older. Elderly patients were less upset than were younger patients by the stories in the paper. Patients who were not a part of England's national health plan were more inclined to view the information favorably.

Resources

Arenberg, I. K., Countryman, L. L., Bernstein, L. H., and Shambaugh, G. E. Vincent's violent vertigo, an analysis of the original diagnosis of Meniere's disease, *Acta Otolaryngol. Suppl.* (Stockh), 1991; 485:84–103.

Baskill, J. L., Bradley, P. J. M., Coles, R. R. A., Graham, R. L., Grimes, S., Handscomb, L., Hazell, J. W. P., and Sheldrake, J. B. Effects of publicity on tinnitus, *Proceedings of the Sixth Tinnitus Seminar,* Hazell, J., ed., Tinnitus and Hyperacusis Centre, London, 1999.

Feldmann, H. Tinnitus in the arts and sciences, *Proceedings of the Third International Tinnitus Seminar,* Harsch Verlag, Karlsruhe, Germany, 1987.

Zorzon, M., Zivadinov, R., Bosco, A., Bragadin, L. M., Moretti, R., Bonfigli, L., Morassi, P., Iona, L. G., and Cazzato, G. Sexual dysfunction in multiple sclerosis: A case-control study. I. Frequency and comparison of groups. *Mult. Scler.,* Dec. 1999; 5(6):418–27.

48

Tinnitus Testing

Rating Tinnitus Severity

Q My long-time tinnitus did not bother me until last January when I awoke with a loud hissing sound in the right ear. I have now seen five health-care professionals, one of whom said the infamous "Go home and learn to live with it." (When are they going to learn to not say that?) At work I wear a hearing aid in my right ear, but when I'm home I wear a masker in my right ear. Both devices give me some relief, each in its own environment. I take Zoloft for depression plus Xanax and some herbs at bedtime to help with sleeping. I want to understand my tinnitus better and how it compares to the tinnitus of others. On a scale of 0 to 10, how do most patients rate the loudness of their tinnitus? (Mine is an 8.)

A The average loudness rating of patients attending the Tinnitus Clinic at Oregon Health Sciences University is slightly over 7, on a scale of 0 to 10. Your rating of 8 is not unusual. It is interesting to note that the actual loudness of a person's tinnitus does not correspond directly to his or her severity rating of it.

We once measured the loudness of a patient's tinnitus and found it to be 25 dB above hearing threshold. This was the loudest tinnitus we had ever measured and yet, on the 0 to 10 loudness scale, he had rated it a 4! We asked him how he was able to rate his tinnitus so low despite it actually being so loud. He answered that originally he would have rated his tinnitus as a 20 on that 0 to 10 scale, but that he started helping other people and soon discovered there were people less fortunate than he.

Q Will my tinnitus get worse as I get older?

A One study compared a group of 353 elderly tinnitus patients with a group of 726 younger tinnitus patients. The senior group (SG) was 65 to 90

How Much Does Your Tinnitus Bother You?

Tinnitus can disrupt your daily living. It can interrupt sleep and work and make concentration difficult. If you have tinnitus, you already know this. But family members, physicians, and friends do not always understand how debilitating tinnitus can be.

In an attempt to quantify the daily experience of tinnitus, researchers at the Oregon Hearing Research Center established the Oregon Tinnitus Data Registry in 1982 to collect information from patients about their day-to-day experience with tinnitus.

The following questions and responses are a sample of those found in the registry. If you see yourself in here, you'll see that you are not alone.

N refers to the number of responses received.

1. Does your tinnitus interfere with your sleep?

	N	%
No	467	28.8
Sometimes	720	44.5
Often	398	24.6
Other answer	33	2.0
TOTAL	1618	100%*

2. Does your tinnitus make you feel irritable or nervous?

	N	%
No	291	18.2
Sometimes	685	42.7
Often	608	38.0
Other answer	18	1.2
TOTAL	1602	100%*

3. Does your tinnitus make you feel tired or ill?

	N	%
No	726	46.5
Sometimes	435	27.9
Often	384	24.7
Other answer	15	1.0
TOTAL	1560	100%*

4. Do you have difficulty relaxing due to your tinnitus?

	N	%
No	290	18.0
Sometimes	558	34.7
Often	730	45.4
Other answer	29	1.8
TOTAL	1607	100%*

5. Has tinnitus made it uncomfortable for you to be in a quiet environment?

	N	%
No	409	25.6
Sometimes	378	23.7
Often	710	44.5
Yes, no further info	98	6.1
TOTAL	1595	100%*

6. Do you have difficulty concentrating because of your tinnitus?

	N	%
No	345	21.5
Sometimes	530	33.0
Often	614	38.2
Yes, no further info	118	7.3
TOTAL	1607	100%

(continued)

How Much Does Your Tinnitus Bother You?, Continued

7. Did you become aware of your tinnitus suddenly or more gradually?

	N	%
Gradually (more than 1 month)	811	50.9
Rapidly (more than 1 week, less than or equal to 1 month)	115	7.2
Suddenly (less than or equal to 1 week)	619	38.8
Unsure	41	2.6
Other	8	0.5
TOTAL	1594	100%

8. Where does your tinnitus appear to be located?

	N	%
Left ear or side	206	12.6
Right ear or side	160	9.8
Both ears	918	56.1
Head	90	5.5
Head + 1 or both ears	160	9.8
Other	102	6.2
TOTAL	1636	100%

9. Does your tinnitus appear to be one sound or more than one sound?

	N	%
1 sound	868	53.3
2 sounds	428	26.3
3 sounds	154	9.5
More than 3 sounds	94	5.8
Unsure	74	4.5
Other answer	9	0.5
TOTAL	1627	100%*

10. Has the location of your tinnitus changed since it started?

	N	%
No change	1373	85.0
Started one side, now both	176	10.9
Now different location	23	1.4
Other answers	66	2.7
TOTAL	1615	100%

11. Loudness match of tinnitus (The sound introduced for the loudness match was at the tinnitus pitch.) LM, dB SL = loudness match in decibels at sensation level of hearing LM, dBSL.

	N	%
0–3	572	40.2
4–6	408	28.7
7–9	212	14.9
10–12	99	7.0
13–15	64	4.5
16–18	30	2.1
19 or more	37	2.6
TOTAL	1422	100%

12. On a scale of 0–10, how would you rate the loudness of your tinnitus?

	N	%
0.0–2.0	20	1.8
2.1–4.0	151	13.8
4.1–6.0	328	30.0
6.1–8.0	377	34.5
8.1–10.0	209	19.1
Too variable to code	9	0.8
TOTAL	1094	100%

*Individual percentages rounded to nearest 0.1%; total percentage rounded to 100%.

years old with an average age of 70. The younger comparison group (CG) was 16 to 50 years old with an average age of 40. These two groups were compared on the basis of the tinnitus pitch, tinnitus loudness, minimum masking level, type of tinnitus (tone or noise), amount of residual inhibition, and subjective severity that they experienced.

Pitch of the tinnitus   SG = 4000 Hz at 4 dB SL   CG = 7000 Hz at 5 dB SL

Minimum masking level   SG = 7.0 dB SL   CG = 10.9 dB SL

Type of tinnitus	Tonal	Noise	Both
SG	72%	19%	9%
CG	86%	5%	9%

Displayed some form of residual inhibition   SG = 92%   CG = 86%

Average duration of residual inhibition after 60 seconds of masking

SG = 156 seconds   CG = 96 seconds

Major problem	Hearing	Tinnitus	Both
SG	12%	59%	33%
CG	6%	69%	25%

Severity index (0 to 36 on a subjective scale)   SG = 18.9   CG = 22.3

Based on these data, the fact (and act) of growing older does not suggest that your tinnitus will become worse. Actually, in some important areas, the seniors' scores were better than the younger group's scores. For example, the average tinnitus pitch of 4000 Hz for the senior group is a more easily tolerated sound compared to the average pitch of 7000 Hz for the younger group. A minimum masking level of 7 dB SL compared to 10.9 dB SL favors the senior group. A greater percentage of the younger subjects have tonal tinnitus, which is a more difficult tinnitus to manage. We must note that this was a cross-sectional study, not a longitudinal study. The older tinnitus patients were not followed from when they were young, and the younger patients are not being followed to see how their tinnitus fares in the future.

Auditory Brainstem Response (ABR), Otoacoustic Emissions (OAE), and High-Frequency Audiometry (HFA)

Q **After having tinnitus for 40 years, I recently went for a hearing test. The technicians wanted to do an ABR test, but I thought it was going to be too loud, so I declined. I didn't want it to worsen my tinnitus. Now I'm wondering if it would have made my tinnitus worse and what they wanted to test for. What does the ABR sound like?**

A A number of patients have complained that ABR tests exacerbated their tinnitus. For most, the exacerbation is temporary, but it is not unusual for the recoveries to take 3 months or more. In a few cases, the exacerbation was permanent. You might have done yourself a favor by following your instincts.

The ABR test (auditory brainstem response) is used to determine if a patient has a tumor, an acoustic neuroma, on the eighth nerve. This test is usually ordered when the tinnitus is one-sided and with no known cause. An ABR test measures hearing in such a way that it can determine if there is a cochlear lesion or a retrocochlear lesion (one that is located between the cochlea and the brain).

In the course of ABR testing, an electrode is placed on the patient's scalp to record the brain's electrical response after a series of clicks and tones is made. These clicks and tones can be quite loud. Knowing this, many doctors still prefer doing the ABR, probably because it can be done in the office quickly. If the ABR test result is positive, an MRI (magnetic resonance imaging) test is usually ordered to give the doctor a better look.

An MRI test is an acceptable option to an ABR test. MRI is the more sensitive of the two tests and can detect an acoustic neuroma as small as 2 mm in diameter. Like the ABR, MRI testing is quite loud. However, you *can* wear earplugs during an MRI test, whereas you cannot wear earplugs during an ABR test.

Before you submit to any test that puts noise in your ears, ask to have your loudness discomfort level (LDL) tested, and then find out the decibel level of the test that your doctor wants you to have. If it is above your sound sensitivity threshold, ask for an alternative test.

Q My audiologist wants to do a variety of hearing tests, including one for otoacoustic emissions and another using HFA. What are they and do I really need them?

A Our ears actually emit their own very quiet sounds, called *spontaneous otoacoustic emissions*. When outside sound is introduced to the ears, they emit a different sound, called *evoked otoacoustic emissions*. Otoacoustic emissions (OAE) testing helps audiologists to see the status of the outer hair cells and the overall functioning of the cochlea.

HFA (high-frequency audiometry) is a way of evaluating the whole auditory system—tinnitus, tinnitus octave confusion, and hearing loss—all the way up to 20,000 Hz. Most audiometric equipment can measure hearing (and tinnitus) up to 8000 Hz, and some can measure up to 12,000 Hz. HFA equipment will give the audiologist as complete a look as possible at your hearing and tinnitus profile.

Pitch and Loudness Matching

Q Can I prove that my tinnitus is as loud as I hear it? I am involved in a Worker's Compensation lawsuit and I need some way to prove that my tinnitus exists.

A The Tinnitus Reliability Test was developed at the Oregon Hearing Research Center to establish a reliable way of measuring the loudness of a patient's tinnitus. In the test, a patient is asked to identify the volume of his or her tinnitus from a range of external pure tone sounds presented. Then, over the course of an hour, the patient is asked six to eight more times to reselect an external tone that is at the *loudness level* of the tinnitus. In further testing, we found that it was not possible for people without tinnitus to repeatedly match a volume without an internal standard of tinnitus in their heads to measure it against. Non-tinnitus test subjects, even those musically trained, could not come up with it. We believe that if patients can repeatedly choose a volume within 3 dB of their established loudness then the test verifies the tinnitus volume unequivocally.

This special tinnitus loudness testing has been accepted as evidence in court to establish the authenticity of tinnitus. If after six or eight tries the sound levels did not vary by more than 3 dB, the court accepted the test as proof that the tinnitus was real. (By the way, the first "tinnitus malingerer" that we caught with the loudness matching technique was a doctor. He thought he knew so much about tinnitus that he could fool anyone.)

To find the pitch, we introduce two separate tones, for example, 1000 and 2000 Hz, to the patient's non- or lesser-tinnitus ear. The patient is then asked to select the tone that is closer to the tinnitus. (All tones are adjusted to match the loudness of the tinnitus first established in the Tinnitus Reliability Test and are then presented in the two-alternative manner.) If 2000 Hz is chosen, we offer that tone again plus 3000 Hz and ask the patient to choose once more. If 3000 Hz is chosen, then that tone and 4000 Hz are offered. If 3000 Hz is reselected at this point, it could be that the tinnitus is around the 3000-Hz range. When a frequency is reselected, patients should be offered another forced choice, this time between the selected frequency and one octave above it, in this case 3000 and 6000 Hz. *Octave confusion* is a fairly common occurrence. (See Figure 48.1 on page 232.) Patients are octave confused about their tinnitus 60% of the time. When given the choice, they usually identify the higher octave tone as the closer match.

We noted that a reliable matching is possible even if the tinnitus fluctuates, since it rarely fluctuates in the span of a testing hour. The loudness matching is the more accurate objectifying test.

Tinnitus severity is a highly individual perception. What is tolerable to one person can be unbearable to another. Tinnitus matching is evidence that people have tinnitus, but it does not indicate how severe it is, if it is permanent, or if it can be relieved.

Q **I have heard about converting tinnitus into a chord. What does this mean and is it something I could try?**

A A long time ago, we tried to convert tinnitus into a chord. It began with a patient whose tinnitus was very easily masked. In fact, she needed to only barely hear the masking sound in order for it to completely cover her tinnitus. While the masking sound was present, however, she complained about

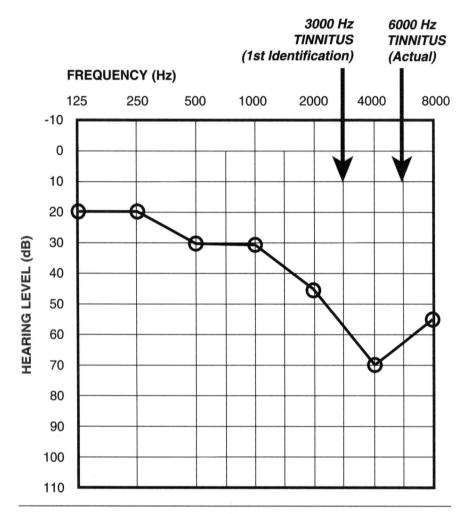

FIGURE 48.1 *Audiogram of Octave Confusion.*

it. She definitely did not like the sound and preferred her tinnitus. This came as a great surprised to us. When we asked her why, she replied, "Because your masking sound is not as melodious as my tinnitus."

We began to think about how tinnitus could be melodious and came up with a theory: She was hearing not one but two tones separated by an octave to produce a chord. When we let her hear two tones an octave apart, the result was an exact match to her tinnitus. We decided to try to convert other people's tinnitus into chords by adding the missing tone, either one octave above or below their tinnitus. Of the nine patients who were offered the "missing" tone, eight immediately rejected the resulting chord, saying that it

Another Tinnitus Malingerer

This is a typical story (though not a typical circumstance) of a tinnitus malingerer, and he was not hard to spot. His inablity to match his own tinnitus was the giveaway clue.

Several years ago, we received a call from the warden of Steilcum Prison, a federal penitentiary on McNeil Island off the coast of Seattle. The warden asked if we would go there to meet and possibly treat a prisoner who claimed to have tinnitus. The prisoner was requesting special privileges, including a private cell, because of his tinnitus. We agreed and went to Steilcum Prison to meet the prisoner.

And meet him we did. "What is that thing?" he asked rudely, referring to the tinnitus sensitizer. "How many other people have you tested? I know I have loud ringing in my ears. Why do you have to test it?" We told him that we had to determine the pitch, loudness, and maskability of his tinnitus so that we could better help him. He let us proceed.

We had him listen to a noise first and then a tone and asked him which of the two sounds was most like his tinnitus. He said it was like both sounds. When we made him choose, he chose the tone. Next, we introduced a 1000-Hz tone that he was able to hear at 15 dB. (He had very good hearing.) We gradually increased the tone until it reached 85 dB. This, he said, was the loudness of his tinnitus. We did the same with the 2000-Hz tone and he gave a similar high-decibel answer. Since no one has ever indicated tinnitus at 70 dB above hearing threshold (25 dB at the most), we knew something was wrong.

We had him listen to the 1000-Hz and then the 2000-Hz tones and asked him which tone was most like his tinnitus. He said the second one was most like his tinnitus. Then we presented the two tones to him again, but this time with the 2000-Hz tone first and the 1000-Hz tone second. Again he chose the second one. Clearly, he was pretending, but we continued the test. In every case, his matches were excessive and irregular. Finally, he selected 4000 Hz as the pitch of his tinnitus and we started a series of loudness measures. His first choice was 40 dB, then 60 dB, then 45 dB, 65 dB, 30 dB, and 10 dB. He appeared to be basing his answers on the speed with which we increased the sound levels on the tinnitus testing equipment. We vary it to catch people who do just what this fellow did. Finally, we asked him when he felt his tinnitus was worse. He replied, "When I smoke marijuana." (The warden had left us alone for the testing.)

This "patient" might actually have tinnitus, but only when he smokes marijuana—a pastime he said he had no intention of giving up. Needless to say, we did not recommend that he be given special quarters. But we did tell him that marijuana is not recommended for tinnitus patients.

---

was worse than their tinnitus and not nearly as good as ordinary masking. The one patient who thought that the chord arrangement was better had tinnitus at the relatively low pitch of 2000 Hz.

Q My tinnitus is excessively loud, which in and of itself is a harsh problem. In addition, the tinnitus prevents me from hearing. I notice it most during conversations. I have normal hearing according to a recent hearing test. Is there any way to improve my ability to hear over the tinnitus?

A Many tinnitus patients indicate that their tinnitus interferes with their ability to understand speech. In actuality, most tinnitus does not interfere with speech signals. Most speech signals are located between roughly 200 and 4000 Hz, whereas tinnitus signals are usually between 7000 and 12,000 Hz. These are two very different signals. Now, although we can hear many different signals simultaneously, we can only *attend* to one sound at a time. When your attention is on tinnitus, you cannot easily attend to other sound, such as speech, at the same time.

To demonstrate the nature of our attentive ability, try this experiment. Count backward by 3's starting with the number 60. When you are done, consider this question: While your attention was on the counting task, did you hear your tinnitus? It is likely that you didn't. We cannot fully attend to two things simultaneously. In the future, when you want to pay attention to someone who is speaking, shift your attention to that speaker. It will undoubtedly take practice to shift your attention away from your tinnitus, but keep at it. The interference that you perceive can be greatly diminished.

Interestingly, tinnitus is not loud. When the loudness of tinnitus is measured, it is, on average, 4.4 dB SL. (The SL stands for the *sensation level* above the hearing threshold of that sound.) Tinnitus is perceived as being loud probably because it is very distinctive. It is usually all alone somewhere in the 7000- to 12,000-Hz region where there are no other sounds to interfere with it.

Q Members of our self-help group have made many comments about the pitch and loudness of tinnitus. I was told that my tinnitus has a loudness level of 70 dB. As interesting as it is to know, what real value is there in knowing it?

A When an audiologist gets accurate, descriptive information about a patient's tinnitus, the audiologist is given the best chance of selecting a workable treatment for the patient. For example, if a tinnitus patient has a hearing loss, and most do, the audiologist needs to know if the tinnitus pitch is low enough to be serviced with hearing aids. In the case of bilateral (two-eared) tinnitus, the audiologist also wants to know if the pitches in the ears are equal to or different from one another. If the pitches are different, then each ear might require different instrumentation to treat. The volume of a patient's bilateral tinnitus is commonly different from one ear to the other. The pitch, however, is usually the same. Patients at the Oregon Hearing Research Center's tinnitus clinic contributed to the following statistics: The average tinnitus loudness was 7 dB above hearing threshold, and the average tonal tinnitus pitch was at 7000 Hz.

Pitch matching is hard to do, even in the best circumstances, even when an experienced clinician tests a musically trained patient who has good hearing. A patient's hearing loss can and often does interfere with his or her ability to hear the external matching tones. A majority of tinnitus patients have a high-pitched tinnitus that necessitates the use of high-frequency testing apparatus. This is another hindrance to the accuracy of the pitch-matching tests, because this kind of high-frequency testing equipment is not commonly available. The testing equipment that *is* used in most cases lacks the frequency range needed to accurately do the job.

Audiologists can use this guide to hone in on their patients' tinnitus pitch: Introduce low-frequency tones and slowly move to high-frequency tones. Chart the perceived loudness of each tone above hearing threshold. The closer you get to the actual pitch of the patient's tinnitus, the quieter the tone will seem to the patient. Remember that 7 dB is the average tinnitus loudness and aim for it.

If a patient identifies 3000 Hz as the tinnitus pitch, but hears the 3000-Hz tone at 20 dB, test some higher frequencies. At 4000 Hz, the patient might match the tone's loudness at 11 dB. At 6000 Hz, the patient might identify that tone as a true match, even better than the first match at 3000. At 6000 Hz, the loudness level of the tinnitus will probably be around 7 dB. (See Figure 48.2.)

It is possible that you have a rather severe hearing loss, perhaps 60 dB at the pitch of your tinnitus. This would make your tinnitus loudness match at 10 dB SL. Tinnitus is a very quiet tone with a very big impact.

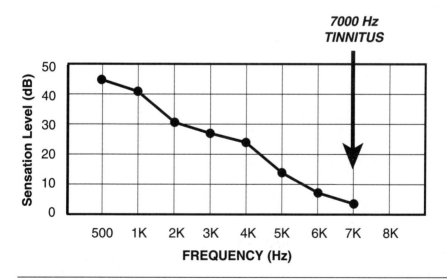

FIGURE 48.2 *Diminishing tinnitus loudness match as a means of identifying tinnitus pitch.*

Resources

Henry, J., Meikle, M. B., and Gilbert, A. Audiometric correlates of tinnitus pitch: Insights from the Tinnitus Data Registry, *Proceedings of the Sixth International Tinnitus Seminar*, Hazell, J., ed., Tinnitus and Hyperacusis Centre, London, 1999.

Meikle, M. B., Johnson, R. M., Griest, S. E., Press, L. S., and Charnell, M. G. Oregon Tinnitus Data Archive #95-01, www.ohsu.edu/ohrc-otda/, 1995.

49

TMJD: Temporomandibular Joint Dysfunction

Q My tinnitus gets much louder when I yawn or grimace. Then sometimes it disappears for a day or two only to return when I yawn or grimace again. No one in my support group has had this experience or even heard of it. Is mine a special form of tinnitus?

A Your tinnitus might be related to a dysfunction of the temporo-mandibular joint (TMJ), the ball and socket joint that allows the mouth to open and close. The upper socket of the joint, called the *fossa,* is part of the temporal bone. (The temporal bone houses the inner ear.) The lower ball, called the *condyle,* fits into the socket and is cushioned by a disk that keeps the ball and socket from rubbing together.

In one study of TMJ patients, 12% had severe tinnitus and 21% had mild or fluctuating tinnitus. When oral appliances, like removable bite plates, were prescribed for these patients, the mild or fluctuating tinnitus disappeared or was reduced by half for all 21%. The severe tinnitus was not changed with the addition of the appliance.

Q My doctor thinks that my headaches and tinnitus are the result of a problem with my temporomandibular jaw joint. If I focus on healing my TMJ, will the tinnitus go away?

A According to Ira Klemons, D.D.S., president of the American Board of Head, Neck, and Facial Pain, the condition of TMJ (or TMJD, temporo-mandibular joint dysfunction) is a dysfunction of the ligaments, muscles, and joints in the neck and head. Tinnitus is an associated symptom of TMJD for nearly half of Klemons's patients. Other studies show similar percentages; usually, between 33% and 50% of TMJD patients also report the presence of tinnitus.

Researchers Wright and Bifano might have identified a way to predict which tinnitus patients will respond to TMJD therapy. In their 1997 study, 40 TMJD patients, whose tinnitus was self-rated as either moderate or severe, were selected to receive TMJD therapy. After treatment, 21 out of the 40 reported that their tinnitus was totally resolved, 12 reported significant improvement, seven reported that their tinnitus was unchanged, and none reported a worsening of tinnitus. These data led the researchers to identify the following TMJD patient profile that was significantly associated with tinnitus improvement:

- The patient is younger in age (although they did not say how young).
- The tinnitus is moderate, not severe.
- The tinnitus began at the same time as the other TMJD symptoms began.
- The tinnitus is related to stress.
- The tinnitus cause is unrelated to loud noise.
- The tinnitus is brought on or intensified by 1 minute of voluntary clenching of the back teeth.

Klemons also points out that patients whose only symptom is tinnitus will probably not find tinnitus relief with TMJD treatment.

You can contact the TMJ & Stress Center (See Appendix I) for a referral to a local dentist who treats TMJ disorders.

Q How can a dysfunction of the temporomandibular joint produce tinnitus? Does the treatment of this dysfunction relieve tinnitus?

A Many researchers have looked at the connection between TMJ dysfunction and tinnitus. The claims and results from the studies are mixed, but it is clear that jaw joint dysfunction and tinnitus are connected for many people.

Dentist John Taddey wrote that "the teeth have a profound influence on the position of the [TMJ] ball and socket as well as on the amount of stress placed on the joint." Eventually, a misaligned bite can cause the ball and socket to grind together and produce significant pain. Poorly fit dentures and missing or worn down teeth can cause this ball and socket degeneration. But what is its relation to tinnitus?

There are several points of interaction between the ear and the jaw joint. In the early 1960s, a researcher named O. F. Pinto discovered a ligament in the TMJ that connects to the malleus, one of the three bones in the middle ear. It was later confirmed that movement of the jaw and therefore this ligament (now named Pinto's ligament) causes movement of the bones in the middle ear. The trigeminal nerve (also called the fifth cranial nerve or facial nerve) runs through the TMJ joint, up to and alongside the auditory nerve on its way to the brain. Other delicate muscles in the auditory system are also structurally connected to the trigeminal nerve.

When a TMJ dysfunction is identified and there is no other cause for the tinnitus, TMJ treatment is indicated. In one such study, 79 TMJ patients were treated and evaluated. Forty-nine of the patients received dental splints, 13 received dental adjustments, 9 were given jaw exercises to do, and 8 received other dental treatments. Twenty-six (33%) out of the 79 patients reported a reduction in their tinnitus, and none reported an increase in their tinnitus. A 2-year follow-up survey revealed that 20 of the 26 still had a tinnitus reduction. All the patients in this study were initially informed that their dental professionals did not believe in a connection between TMJ dysfunction and tinnitus. This statement served to reduce the placebo effect.

Many people have noticed that muscle movements of all sorts, including the tensing and untensing of muscles in the jaw, head, neck, and the extremities, can make existing tinnitus temporarily louder. Researcher Robert Levine, M.D., believes that the connection between tinnitus and muscle contractions is more than physical. His new research suggests that there is an interaction between the auditory center and somatosensory (sense of touch and pressure) center in the brain. We are complicated creatures indeed.

Resources

Gelb, H., Gelb, M., and Wagner, M. L. The relationship of tinnitus to craniocervical mandibular disorders, *J. Craniomandibular Practice*, Apr. 1997; 15(2).

Klemons, I. M. Successful treatment of tinnitus in patients with TMJ dysfunction, *Tinnitus Today*, June 1999; 24(2):17–18.

Melcher, J. R., Sigalovsky, I. S., Guinan, J. J. Jr., and Levine, R. A. Lateralized tinnitus studied with functional magnetic resonance imaging: Abnormal inferior colliculus activation. *J. Neurophysiol.*, Feb. 2000; 83(2):1058–72.

Tabachnick, B. TMJ—A profile, *Tinnitus Today*, Sept. 1994; 19(3):6–9.

Taddey, J. *TMJ—The Self-help Program*, Surrey Park Press, La Jolla, CA, 1990.

Wright, E. F., and Bifano, S. L. The relationship between tinnitus and temporomandibular disorder (TMD) therapy, *Int. Tinnitus J.*, 1997; 3(1):55–61.

50

TRT: Tinnitus
Retraining Therapy

Q What is the theory behind tinnitus retraining therapy (TRT)?

A TRT is based on the premise that a person cannot be bothered by noises that he or she does not consciously perceive. TRT clinician, Stephen Nagler, M.D., says, "If sound does not reach the part of the brain responsible for the conscious perception of sound, then for you there is no sound." The principle holds true for tinnitus: If you are not hearing the tinnitus, there is no tinnitus.

There are multiple steps in the TRT process, and it begins first with patient education. Patients are taught about the "benign-ness" of their tinnitus, that it is not their enemy, and that it is instead something neutral, even unimportant. TRT often requires that patients change their ways of thinking about their tinnitus. This is accomplished through an interactive educational process called *directive counseling*.

The next step in the TRT process is the introduction of sound to the patients' environment, a steady, low-level, meaningless sound for the ears (and the brain) to hear and then slowly habituate, or become unaware of. The recommended sound stimulus is a broadband of noise from 250 to 5500 Hz set at a volume that does not cover up the tinnitus. This sound is used to decrease the contrast between the tinnitus and the background sounds. The TRT community refers to the devices they use as *white noise generators*, although they acknowledge that they are mislabeled. White noise is the full spectrum of sound audible to humans, from 20 to 20,000 Hz.

Authors Kellerhals and Zogg write that TRT's goal is not the elimination of tinnitus, but the diminishment of its importance and the patients' awareness of it. They explain that, through the process of TRT, tinnitus will not actually get quieter. Instead, the patients will become aware of their tinnitus less frequently and will be less annoyed by it when they *are* aware of it. The protocol of TRT instructs patients to avoid silent environments, moreover to constantly enrich their background with sound.

TRT can provide tinnitus relief, although usually after an interval of time. For some people it can take several months. For others, it can take 1 to 2 years to achieve the desired goal of habituation.

Q **I have been using a masker/sound generator for 3 months. I'm trying to adapt to it, but I'm having poor results. Should I continue to try for a longer period of time?**

A Patients often need a month or two to adapt to having devices in their ears every day, whether the devices are hearing aids or maskers or white noise generators. As for tinnitus retraining therapy (TRT) itself, patients generally need a bit of time—sometimes 6 months, sometimes longer—before they begin to see changes in their tinnitus. If you are attempting this therapy, it is important to stay in verbal contact with the audiologist or doctor who is guiding you through it. Your ongoing interaction is a kind of counseling and is a part of the TRT protocol. Sound generators, as TRT devices are called, are always used in pairs for this treatment. Therefore, you might find that wearing two devices would speed your habituation process.

If you are on a masking program, it might be that the masker is improperly fitted. Also, if you have some hearing loss, it is possible that a tinnitus instrument would help you more than a simple masker. If you have no hearing loss, but have bilateral (two-sided) tinnitus, it is likely that you need to have two maskers instead of one. Many hearing aid dispensers will fit a single hearing aid on a patient with dual hearing losses. This thinking often spills over to the fitting of tinnitus maskers. They incorrectly reason that adapting to one unit is easier than adapting to two units. In many cases, patients need two maskers in order to get the relief they seek.

Q **I have heard about tinnitus retraining therapy (TRT). What does it actually entail? Are there pills to take or hearing aids to wear?**

A TRT clinicians use directive counseling with their patients in order to help to demystify tinnitus for their patients. Through this demystification process, patients learn that the brain is interpreting a nonthreatening meaningless sound (their tinnitus) as a threat.

In a majority of cases, TRT patients are fitted with ear-level noise-generating devices that look like hearing aids with open molds so that the ear canals are not obstructed. A hearing aid is sometimes used as the tool for bringing in the required low-level background sound. In some cases, table-top environmental sound-making machines or CDs with nature sounds are all that is required.

TRT patients are instructed to wear the maskerlike devices in their ears for 8 or more hours per day. Every morning the patients set their devices at the *mixing point,* the point at which the sound emitted from the device just begins to blend with the tinnitus. Patients have to clearly detect both the tinnitus and the noise generator sound. In a few cases, the noise generators are set at the lowest audible sound.

Although it can take 18 months before results are seen with TRT, often the results are favorable and patients can discontinue wearing the devices. As a rule, medication is not a part of the TRT protocol.

Q If both TRT and masking treatments use maskers, aren't they really the same treatment?

A There is no question that these two therapies look alike. But they are not the same. Here's what *is* the same: Both treatments introduce sound to the tinnitus patient as a way of relieving tinnitus. Masking treatment involves the use of devices called *maskers* and TRT involves the use of devices called *sound generators*. These devices, which are available in either in-the-ear or behind-the-ear styles, produce broadband sounds, like that of running water or a "shhhh" sound. The masker is usually set to include a higher-frequency bandwidth of sound than is the noise generator. There is another similarity: Both treatments are helpful for some and not helpful for others. Table 50.1 shows one way to look at the differences and similarities.

Two things seem to influence the success rates: the degree of professional training and the degree of the professional's empathy for the problem and the patient. When a health provider is trained and caring, his or her patients generally have a high rate of success. James Henry, Ph.D., and Martin Scheckley, Ph.D., from the Portland VA Medical Center, and Richard S. Tyler, PH.D. from the University of Iowa, have begun studies to scientifically compare the success rates of these two workhorse tinnitus treatments.

Q Who developed TRT and what is the rationale for its effectiveness?

A TRT is the brainchild of Pawel J. Jastreboff, Ph.D., Sc.D., now at Emory University in Atlanta (404-778-3109, www.tinnitus-pjj.com). This treatment applies known scientific principles to tinnitus alleviation. We already know that the brain has the ability to habituate non-threatening and non-information-bearing sounds. For example, we notice when the refrigerator motor goes on, but within a minute or so we are no longer aware of the sound. This is habituation. As a therapeutic approach to tinnitus, TRT offers the possibility of eventual remission of tinnitus without the patient having to rely on continued use of medications or sound-making devices. Remission in this context does not mean a cure, but instead the absence of awareness of the offending tinnitus.

Not all patients want to wait the long time (sometimes up to 2 years) that TRT can require to be effective. Some clinicians who offer TRT know this and are prepared to offer a variety of more immediate treatments approaches to their tinnitus patients.

TRT is also helpful for hyperacusis, a supersensitivity to everyday sounds. Dan Malcore, founder of the Hyperacusis Network, sent a survey to members of his organization and asked them about their experiences with

TABLE 50.1   *Comparing Masking and TRT*

Masking	TRT
Maskers are set at a level loud enough to provide relief from the tinnitus. This means that the tinnitus is either entirely covered by the masker or partially covered by the masker.	Noise generators are set at a low volume that allows the tinnitus to still be heard. Noise generators do not cover the tinnitus.
The goal of masking is to give the patient immediate relief from the tinnitus. Seventy-eight percent of a group of 1758 patients with maskable tinnitus experienced short periods of residual inhibition (total cessation of tinnitus) when their maskers were removed.	The goal of TRT is to retrain the brain to no longer notice the tinnitus sound so that in time the tinnitus is no longer an issue in the patient's life. Tinnitus relief with TRT can take as long as 24 months to be achieved.
Masking gives patients the opportunity to put the devices in and mask out the tinnitus sound whenever they want to.	TRT patients wear the devices every day for a minimum of 8 hours. The goal of TRT is for patients to outgrow the need for the devices.
One-time informal counseling is offered at the beginning of treatment. Some masking clinicians offer follow-up care.	Directive counseling is an intensive educational aspect of TRT. Patients are taught about the brain's involvement in their perception of tinnitus.
The masker sound bandwidth is usually 3000 to 12,000 Hz, a setting that captures the pitch of the tinnitus.	The noise generator sound bandwidth is in the approximate range of 250 to 5500 Hz, a setting usually lower than the pitch of the tinnitus.

TRT. Of those who have tried it, more than 90% reported some degree of hyperacusis and tinnitus improvement. Unfortunately, Dan's survey was not as specific as it could have been, so we don't know how many had "some improvement" or "95% improvement." We also don't know how many people in the survey attempted the treatment. Malcore concedes that TRT is a marathon treatment protocol and that it "takes a marathon mentality to complete it." Still, the word *improvement* is a word we like to see.

References

Kellerhals, B., and Zogg, R. *Tinnitus Rehabilitation by Retraining*, Karger, Basel, Switzerland, 1999.

Malcore, D. *Hyperacusis Network Newsletter*, Mar. 2000, p. 13.

Nagler, S. *Tinnitus: Learn to live without it—thoughts on tinnitus retraining therapy* (videotape), Alliance Tinnitus and Hearing Center, Atlanta, GA, 2000.

Nagler, S. Tinnitus retraining therapy and the neurophysiological model of tinnitus, *Tinnitus Today*, Mar. 1998; 23(1).

Sandlin, R. Treatments for subjective tinnitus, *Tinnitus Today*, Mar. 1997; 22(1):13.

Epilogue

Our remedies oft in ourselves do lie.
—William Shakespeare
All's Well That Ends Well

This book is a slice out of time. Our decision to include Internet addresses was one made with a twinkle in the eye. We verified them monthly as we compiled the book, and we laughed about it monthly, too, as Web addresses came and went. We realize the folly of our ways. But folly or not, we decided that some might stick around long enough to be of service to you and so they are here. It is probably more important for you to learn how to find this information yourself.

The National Library of Medicine has a phenomenal online database, called PubMed. Search for it on the Internet that way. It is sponsored by the National Institutes of Health and available to everyone. When you are in PubMed, you can search on the word *tinnitus* alone or with other words like *TMJ* or *acupuncture* or a researcher's name. The study titles will appear in a list with the most current study at the top. If you click on the title of the study, it will send you to an abstract, or short synopsis, of the research. Some PubMed abstracts are very thorough. This Web site lists authors, publication names, article titles, and dates, so you can find the full articles if you need to.

The Internet has many other useful medical resources. We found www.drugstore.com to be a big help in deciphering over-the-counter and prescription drug names and for hunting for side effects and dosages. Of course, this is intended only as an educational tool, not as a substitute for medical advice.

If you have an interest in participating in a research study, go to www.clinicaltrials.gov and type in "tinnitus" or "sleep" or "Ménière's" or your topic of choice. As of this writing, there are no posted clinical trials on tinnitus. But the Web site is relatively new. More research opportunities are posted weekly. This is a site we will follow closely.

When you search on the Internet for scientific information, look for site addresses that end in ".edu" over others. Only educational institutions like universities and hospitals can qualify for such an extension. There are no guarantees on the Internet, but at least this will increase your odds of finding legitimate scientific data. The Web site extension of ".org" will send you to nonprofit agency sites. Most are worth the trip. The ".gov" extensions are used by governmental offices and can also steer you to factual information. The ".com" extension indicates a commercial enterprise (products or services for sale) or an individual's posting of a personal opinion. We want you to go into an online search with this foreknowledge so that you can choose your information mindfully.

Your doctor is another source of tinnitus information. Yes, too many of them tell tinnitus patients to go home and learn to live with it and then fail to tell them how to accomplish this Herculean feat. If you anticipate this response, you can prepare for it. Ask the easy questions first, the ones that your doctor *can* answer.

What is your exact diagnosis of my condition?

What tests do you think I should have?

How much will each test cost?

If the test is loud, I want to have a quieter test. What do you recommend?

What are the exact instructions for taking this medication?

How will the medication affect my tinnitus?

If you can't help me with my tinnitus, do you know of an audiologist (or ENT, neurologist, psychologist, TMJ dentist, or biofeedback specialist) who can?

Compile your list of questions before you visit the doctor. During your visit, write down the answers that you get, or bring someone along who will write down the answers for you. If your doctor is worth seeing again, he or she will answer your questions on the spot or get back to you with the answers soon.

Health professionals have an obligation to be of service, to remember that each patient is an individual with a life and a problem, and to do no harm. They also have an obligation to work within their health-care systems so that desperate people are not turned away at the door because of Medicare or HMO limitations. Patients are consumers. Doctors are service providers. Shop around until you find one that fits.

When you do find a doctor who knows and cares about tinnitus and the people who have it, the sky is the limit. Ask everything. Even if you think that your questions are farfetched, ask them anyway. Dr. Ross Coles once wrote regarding tinnitus, "There is still plenty of room for the unexpected and the unexplained." Those farfetched questions are the ones that push our scientific thinkers into thinking differently and innovatively.

Stand back and look at the dominating discoveries in science today. It is hard to grasp the potential of all of them, such as the Human Genome

Project—the plotting of our genetic sequencing in order to predict and prevent disease. It very well could point the way out of this disorder in a few short years.

This is the Information Age. We now have the tools to turn over and examine every research and treatment stone, to share discoveries globally and instantly, and, we believe, to silence tinnitus in our lifetime. We are brimming with hope.

You can write to Dr. Jack Vernon with questions about tinnitus at the American Tinnitus Association, P.O. Box 5, Portland, Oregon 97207-0005.

Appendix A

PDR Companion Guide, 2000, Tinnitus Drug Interaction List

The following drugs produced tinnitus in a small percentage of patients. The asterisk symbol (*) indicates that the drug produced tinnitus in 3% or more of patients. Look in the PDR for more information about these listed drugs. The PDR page numbers follow the drug names on this list. *Note: These drugs were not specifically tested on people who already had tinnitus. Consult your physician before you make any change in medication.*

Abelcet Injection, 1653
Accutane Capsules, 2610
Aceon Tablets (2, 4, 8 mg), 3057
Achromycin V Capsules, 1528
Actiq, 405
*Actonel Tablets, 2504
Adalat CC Tablets, 673
Agrylin Capsules, 2584
Alferon N Injection (Interferon), 1439
Alka-Seltzer Cherry Effervescent Antacid and Pain Reliever, 603
Alka-Seltzer Extra Strength Effervescent Antacid and Pain Reliever, 603
Alka-Seltzer Lemon Lime Effervescent Antacid and Pain Reliever, 603
Alka-Seltzer Original Effervescent Antacid and Pain Reliever, 603

Alka-Seltzer PM Pain Reliever & Sleep Aid Medicine Effervescent Tablets, 606
Altace Capsules, 1928
Alumadrine Tablets, 1068
Ambien Tablets, 2884
Amerge Tablets, 1148
Amicar Syrup, Tablets and Injection, 1412
*Anaprox DS Tablets, 2631
*Anaprox Tablets, 2631
Anzemet Injection, 1349
Anzemet Tablets, 1352
Aralen Hydrochloride Injection, 2733
Aralen Tablets, 2734
Aricept Tablets, 1009, 2322
Arthrotec Tablets, 2888
Asacol Delayed-Release Tablets, 2511

Appendix B

Hearing-related Organizations

Acoustic Neuroma Association (ANA)
P.O. Box 12402
Atlanta, Georgia 30355
404-237-8023
Fax: 404-237-2704
E-mail: ANAusa@aol.com
Web: http://anausa.org

American Academy of Audiology (AAA)
8300 Greensboro Dr., # 750
McLean, Virginia 22102
800-AAA-2336
703-790-8466
Fax: 703-790-8631
(For e-mail, go to their Web site, then "Contact us")
Web: www.audiology.org

American Academy of Neurology (AAN)
1080 Montreal Ave.
St. Paul, Minnesota 55116
651-695-1940
E-mail: web@aan.com
Web: www.aan.com

American Academy of Otolaryngology (AAO)
One Prince St.
Alexandria, Virginia 22314-3357
703-836-4444
Web: www.entnet.org

American Hyperacusis Association
P.O. Box 4229
Vancouver, Washington 98782
Web: www.hyperacusis.org

American Speech–Language–Hearing Association (ASHA)
10801 Rockville Pike
Rockville, Maryland 20852
800-498-2071
TTY: 301-897-5700
Fax: 301-571-0457
Web: www.asha.org

American Tinnitus Association (ATA)
P.O. Box 5
Portland, Oregon 97207-0005
800-634-8978
503-248-9985
FAX: 503-248-0024
E-mail: tinnitus@ata.org
Web: www.ata.org

**Association of Late-Deafened
   Adults, Inc. (ALDA)**
1145 Westgate St., #206
Oak Park, Illinois 60301
877-348-7537 (U.S. only)
TTY: 708-358-0135
Web: www.alda.org

Autism Society of America
7910 Woodmont Ave. # 300
Bethesda, Maryland 20814-3015
800–3AUTISM
301-657-0881
Fax: 301-657-0869
Web: www.autism-society.org

Better Hearing Institute
800-EAR WELL
E-mail: mail@betterhearing.org.
Web: www.betterhearing.org

**Hearing Education and Awareness
   for Rockers (H.E.A.R.)**
P.O. Box 460847
San Francisco, California 94146
415-409-3277
E-mail: hear@hearnet.com
Web: www.hearnet.com

Hear Now
4001 S. Magnolia Way
Denver, Colorado 80237
Voice/TTY: 303-756-5814
Or: 800–648-HEAR
Fax: 303-695-7789
E-mail: bdinner@compuserve.com
Free hearing aid/masker program

The Hyperacusis Network
444 Edgewood Dr.
Green Bay, Wisconsin 54302
E-mail: malcore@netnet.net
Web: www.hyperacusis.net

The Ménière's Network
EAR Foundation
1817 Patterson St.
Nashville, Tennessee 37203
Voice/TDD: 800–545-HEAR
or: 615-329-7807
Fax: 615-329-7935
Web: www.theearfound.org/
   menieres.html

**National Center for
   Complementary and Alternative
   Medicine**
NCCAM Clearinghouse
P.O. Box 8218
Silver Spring, Maryland 20907-8218
888-644-6226
TTY/TDY: 888-644-6226
Fax: 301-495-4957
Web: http://nccam.nih.gov/

**National Hearing Conservation
   Association (NHCA)**
9101 E. Kenyon Ave., #3000
Denver, Colorado 80237
303-224-9022
Fax: 303-770-1812
Web: www.hearingconservation.
   org/index.html

**National Institute on Deafness and
   Other Communication Disorders
   (NIDCD)**
National Institutes of Health
31 Center Drive, MSC 2320
Bethesda, Maryland 20892-2320
301-496-7243
TTY: 301-402-0252
Fax: 301-402-0018
Web: www.nih.gov/nidcd

Oregon Tinnitus Data Archive
Tinnitus Data Registry, NRC04
3181 SW Sam Jackson Park Rd.
Portland, Oregon 97201-3098
E-mail: ohrc@ohsu.edu
Web: www.ohsu.edu/ohrc-otda/

**Self-Help for Hard of Hearing
   People, Inc. (SHHH)**
7910 Woodmont Ave. #1200
Bethesda, Maryland 20814
301-657-2248
TTY: 301-657-2249
Fax: 301-913-9413
E-mail: national@shhh.org
Web: www.shhh.org

Starkey Hearing Foundation
6700 Washington Ave. S.
Eden Prairie, Minnesota 55344
800-328-8602
612-941-6401
Fax: 612-828-9262
E-mail: talk_to_us@starkey.com
Web: www.hearinfo.com
Free hearing aid/masker program

**Vestibular Disorders Association
   (VEDA)**
P.O. Box 4467
Portland, Oregon 97208-4467
503-229-7705 (answering machine)
Fax: 503-229-8064
E-mail: veda@vestibular.org
Web: www.teleport.com/~veda

Appendix C

Publications of Interest

Hearing Health magazine
  (published 6 times a year)
P.O. Drawer V
Ingleside, Texas 78362
Voice/TTY: 361-776-7240
Fax: 361-776-3278
Web: www.hearinghealthmag.com

International Tinnitus Journal
  (published 2 times a year)
The Tinnitus Center, State
  University of New York
Health Science Center at Brooklyn
Box 1239
450 Clarkson Ave.
Brooklyn, New York 11203
718-773-8888
Fax: 718-465-3669
Web: www.tinnitus.com

Quiet
British Tinnitus Association
4th Floor, White Building
Fitzalan Square
Sheffield S1 2AZ
(0114) 279 6600
Fax: (0114) 279 6222
E-mail: bta@tinnitus.org.uk

Steady
  (published 4 times per year)
The Ménière's Network
1817 Patterson St.
Nashville, Tennessee 37203
800-545-HEAR
Or: 615-329-7807
Fax: 615-329-7935
Web: www.theearfound.org/
  menieres/html

Tinnitus Today
  (published 4 times per year)
American Tinnitus Association
P.O. Box 5
Portland, Oregon 97207-0005
503-248-9985
800-634-8978
E-mail: tinnitus@ata.org
Web: www.ata.org

Appendix D

Masking, Environmental, and Self-hypnosis Sound Devices, CDs, and Audiotapes

General Hearing Instruments
P.O. Box 23748
New Orleans, Louisiana
  70183-0748
800-824-3021
E-mail: information@generalhearing.
  com
Web: www.generalhearing.com
*Ear-level tinnitus masker,
  tinnitus instrument, noise
  generator*

Hearing Innovations, Inc.
9040 S. Rita Rd., #2250
Tucson, Arizona 85747
520-663-0544
TTY: 520-574-7836
Fax: 520-663-0018
E-mail: info@hearinginnovations.
  com
Web: http://hearinginnovations.
  com
*HiSonic® bone conduction hearing
  instrument*

Marpac Corporation
P.O. Box 3098
Wilmington, North Carolina
  28406-0098
910-763-7861
800-999-6962
Web: www.marpac.com/
  sound_cond.asp
*Marsona® TSC-330 and
  TSC-350 bedside
  environmental sound
  conditioners*

**Oregon Hearing Research
  Center**
3181 SW Sam Jackson Park Rd.,
  NRC 04
Portland, Oregon
  97201-3098
503-494-8032
*Moses/Lang pink noise
  CD for hyperacusis
  (with tinnitus masking
  tracks)*

Personal Growth Technologies
404 East Ten Mile Rd.
Pleasant Ridge, Michigan 48069
248-547-4177
800-511-0364
Fax: 248-547-1256
Web: www.tinnitus-relief.com
Tinnitus Relief Systems,
  masking/relaxation CDs

Petroff Audio Technologies
23507 Balmoral Lane
West Hills, California 91307
818-716-6166
E-mail: sales@tinnitushelp.com
Web: www.tinnitushelp.com
Dynamic Tinnitus Mitigation™,
  multi-CD masking/relaxation system

Phoenix Productions
1410 Horizon Circle
San Antonio, Texas 78258–3152
210-497-1611
877-846-6488
Fax: 210-497-1612
E-mail: phoenix@newpro.net
Web: www.soundpillow.com
Sound Pillow™

Sharper Image
800-344-4444
650-344-4444 (outside the U.S.)
Web: www.sharperimage.com
(click on product categories,
  search on "soother")
Sound Soother® tabletop masking
  devices

Shultz and Shultz Enterprises
12440 N. 103rd Ave., PMB #56
Sun City, Arizona 85351
E-mail: quietmind@juno.com
Quiet Mind Tinnitus Hypnotherapy
  Tapes

Starkey Laboratories, Inc.
6700 Washington Ave. S.
Eden Prairie, Minnesota 55344
800-328-8602
612-941-6401
Fax: 612-828-9262
E-mail: talk_to_us@starkey.com
Web: www.hearinfo.com
Ear-level tinnitus maskers,
  tinnitus instruments

Appendix E

Implantable Hearing Aids and Hearing Restoration Systems

Entific Medical Systems USA, Inc.
3944 North Hampton Dr.
Powell, Ohio 43065
888-825-8484
614-799-3485
Web: www.entific.com
Semi-implanted bone anchored hearing aid, BAHA®

IMPLEX America Hearing Systems, Inc.
P.O. Box 58397
Raleigh, North Carolina 27658
919-876-4327
Fax: 919-876-6800
Web: www.implexhearingsystems.com
Totally integrated cochlear amplifier, TICA®

SOUNDTEC, Inc.
2601 NW Expressway #203W
Oklahoma City, Oklahoma 73112
405-842-5045
Fax: 405-842-6339
Implantable SOUNDTEC, Inc.™ DDHS, direct drive hearing system

St. Croix Medical
5301 East River Rd.
Minneapolis, Minnesota 55421
612-574-0570
Fax: 612-574-0554
E-mail: info@StCroixMedical.com
Web: www.stcroixmedical.com
Totally implantable Envoy™ hearing restoration system

Symphonix Devices, Inc.
2331 Zanker Rd.
San Jose, California 95131-1109
408-232-0710
408-232-0720
Web: www.symphonix.com
Semi-implantable Vibrant Soundbridge™

Appendix F

Educational Videos

Mid-Atlantic Tinnitus Conference

What's new in tinnitus research, brain-imaging techniques—PET scanning, medical intervention for tinnitus, and hypnosis

3 hours, 45 minutes, VHS (2 videos)

featuring Richard Salvi, Ph.D., Max Ronis, M.D., and James Sumerson, M.D.

American Tinnitus Association
P.O. Box 5
Portland, Oregon 97207–0005
503–248–9985
800–634–8978
E-mail: tinnitus@ata.org
Web: www.ata.org

Tinnitus: Learn to Live WithOUT It

Thoughts on Tinnitus Retraining Therapy

2 hours, VHS

by Stephen M. Nagler, M.D.

Alliance Tinnitus and Hearing
    Center
980 Johnson Ferry Rd., NE, #760
Atlanta, Georgia 30342
404-531-3979
Web: www.tinn.com

Tinnitus: Ringing in the Ears

Masking applications and origins of tinnitus treatments

1 hour, VHS

by Jack A. Vernon, Ph.D.

American Tinnitus Association
P.O. Box 5
Portland, Oregon 97207-0005
503-248-9985
800-634-8978
E-mail: tinnitus@ata.org
Web: www.ata.org

Appendix G

Hearing Protection Devices

Aearo Company Safety Products
8001 Woodland Dr.
Indianapolis, Indiana 46278
800-327-3431
Fax: 800-488-8007
E-mail: aearo@mmcweb.com
Web: www.aearo.de
*Foam and molded earplugs, earmuffs,
   other devices*

Bose Corporation
The Mountain Road
Framingham, Massachusetts 01701
800-242-9008
Web: www.bose.com
Active noise cancellation devices

Cirrus Healthcare Products
P.O. Box 469
Locust Valley, New York 11560
516–759–6664
800-EAR-6151
Fax: 516–759–5832
E-mail: info@cirrushealthcare.com
Web: www.cirrushealthcare.com
EarPlanes® filtered earplugs

Etymotic Research
61 Martin Lane
Elk Grove, Illinois 60007
847-228-0006
Web: www.etymotic.com
Musicians Earplugs™

**FHI-Digital Hearing
   Instruments**
Jim Fenwick, M.S.
2888 NW Westover Rd.
Portland, Oregon 97210
503-464-9441
800-464-9714
E-mail: fhi@spiritone.com
*Star 2001 electronic earplugs
   for hyperacusis*

Howard Leight Industries
7828 Waterville Rd.
San Diego, California 92173
800-543-0121
Fax: 800-322-1330
Web: www.howardleight.com
*Foam earplugs, Thunder 29
   earmuffs*

Micro-Tech
3500 Holly Lane North, #10
Plymouth, Minnesota 55447
800-745-4327
Web: www.hearing-aid.com/
   rfh.htm
*Refuge Hyperacusic™
   electronic earplugs*

Noise Cancellation Technologies
20 Ketchum St.
Westport, Connecticut 06880
800-278-3526
203-226-4447
Fax: 203-226-3123
E-mail: sales@nct-active.com
Web: www.nct-active.com
Active noise cancellation devices

Westone Laboratories, Inc.
P.O. Box 15100
Colorado Springs, Colorado 80935
719-540-9333
800-525-5071
Fax: 719-540-9183
E-mail: westone@earmold.com
Web: www.earmold.com
Custom earplugs

Appendix H

International
Tinnitus Organizations

Australia
Australian Tinnitus Association
P.O. Box 660
Woollahra, NSW 2025
(6102) 93617331
Web: www.tinnitus.asn.au/
  home.htm

Canada
Tinnitus Association
  of Canada
23 Ellis Park Rd.
Toronto, ON M6S2V4
416-762-1490
E-mail: chasm@pathcom.com
Web: www.kadis.com/ta/
  tinnitus.htm

England
British Tinnitus
  Association
4th Floor, White Building
Fitzalan Square
Sheffield S1 2AZ
(0114) 279 6600
Fax: (0114) 279 6222
E-mail: bta@tinnitus.org.uk

France
France Acouphenes
11 Rue Ernest Cresson
Paris, 75014
(33) 0145435046

Germany
Deutsche Tinnitus-Liga e.v.
AM Lohsiepen 18
Wuppertal, D42369
(49) 202–2465235

Ireland
Irish Tinnitus Association
35 N Frederick St.
Dublin, 1
(3531) 8723800

New Zealand
New Zealand Tinnitus Association
P.O. Box 100734
No. Shore Mall Center
Auckland, 10
(6409) 486–5359

Spain
Associacion de Personas Affectatos
  por Tinitus
Apart Ado De
Correos #57
Barcelona
08320-Masnou
(3493) 555–4955

Switzerland
Schweizerische Tinnitus-Liga
Landliweg 12
Baden, Ch-5400
(4156) 2228140

Appendix I

Alternative Therapies

Biofeedback
Association for Applied
  Psychophysiology
  and Biofeedback
10200 W. 44th Ave., #304
Wheat Ridge, Colorado 80033
800-477-8892
303-422-8436
Fax: 303-422-8894
E-mail: aapb@resourcenter.com
Web: www.aapb.org

Chiropractic
American Chiropractic Association
1701 Clarendon Blvd.
Arlington, Virginia 22209
800-986-4636
703-276-8800
Fax: 703-243-2593
Web: www.amerchiro.org/
  index.html
*Online directory of U.S. doctors
  of chiropractic*

Craniosacral Therapy
The Upledger Institute, Inc.
11211 Prosperity Farms Rd.
Palm Beach Gardens, Florida 33410
800-233-5880
561-622-4334
Fax: 561-622-4771
E-mail: Upledger@upledger.com
Web: www.upledger.com
*Online directory of international
  practitioners*

Homeopathy
National Center for Homeopathy
801 N. Fairfax St., #306
Alexandria, Virginia 22314
703-548-7790
Fax: 703-548-7792
E-mail: info@homeopathic.org
Web: www.healthy.net/pan/pa/
  homeopathic/natcenhom

Hyperbaric Oxygen
Undersea and Hyperbaric
  Medical Society
10531 Metropolitan
Kensington, Maryland 20895
301-942-2980
Fax: 301-942-7804
E-mail: uhms@uhms.org
Web: www.uhms.org

Hypnosis
American Board of Hypnotherapy
16842 Von Karman Ave. #475
Irvine, California 92606
949-261-6400
800-872-9996
E-mail: mind@hypnosis.com
Web: www.hypnosis.com

  Or

American Society
  of Clinical Hypnosis
33 W. Grand Ave.
Chicago, Illinois 60610
312-645-9810

Naturopathy
American Association
  of Naturopathic Physicians
601 Valley #105
Seattle, Washington 98109
206-298-0126
Fax: 206-298-0129
Web: www.healthy.net
Access to U.S. and Canadian directory
  of naturopathic physicians

Temporomandibular
  Joint Disorder
TMJ & Stress Center
P.O. Box 89698
Tucson, Arizona 85752
520-744-8000
E-mail: tmjinfo@myodata.com

Transcendental Meditation
17301 Sunset Blvd.
Pacific Palisades, California 90272
(310) 459–3522
(800) 888–5797
Web: www.tm.org

Yoga
Himalayan International Institute
  of Yoga
Science and Philosophy
RR 1, Box 400
Honesdale, Pennsylvania 18431
(800) 822-4547
Web: www.himalayaninstitute.org

Index

ABR (auditory brainstem response), 1, 229–30
Acoustic damage as time-intensity function, 172, 173
Acoustic neuroma, 1, 9–14, 124, 188, 191, 192, 193
 ABR test to diagnose, 230
 radiation therapies for, 13
 vestibular schwannoma, 12–14
Acoustic Neuroma Association (ANA), 14, 254
Acoustic stress, glucocorticoid reaction to, 130
Acupuncture, 25–26, 189, 190, 191, 192, 193
Addictive drug, 1
Advil (ibuprofen), 77
Aearo Company Safety Products, 262
Aerobics activities, 103
Afferent nerves, 1, 138
Aging
 choices of tinnitus relief and, 153
 tinnitus perception and, 120
 tinnitus severity and, 226–29
Airbag Options, Inc., 17
Air bags, 15–18, 192, 193
 auditory injuries from, 15
 on-off switch for, 15–17
 sound level of exploding, 15–16
Airbag Service, Inc., 17
Airbag Systems, Inc., 17
Air conduction hearing test, 176, 218
Air pressure, effect of changing, 34–35, 104
Air travel, 104–7
Alcohol
 effect on tinnitus, 179
 insomnia and, 203
 interaction with Xanax, 78, 79
Alka Seltzer, 76
Allergy(ies)
 food, 29
 Ménière's disease and, 163, 192
 tinnitus and, 29, 211
Alprazolam. See Xanax
Alternating current (AC), 97, 100
Alternative treatments, 19–33
 acupuncture, 25–26
 auditory training, 32
 Carbo vegetabilis 6C, 31
 Chinese medicines, 23–24, 29
 Cimicifua 6C, 31
 diet, 28–29
 DMSO, 21–22
 Dr. John's Special Ear Drops, 27
 Ginkgo biloba, 23–24
 heating pad, 24–25
 homeopathy, 5, 30, 31

hyperbaric oxygen, 22–23, 187
 in Israel, 22
 lasers, 20
 magnesium, 28
 niacin, 31–32, 175
 organizations for, 265–66
 taurine, 20–21
 Tinnitabs, 30–31
 Transderm Scop, 20
 Wobenzyme-N, 25
 zinc, 27, 28
Altitude, effect of, 34
Amalgam dental fillings, 63
Amedee, R., 80–81
American Academy of Audiology (AAA), 254
American Academy of Neurology (AAN), 254
American Academy of Otolaryngology (AAO), 254
American Hyperacusis Association, 254
American Medical Association (AMA), 19
American Speech-Language-Hearing Association (ASHA), 254
American Tinnitus Association, 41, 56, 102, 119, 136, 185, 214, 223, 254
Amifostine pretreatment, 73
Aminoglycosides, 70, 81, 88
Amitriptyline, 204
Amplification, 1
Anacin, 76
Analog hearing aids, 114
Anecdotal report, 1
Anodal monophasic pulse, 100
Antibiotics, 72–73, 87–88
Antidepressants, 1, 64–65
Antiepileptic/anticonvulsant medications, 88–89
Anti-inflammatories, 74–75, 77
 prostaglandins reduced by, 88
 Wobenzyme-N, 25
Antioxidant drugs, perfusion into inner ear of, 70
Anxiety, 202
Anxiolytic (antianxiety) medications, 1–2. See also Xanax
Appliances, noise level from, 173
Aran, J.-M., 98, 187
Aristotle, 223
Arthritis, 80
Artificial food flavorings, sodium salicylate in, 76
Ascaridole *(Chenopodium anthelminticum)*, 30
Ascriptin, 76
Aspartame (Nutrasweet), 211
Aspergum, 76

267